WHEN DEATH ENTERS THE THERAPEUTIC SPACE

Although it is a natural and inescapable part of life, death is a subject that is often neglected in psychotherapeutic literature and training. In *When Death Enters the Therapeutic Space* Laura Barnett and her contributors offer us insights into working with mortality in the therapeutic encounter.

Taking an existential perspective, the book brings together a variety of client groups, all of whom have experienced a confrontation with mortality, and encourages the reader to engage with and reflect upon the subject of death. Although this may initially evoke anxiety and distress, Barnett and her contributors introduce the reader to the 'vitality of death' (Koestenbaum): an energy and focus that can come from confronting our greatest fears and anxieties, including the anxiety aroused by our own mortality. Topics covered include:

- philosophical roots and principal approaches to existential therapy
- health related issues including cancer, HIV and Intensive Care
- surviving violent trauma
- creating a safe space for the client
- short prognosis and palliative care
- bereavement.

When Death Enters the Therapeutic Space presents therapists with an understanding of what it means to experience such traumas and prepares them for helping the client. It will be useful for trainee counsellors and experienced therapists alike.

Laura Barnett is an existential psychotherapist and supervisor working in the NHS and in private practice. She manages the Cancer Counselling Service and the Psychological Aftercare Service for Intensive Care Patients, which she set up at Mayday University Hospital, Croydon.

WHEN DEATH ENTERS THE THERAPEUTIC SPACE

Existential Perspectives in Psychotherapy and Counselling

Edited by Laura Barnett

Foreword by Emmy van Deurzen

Routledge
Taylor & Francis Group

LONDON AND NEW YORK

Published 2009 by Routledge
27 Church Road, Hove, East Sussex BN3 2FA

Simultaneously published in the USA and Canada
by Routledge
711 Third Avenue, New York, NY 10017, USA

*Routledge is an imprint of the Taylor & Francis Group, an
informa business*

Typeset in Times New Roman by
RefineCatch Limited, Bungay, Suffolk
Paperback cover design by Jim Wilkie

British Library Cataloguing in Publication Data
A catalogue record for this book is available from the British Library

Library of Congress Cataloging-in-Publication Data
When death enters the therapeutic space : existential perspectives in
psychotherapy and counselling / edited by Laura Barnett.
p. ; cm.
Includes bibliographical references and index.
ISBN 978–0–415–41654–2 (hardback) – ISBN 978–0–415–41655–9
(pbk.) 1. Existential psychotherapy. 2. Counseling. 3. Death –
Psychological aspects. I. Barnett, Laura, 1953–
[DNLM: 1. Attitude to Death. 2. Psychotherapy – methods.
3. Bereavement. 4. Counseling – methods. 5. Existentialism – psychology.
6. Hospice Care – psychology.
WM 420 W567 2008]
RC489.E93W48 2008
616.89′14–dc22   2008010333

ISBN: 978–0–415–41654–2 (hbk)
ISBN: 978–0–415–41655–9 (pbk)

Indeed, it is not impossible . . . to define a 'person' by their dead
− . . . by the roads and paths which they have traced [in their
necropolis], by the teachings which they have decided to obtain
for themselves, by the 'roots' which they have put down there.

(Sartre 1996: 587)

To my clients and clinical supervisors, the living and the dead,
For what they have taught me,
And to the other dead in my 'necropolis', in remembrance and
   gratitude,
For the 'roots' they have given me.

To all of them, this book owes its existence.

CONTENTS

CONTENTS

CONTRIBUTORS

Laura Barnett (Editor) is an existential psychotherapist and supervisor working in the NHS and in private practice. She manages the Cancer Counselling Service and the Psychological Aftercare Service for Intensive Care Patients, which she set up at Mayday University Hospital, Croydon.

Dick Blackwell is a group analyst, family therapist and organization consultant in private practice who has for the past 20 years worked as psychotherapist and supervisor at the Medical Foundation for the Care of Victims of Torture. He is the author of *Counselling and Psychotherapy with Refugees* (Jessica Kingsley Publishers 2005) and a number of articles on psychotherapy in political contexts.

Ann Chalmers is Chief Executive of the Child Bereavement Charity, which supports families and educates professionals both in situations of baby and child death, and where children are bereaved of someone important in their lives. Ann is a trained integrative counsellor.

Emmy van Deurzen, Professor, Schiller International University, founded the School of Psychotherapy and Counselling (SPC) at Regent's College and the New School of Psychotherapy and Counselling (NSPC) at Schiller. She is also co-founder of the Centre for the Study of Conflict and Reconciliation, Sheffield. Her numerous books and articles on existential therapy include: *Existential Counselling and Psychotherapy in Practice*; *Paradox and Passion in Psychotherapy*; *Psychotherapy and the Quest for Happiness* (2008).

Alison Diffley is a clinical nurse specialist in palliative care and has been working in that field for almost 20 years. She is also a trained integrative counsellor and practices part time in primary care and in a hospital setting.

The Revd Hilary Fife is Senior Chaplain at Mayday University Hospital and was formerly chaplain at Marie Curie Hospice. She has many years' experience of working with the dying and the bereaved.

John Heaton is a psychiatrist who has been practising psychotherapy for some 40 years. He worked in the Philadelphia Association as a colleague of R.D. Laing and was Chair of the Training Committee. He is an editor of *Existential Analysis*. He has written three books: *The Eye: Phenomenology and Psychology of Function and Disorder*; *Introducing Wittgenstein*; *Wittgenstein and Psychoanalysis*.

David Horne is a registered existential psychotherapist and supervisor working in private practice and the public sector. He has worked for almost a decade as a supervisor for London Lighthouse/Terrence Higgins Trust. David is also a tutor and supervisor at the NSPC.

Melanie Lockett runs an independent practice as an integrative counsellor, supervisor and trainer. For the last 20 years she has supported people affected by cancer. She is employed in a variety of health settings, facilitating cancer support groups and offering clinical supervision to health professionals and counsellors.

Sanja Oakley trained as an existential psychotherapist and works as a therapist for Transport for London, as well as in private practice, using a range of body-oriented approaches to therapy. Sanja lectures and supervises at the NSPC and SPC.

Paul Smith-Pickard is an existential psychotherapist and supervisor in private practice, formerly a psychotherapist at King's College Hospital, working in acute healthcare. Paul has lectured at the SPC and NSPC and is a former Chair of the Society for Existential Analysis.

Bernice Sorensen is a psychotherapist, supervisor and trainer in private practice who has become increasingly involved in using narrative for research. She has written several articles and books, including *Counselling Young People* (with Judith Mabey, OUP 1995) and *Only Child Experience and Adulthood* (Palgrave 2008).

Sarah Young is an existential psychotherapist and supervisor in private practice. She also works as a volunteer for a hospice bereavement counselling service. Sarah has lectured and supervised at various institutions over the years, including the SPC and NSPC.

FOREWORD

Emmy van Deurzen

Memento mori.
Remember that you will die.

What does it mean to be faced with our mortality? For millennia philosophers have debated the brevity of human life. They have shown that our capacity for facing our own demise is a fundamental aspect of the human condition. They have argued that it is an advantage rather than a disadvantage to be able to reflect on death and they have shown us how we can live with the knowledge of our impermanence. But how do we apply such ideas to therapeutic work?

We know from the start that we all must die. Yet this obvious fact remains the object of much denial. Some argue that such denial may be a good thing and that it helps us to get on with our everyday lives. There is no doubt that death is the cause of much human suffering and yet the denial of death is also the root of much misery and pain. And there is a paradox here: for the less we let ourselves know about death, the harder it becomes to live life to the full. By the same token, the more we face up to death resolutely, the stronger we are for it.

This too has been noted by philosophers: that a constructive and courageous approach to death is probably one of the surest ways of living well. The existential approach to therapy, which is directly based in philosophy, takes the view that awareness of death, our limitations and our weaknesses is as important as awareness of our strengths and possibilities. To remember our mortality is the key to wisdom, as well as to a fuller life.

It is all very well and good to think philosophically about death as long as life can still be taken for granted. But what happens when we do not have a choice in the matter and are confronted with our mortality by force? What if our world has been turned upside down by a diagnosis of cancer or the loss of a loved one? What if we wake up in Intensive Care after a life-threatening accident? What if we are in refuge from the ravages of genocide, which have ripped apart our family and community?

What happens when death enters the therapeutic space? This book does not shy away from the realities of the threat, the pain and the tragedy that ensue from such confrontations with mortality. Here is a collection of the writing and observations of a wide range of experienced and considerate professionals who work with people in these predicaments. Their words open up a new vista on mortality that does not idealize or catastrophize. We get some rare glimpses into the abyss and what we see is much more promising than frightening.

Not all those who encounter death in life do so from the same perspective. The book shows the clear differences between encounters with death that are the result of loss, accidents, disasters, social upheavals, physical illness or personal choice. It also makes the distinction between those who welcome the image of death and those who abhor it. Yet while a suicidal person may experience death as a potential place of sanctuary and safety, the consequences for others may still be catastrophic and destructive for many years to come. Every death has many long-term effects that are often unspoken and unseen. Reading about these will open your eyes to a dimension of life not usually within our ken.

This book demonstrates the wide array of skilful interventions and considerate interactions employed by professionals working in a variety of therapeutic arenas. What happens to human beings when they are challenged to the limit and all their usual ways of coping and hiding defeat them? And what happens to those who work with people on the cliff face in this way? Much can be learnt from this book about what has been said on this topic by philosophers and practitioners alike. The subject is not approached with superficial gimmicks or quick fixes. This simply would not work. When the chasm of the ultimate situation is faced, only reality and truth will provide safe ground underfoot.

It is no mean feat to try to meet the other's distress in this situation. Is it equanimity and strength the therapist needs, or rather a willingness to be touched and remain in doubt about life and death?

The counsellor and therapist who are confronted with clients who have been faced with their mortality will find exactly what they need to approach this challenge with due care, consideration and philosophical clarity. This book is not just for those who work in extreme situations: death is relevant to us all. In looking down into the void we come face to face with our own limitations and limits and, in doing so, we recalibrate ourselves and our work to the critical level required of us. If we let ourselves be met and measured by death we will gain the depth of soul that therapeutic work requires. Remember, you too will die. What you learn about dying now will not only enhance your therapeutic work, but it may also make your personal life a better place to be. You may be surprised to find that reading about death can be a superbly uplifting and encouraging experience. This book recounts some very moving personal journeys which will inspire you and which may change the way in which you approach your own life, as well as its ultimate ending.

ACKNOWLEDGEMENTS

My thanks go to all the contributors to this book, for their contributions and their generous cooperation with me in my editorial capacity.

To Anthony Stadlen, for offering me the reassurance of his knowledge and critical acumen in agreeing to read my theoretical chapters; to Benjamin Barnett, Sara Brown and Melanie Lockett for their reactions to the theoretical 'inserts' and their helpful suggestions.

To Joanne Forshaw, Jane Harris and Kate Moysen at Routledge, and Penelope Allport, freelance copy-editor, for their accessibility, friendliness and helpfulness.

To Jane and Cyrille Cahen, my mother and stepfather, for so much and, more relevantly: for listening to my various drafts; for the pleasure of mutually enriching conversations about Dielian and existential therapy; and for puzzling with me over complex passages of existential philosophy – who would have thought that Heidegger could create such hilarity?

To my youthfully elderly father, for modelling astounding vitality, passion and commitment, while conscious of his mortality.

And finally to my husband Christopher, for being fully behind this project and giving me space for it; and for the privilege of our marriage, our children and our grandchildren.

HOW TO USE THIS BOOK

There are two main threads to this book – the dialogue between existential thought and therapeutic practice, and the theme of mortality. I have therefore directed the book at two different (yet overlapping) groups of readers – those with a special interest in the existential perspective and its philosophical roots, and those who are primarily concerned with the theme of working with clients who have been faced with their mortality.

Chapters 1 and 13 represent the theoretical foundation of the book. They are aimed at existential therapists and are likely to be difficult, in parts, for the reader approaching the philosophical roots of existential therapy for the first time.

There are, however, between chapters, brief theoretical 'inserts' that summarize in an accessible form the main concepts of existential thought and therapeutic practice. *These inserts do not refer specifically to the chapters which they precede or follow*: each one, as an aspect of existence, is present as an issue, whether directly addressed or not, in every counselling room.

Finally, this is not a 'how-to-do-it' book, but a 'what-it's-like' book. (All case vignettes in the book are either composite characterizations or based on specific clients whose identifying features have been removed.) However, as we enter the worlds of these different client groups, we need to be mindful of the dangers of overgeneralization and 'normalization': let us not forget that each client's experience is unique.

INTRODUCTION

Laura Barnett

Cellular death sculpts our internal and external form ... We are, at every moment, partly dying and partly being reborn.
(Ameisen 2003: 29–30)[1]

Intimations of mortality

Death is the inescapable end-game of our life: if it fills us with terror, how can we possibly take a step forward without inner turmoil. The conventional remedy is to avoid thinking about it.
(Montaigne 1946, I: XX, 96)

Satish Kumar was four when his father died and it filled him with the terror of death. He used to listen to the travelling Jain monks speak of the cycle of life and death, and of conquering death, and he dreamt of joining their order. When he was nine, his mother relented. Yet, by the age of 17, Satish had come to realize that in his attempt to overcome death he was in fact avoiding life; he ran away from the order and threw himself into the world. He continued to devote himself to his spirituality and his ideals of non-violence, but discovered life, and its limitations, in all its richness (Kumar 2006).

Death is a natural and inescapable part of life, we are born to die. Both therapist and client one day will die; it may even be before their contracted time for therapy is over. Death may suddenly irrupt into the therapeutic space – through the loss of a relative or friend, through a diagnosis of life-threatening illness, through a natural or man-made disaster on a vast scale (tsunamis and hurricanes, bombings and train crashes, etc.). To avoid thinking about death is not the remedy: death has an important place in the therapeutic encounter. But thinking about death, making it an integral part of our therapeutic work, does not mean a therapy of doom and gloom: paradoxically, a focus on death in therapy is a focus on life. For, 'To be mindful of death is to be mindful of freedom' (Montaigne 1946: 99).

Existential philosophy is often thought of, in the UK, as a gloomy, angst-permeated philosophy; but that is to ignore its strong emphasis on anxiety as

1

a catalyst for exploring the possibilities that are open to us – for better engaging with our lives. To see but the dark side of existentialism can be likened to Christians who speak only of sin and punishment and have forgotten Christianity's message of love and forgiveness – a very common occurrence among my Christian cancer and Intensive Care clients.

Although death is culture-bound in terms of the attitudes, customs and rituals that surround it, it is an undisputed universal given of existence. It is the subject of countless sayings and proverbs, poems and novels in every language, yet it occupies a relatively small place in psychotherapeutic literature and training. Did you ever have a module on death? How often in your training did you talk about death – not death in general or death as a philosophical topic, but death as it affected you personally? Did death ever enter your 'personal and professional development group' hour – and how was it dealt with? Did you each allow it to challenge you to the core or was it, conveniently, someone else's affair? For every one of you who can answer these questions in the affirmative, I know that there are others who cannot. This is not a matter for criticism, but for reflection.

In the face of death, therapeutic work is not one-sided (is it ever?): unless professional boundaries have become barriers, when death enters the therapeutic space it touches both therapist and client.

Existential perspectives

There is no such thing as '*the* existential perspective' in psychotherapy and counselling. Not only are there as many existential perspectives as there are existential therapists, but 'existential' can refer to different orders of reflection:

1   Our personal reflections, as human beings, on questions of life and death and what it means to 'exist'.
2   The reflections of specific 'existential' philosophers on those themes.
3   Our personal dialogues, as therapists, with the work of (some of) these existential philosophers.
4   Personal dialogues with the thought and practice of other therapists who define themselves as 'existential' and have engaged in personal reflection with existential philosophy.

While I define an 'existential therapist' quite strictly, as one who engages with both the first and the third form of reflection, I believe that therapists of differing theoretical orientations can have an existential stance in their practice; what is more, through the very process of integrating that stance into their original way of working, they have something of value to offer us existential therapists.

What can be said to underpin an existential perspective in therapy? The therapist's personal dialogue with what it means to 'exist'; a holistic and non-deterministic view of human existence; a lifelong questioning of one's assumptions; a person-to-person way of being as therapists with our clients that is not pathologizing and not based on taking the position of an expert dispensing interpretations; an openness to be challenged by our clients to the core of our personal and professional belief system.

Some of the contributors to this book refer to themselves as 'existential therapists', others as 'integrative'; all have allowed themselves to be touched, challenged and called into question by their confrontation with death, in their lives and in the counselling room. Each in their way has experienced the creative potential of facing up to their own mortality and they give voice to it, directly or indirectly, in these pages.

Book outline

Chapter 1 explores some of the philosophical roots of existential therapies and summarizes the principal approaches to existential therapy. It concludes by examining the diagnosis of post-traumatic stress disorder and contrasting it with an existential perspective. Chapters 2, 3 and 4 deal with health-related issues.

In Chapter 2 Melanie Lockett movingly weaves her own story into that of her clients, as she explores the impact of her recent experience of breast cancer on her therapeutic and supervisory practice as a cancer counsellor. Yalom's 'ultimate concerns' provide the chapter's backdrop.

In Chapter 3 David Horne tackles the emotive subject of HIV. He shows how clients can be overwhelmed by a sense of catastrophe, yet also discover the 'vitality of death': they can learn to re-engage with life in a fuller and more satisfying manner.

In Chapter 4 I describe the disruption to a person's whole being-in-the-world that can follow a stay in Intensive Care. It draws attention to the phenomenon of 'lost time' and to the importance of Intensive Care dreams and hallucinations.

In Chapter 5 Sanja Oakley's journey has taken her away from a strong existential position to a firm belief in 'trauma therapy' as a specialized field. Using examples derived from her work in the immediate aftermath of the 'London 7/7 bombings', she warns us that our clients may be too overwhelmed by traumatic shock to engage immediately with existential explorations.

Next, Dick Blackwell opens up before us the world of refugee survivors of torture and organized violence in Chapter 6. He describes how 'the fragility of human existence, the uncertainty of life and the threat of death are central to the experience of becoming a refugee'.

In Chapter 7 John Heaton takes Kierkegaard's *Sickness unto Death* as the starting point for his philosophical reflections on suicide and despair. Heaton stresses the dangers of applying learnt theory and skills to the suicidal client.

He also reflects on the problems of language as a means of communicating and appropriating the experience of despair. Important considerations in therapeutic work with suicidal clients follow his chapter.

The next two chapters deal with the end of life. In Chapter 8 Paul Smith-Pickard depicts three encounters with patients who have been given a short prognosis. He lets us sense the shift in relation from that of the 'healthcare professional' approaching the hospital patient's bedside to a meeting between client and therapist. 'This is raw psychotherapy', leaving behind 'the comfort of the consulting room' and of a firm time frame. Merleau-Ponty is Smith-Pickard's principal philosophical reference here.

Chapter 9 brings together a palliative care clinical nurse specialist (Alison Diffley), a hospital chaplain (The Revd Hilary Fife) and a counsellor (Melanie Lockett), as they relate to 'Kate'. It explores 'all there is to be done when there is nothing left to do' (Saunders, cited in Hirsch 2003: 168). Their moving and intimate chapter will be of interest to nurses, chaplains and counsellors alike.

In the first of two chapters on therapy with the bereaved, Sarah Young offers a brief overview of the history of 'bereavement therapy' in Chapter 10. She follows this with an alternative, existential (Heideggerian) perspective, which explores bereavement within the context of the person's whole life.

In Chapter 11 Ann Chalmers uses her personal and professional experience to help us understand the world of bereaved parents. This is a loss that goes 'against nature' and, like our clients, we may feel overwhelmed by it and powerless to help – as indeed they felt powerless to protect their child from death. Both Young and Chalmers stress the tension between the clients' need for a 'continuing bond' with the person they are mourning, assumptions about their need to 'move on' and anxiety that they can never do so.

Chapter 12 arose out of congruence: therapists too are mortal! Bernice Sorensen reminds us that, whatever our present circumstances, we may need to think about preparing our clients and supervisees for the possibility of our death.

In Chapter 13, I further develop the book's theme of 'dialogue' with reference to Buber, Rogers and Lévinas.

Finally, in the Conclusion, I draw the themes of the book together and look at the therapeutic relationship, where death has entered the therapeutic space.

Note

1   In my chapters, all translations from the French are my own.

References

Ameisen, J.-C. (2003) Dialogues entre la vie et la mort, in Ameisen, J.-C., Hervieu-Léger, D. and Hirsch, E. (eds) *Qu'est-ce-que mourir?*, Paris: Editions le Pommier.

Hirsch, E. (2003) Face à l'autre qui va mourir, in Ameisen, J.-C., Hervieu-Léger, D. and Hirsch, E. (eds) *Qu'est-ce-que mourir?*, Paris: Editions le Pommier.

Kumar, S. (4 March 2006) BBC Radio 4.

Montaigne, M. (1946 [1580]) *Essais*, Paris: Bibliothèque de la Pléiade, Nouvelle Revue Française.

1

THE PHILOSOPHICAL ROOTS OF EXISTENTIAL THERAPIES

Laura Barnett

The expressions 'existentialism' and 'existential philosophy' are used to refer to a number of nineteenth- and twentieth-century philosophers, most of whom would not have categorized themselves in this way. Its central figures were Kierkegaard and Nietzsche, Heidegger, Sartre and Merleau-Ponty. While the first two were major influences on the other three and on many existential therapists, I shall be focusing in this chapter on Heidegger, whose work has had, without doubt, the greatest impact on existential therapy. His philosophy could be said to underlie every one of the characteristics of an existential perspective in therapy, as summarized in the Introduction.

When I say that many of the concepts which Heidegger articulated are fundamental to existential practice, I do not mean that we should apply them to our work like a theory, skills or a tool: rather, they offer us new ways of understanding human existence and this can have an immense impact on our therapeutic practice. Heidegger sees philosophy as:

> a questioning in which we inquire into beings as a whole, and inquire
> in such a way that in so doing we ourselves, the questioners, are
> thereby also . . . placed into question . . . It deals with the whole and
> it grips existence through and through.
>
> (Heidegger 1995: 9)

I have also found that reflecting on my clients has thrown a different light on some of Heidegger's ideas; thus a two-way dialogue has emerged for me between existential thought and therapeutic practice.

Heideggerian thought and its relevance to existential therapy

(In this section, all references, otherwise specified, are to Heidegger. For *Being and Time*, the first page number refers to the English translation, the second, to the German edition.)

Context

Heidegger (1889–1976) spent most of his life in the Black Forest area of South West Germany. There he became professor of philosophy at the University of Freiburg, later turning down the opportunity of a professorial chair in Berlin. (Roots have an important place in Heidegger's philosophy.) In relation to his philosophical heritage, Heidegger's thought is marked by his 'deconstruction'[1] of traditional metaphysics, his opposition to Cartesian dualism[2] and a return to Ancient Greek philosophy.

For his method of 'hermeneutic phenomenology', he is indebted both to Dilthey's theory of interpretation (hermeneutics) and to his former professor, Husserl, whose method he crucially modified. Like Husserl, Heidegger sought to rid himself of the baggage of traditional philosophy and to get back 'to the things themselves' as they appear to us.[3] But they disagreed fundamentally about what these things were:

> What must be experienced as 'the things themselves' in accordance with the principle of phenomenology? Is it consciousness and its objectivity [the aim of Husserl's 'transcendental phenomenology'] or is it the being of beings in its unconcealedness and concealment?
>
> (2003c: 74)

Unlike Husserl, Heidegger does not seek to observe phenomena in a void, suspending all personal assumptions, for in any enquiry we 'must be guided beforehand by what is sought.' (1962: 25; 5) Heidegger wants to uncover the very ground of these assumptions, to discover what it is about us and the world that enables us to encounter the world. Such a project cannot proceed in a void, only in the midst of beings. However, as Heidegger likes to remind us, 'being intrinsically inclines toward self-concealment'[4] (2000: 121). Hence there is always a more primordial and more universal aspect of being to uncover and the process of interpretation (hermeneutics) is never ending. His attempt to elucidate the 'meaning of being' became Heidegger's lifelong quest, which he approached from a number of different angles.

The question

'For manifestly you have long been aware of what you mean when you use the expression "being". We, however, who used to think we understood it, have now become perplexed' (1962: 19; 1). It is with this quote from Plato that Heidegger opens his book *Being and Time*, one of the most influential philosophical works of the twentieth century. First, we need to clarify what Heidegger means by 'being' and 'beings'. The word 'beings'[5] does not simply refer to animals and human beings, but to 'any entity, physical or otherwise with which we may have dealings, whether real, illusionary or imagined'

(Fried and Polt 2000: x); that includes 'products of human work', such as 'Bach's fugues' and 'the cathedral of Strassburg' (2000: 81). In other words, while the above are *'fundamentally diverse "kinds" of beings'* (1995: 275), what all these things have in common is that they *are*.

What Heidegger is enquiring into is the 'being' of these varied beings – what do we mean by it, how can we discover it, can it reveal itself to us? Why does the very question of the meaning of being seem so strange to us? Heidegger argues that this question is at the core of our Western philosophical tradition, from Early Greek philosophy to Plato and Aristotle, for whom it constituted the 'first philosophy'. However, according to Heidegger, with the development of philosophy as an academic discipline in ancient and medieval times, the question of being became misunderstood, 'covered over' and forgotten. Heidegger's aim is to 'uncover' being and bring it into 'unconcealment'; this involves returning to the sources of Western philosophical thought, engaging with that thought and allowing it to challenge us personally. For the question of 'being' is not some intellectual debate that happens to have interested philosophers of Ancient Greece, it is, Heidegger insists, a question that concerns each and every one of us. We have lost our sense of wonderment (*thauma*, which characterized the attitude of the Ancient Greeks). We no longer ask ourselves (as Leibniz once did): 'Why are there beings at all instead of nothing?' (2000: 1, first line).

A few years ago, my husband and I spent the night in a refuge on a mountain in Switzerland which was famed for its stunning sunrise views. We got up at 4.30 am; when the sun began to rise, we were so overwhelmed by the magical splendour of this sight that, most uncharacteristically for us, our impulse was to embrace the other people who were watching with us. It was a while before I reminded myself that this sunrise was a daily occurrence! Science fiction or thoughts of a nuclear disaster can also bring us to question our daily experience of beings and being: imagine a post-nuclear explosion – desert, wasteland, a leaden sky, nothing; and then one day a blade of grass, a cloud, a birdsong. How this blade of grass, this cloud, this birdsong, why is it that they *are* now or at all? Where have they come from? What are they to us? Likewise, clients remind us how life-threatening events can reawaken this sense of wonder in us; for example, T recalled with tears in his eyes the unforgettable day he was able to touch his nose again.

The quest for the meaning of being: Being and Time *(1927)*

In *Being and Time*, Heidegger's aim is 'to work out the question of the meaning of being and to do so concretely' (1962: 19; 1), through a study of one particular kind of being, namely human being. He does not use the German equivalent of 'human being' or 'man', but prefers the word *Dasein*, a common German word for 'existence' (made up of *da* 'there' + *sein* 'to be'); his reasons for doing so will emerge from what follows. (It is the custom to keep the German word Dasein in English translations of Heidegger. However, to avoid the danger of Dasein becoming a sort of neuter person, I shall at times use 'human existence' and Heidegger's own later term 'ek-sistence'.)

Why does he choose to approach the question of being through Dasein? Because, he argues, it is the only being for whom 'in its very being, that being is an issue for it' (1962: 32; 12). However intelligent some animals may be, they do not have (as far as we know) the capacity to ask themselves about the meaning of their being, their place in the universe, the purpose of their existence. We do; and the very fact that we can formulate these questions for ourselves, Heidegger argues, points to our having a privileged relationship to being: '*Understanding of being is itself a definite characteristic of Dasein's being*' (1962: 32; 12). That is why human existence can be questioned about its being. Its characteristics are not of the same kind as the properties of a table or a tree. Rather: '*The essence of Dasein lies in its existence*' (1962: 67; 42). My *being*, the way I *am*, depends on the way I live my life and the choices I make from among the possibilities before me. It is therefore through a concrete exploration of Dasein's everyday way of existing that the search will have to proceed. These concrete examples will throw light on characteristics of individual Daseins ('ontic', 'existentiell' characteristics) and on Dasein's essential characteristics ('ontological' characteristics or 'existentialia'). The distinction between beings and being, between ontic and ontological is usually referred to as the 'ontological difference'; it is fundamental to Heidegger's thought and also has its place in existential therapy (Cohn 2002).

Being-in-the-world

Heidegger defines human existence's specific way of being as 'being-in-the-world'. That concept is one of the lynchpins of his thought and it underpins philosophically the holistic character of existential therapy. What does Heidegger mean by 'being-in-the-world'? The hyphens indicate that this is a 'unitary phenomenon' (1962: 78; 53) and the richness and innovative character of this concept lies in the very fact that one cannot separate its three elements – 'being', 'in' and 'world'. This makes 'being-in-the-world' difficult to clarify, as none of its elements can be viewed on its own and defined in isolation. Instead, Heidegger approaches being-in-the-world from different perspectives. One overarching way of describing the being-in-the-world of human existence is 'care'.[6] 'Care', *Sorge*, for Heidegger, does not mean 'caring for' and is more basic than 'caring about'. Ek-sistence cares in that it *cares that* there are beings rather than nothing; that fact is meaningful to it. Heidegger goes on to illuminate from different angles the ways ek-sistence 'cares': its relationship to objects, to other ek-sistences, to itself, its life and its possibilities, including that of its death.

In what way is ek-sistence 'in' the world and what is meant by 'world'? It is easiest to start with what '*in*' does not mean: ek-sistence is not *in* the world like an apple is in a bowl, '*in*' does not express being contained; nor does it express some form of participation in a totality of beings. Rather, 'in' refers to ek-sistence's 'dwelling' in a 'system of meaningful relations' (1962: 160; 122). For example, a hammer is not first and foremost a wooden stick with a metal end-piece, it is an implement, which most of us recognize as a tool for banging in nails – one which I mainly use for hanging up pictures, but which P, my client's father, likes to put beside his pillow for his protection when he goes to sleep at night. From this example, it is clear that our relationship to a hammer is based on both its common use and its personal associations[7] – we have both shared meanings and individual meanings. 'Meaningfulness' and what we *understand* something *as* are fundamental to the elucidation of Heidegger's concept of 'world'. This is the essential way, for Heidegger, in which ek-sistence's relationship to its 'world' differs from an animal's relationship to its 'environment' (1995: 343).

Heidegger's metaphor for ek-sistence is that of a light clearing (*Lichtung*) in a dark forest 'illuminated' (*erleuchtet*) by the sun's rays (1962: 171; 133).[8] He believes that what enables ek-sistence to perceive its world and attach meanings to it is its 'character of having been laid open' (1962: 105; 75). He calls it Dasein's 'disclosedness'. This concept has a central place in Heidegger's thought. It expresses ek-sistence's ontological openness and receptivity to being and to the world, as well as its capacity to open up and disclose the world and itself to itself.

These characteristics of disclosedness and meaningfulness underpin philosophically fundamental elements of existential therapeutic practice. They highlight the importance of meaning and the fact that, while our shared meanings offer us sufficient common ground to enable us to communicate, we constantly need to clarify what our clients are saying and ascertain what, for them, is the significance of it. These concepts underlie our need to constantly question our assumptions about our clients and their world, together with our assumptions about our own world. Also, while some of our clients may present as 'closed' to experiences and to the views of others, we must remember that openness and receptivity are existential characteristics of human existence, which may become 'existentielly' (see p. 10) obscured and closed off to a certain extent.

Heidegger shows how our 'moods' or 'attunement', *Befindlichkeit, Stimmung* affect our understanding of our world: that understanding changes with the way we feel disposed towards it (the literal meaning of *Befindlichkeit*) and how we tune into it (the literal meaning of *Stimmung*) at any given moment. When we speak of seeing things 'through rose-tinted spectacles', the glass as being 'half full' or 'half empty', our idioms attest to the power of our optimistic and pessimistic attunements. Whatever the mood, it colours the way we perceive and understand the world. Heidegger's originality, however, is to develop this much further. We are, he explains, always 'attuned' in some way, we cannot not be so – what may feel like no mood at all, may be a 'pallid' mood or a form of indifference. To find ourselves 'always already' disposed in a certain way is an 'existentiale', an essential characteristic of Dasein's 'disclosedness'.

Heidegger views some moods, such as anxiety, boredom, despair and joy, as being 'fundamental attunements' (*Grundstimmungen*). These moods are better able to cast light on both our finitude and our 'thrownness' (the fact that, from the moment of our birth, we always find ourselves 'already' in a certain situation). We are 'thrown' into a particular era, country, locality, socio-economic category, into particular family dynamics, with particular sets of genes. We have no control whatsoever over our own birth. These are the 'givens' of our existence and there is nothing that we can do about them. This 'thrownness' (also called 'facticity') is an essential characteristic of Dasein's being and existence, it is one of its *existentialia*'. Our 'thrownness' does not simply refer to the circumstances of our birth, but to every situation that we find ourselves already in – such as the situation you are in right now as you read this. Much of the work of therapy deals with helping clients realize that they cannot change what has already happened (the givens of their situation), but that they can change the way they look at what has happened and, by changing their perspective, uncover other meanings and possibilities. Meanings and possibilities depend on how we understand our present situation, our past and our plans for the near and distant future:

> T sustained severe injuries as a result of a car accident; his condition had been critical. T's anger and disbelief, that something like this could have happened to him through no fault of his own, were mixed with a sense of his own possibilities and of what he saw as his responsibility towards himself.

'Dasein is . . . *thrown possibility* through and through. Dasein is the possibility of being-free for its ownmost potentiality-for-being. Its being-possible is transparent to itself in different possible ways and degrees' (1962: 183; 144). Or as T put it: 'I didn't fucking ask for this, it's not my fault . . . but I'm not fucking going to curl up in a corner and be a victim.' T 'projected himself upon' the possibilities before him. He was able to understand some of these possibilities as being still open to him, as paths to follow, as choices to make, while many others in his situation would have seen most of these paths as now being closed to them. In that sense, our freedom is closely linked to how we understand the world and our possibilities: 'The kind of being which Dasein has, as potentiality-for-being, lies existentially in understanding' (1962: 183; 143).

Hence, for Heidegger, the three fundamental aspects of ek-sistence's openness to itself and its world are: attunement, understanding and its ability to express the intelligibility of being-in-the-world, namely 'discourse'. They are aspects of our relationship of 'care' towards the world, ways in which we let other beings, other ek-sistences, other possibilities etc. matter to us. They are a way of characterizing the 'in' of our being-*in*-the-world. Understanding, attunement and discourse 'together constitute Dasein's "existentiality", the being of the "there" [the "sein" of the "Da" of Da-sein]' (1962: 203; 161). All three are central to therapy.

Authenticity and falling

There are many aspects to our being-in-the-world. In *Being and Time*, Heidegger makes a distinction that has been very influential in the world of therapy: we can be 'authentically' or 'inauthentically' in-the-world. Or rather, we are most of the time 'inauthentic', but may have decisive moments of authenticity. The word 'authentic', like the German 'eigentlich' which it is translating, is based on its etymological sense of 'one's own' (German 'eigen' and Greek 'autos': own, self). Unfortunately 'authentic' has taken on a life of its own in therapeutic and common parlance and lost its original etymological, philosophical and therapeutic meaning of making our lives our own.

Our average everyday existence is inauthentic. We tend to live according to the customs of our era and country (whether in agreement or in rebellion); we hold received values, beliefs, expectations and opinions, all handed down to us by the indeterminate *das Man*,[9] the 'they' – society, the Church, the media, our family, our peers, etc. As human existence is always in relation to others – even a recluse is in a relation to others (albeit in one of avoidance) – we fall with ease into this way of living according to what the 'they' dictates. To a large extent we need to, for we need a shared basis of customs, values, meanings, etc. to be able to live with others. However, when ek-sistence relies on the opinion of the 'they' in all things, it can be said to have 'lost' its own voice, its own self and adopted a 'they-self'. Heidegger refers to this state as 'falling'. 'Fallen' ek-sistence 'in its average everydayness' is 'amidst' the world, 'at home' in the world, so 'fascinated by' it, that it does not seek the opportunity to stop and take stock, to think for itself about itself:

> The self of everyday Da-sein is the *they-self*, which we distinguish from the *authentic*, that is to say the expressly grasped *self*[10]. . . . *Nearly* always, it is not 'I', in the sense of my own self, that 'am', but rather the others, in the guise of the 'they'.
>
> (2006: 129, my translation)

Being inauthentic and 'in thrall' to the 'they' is just as much part of ek-sistence as being authentic: falling is an existential characteristic of ek-sistence. For Heidegger, the difference between authentic and inauthentic existence is linked to the way we relate to our own death. Every ek-sistence is characterised by 'mineness' – it is always the ek-sistence of one particular 'I', but death is one's 'ownmost possibility' and is non-transferable. While Dasein can live without fully owning its life, it alone can await and die its death. The 'they' seeks to put our mind at rest by first shifting the focus from mortality to the event of death, then passing death off as a common occurrence that comes to us all one day. By expressing ourselves in proverbs and generalities, using plural or indefinite pronouns ('we', 'us', 'one') we do not allow ourselves to engage with the 'mineness' of death: there is a world of difference between saying 'death comes to us all' and 'I shall die'. The former utterance is fallen ek-sistence's 'ambiguous' response, lulled by the 'tranquil-lizing' words of the 'they' ('death may well come to us all, but it does not concern me, or not for a while yet'). Dying has become 'perverted into an event of public occurrence which the "they" encounters' (1962: 297; 253). Saying 'I shall die' expresses my awareness of *my own* mortality – death, not so much as an event in the future, but as a certain yet indefinite possibility of my present existence (I know it will happen, but I don't know when).

> Pete had been stationed as a soldier in Afghanistan and had fought in Iraq, but when his mother was diagnosed with terminal cancer, his world fell apart. With the realization that his mother was going to die, he was suddenly faced with his own mortality, which, he felt, he had kept hidden 'behind an iron curtain'.

How could Pete not be aware of his mortality, when his life had been so seriously and repeatedly threatened and what had brought about his sudden realization? From a Heideggerian perspective, while he may have feared specific threats, such as the possibility of an ambush or a bombing, he did not allow himself to face the overwhelming anxiety that accompanies the thought of one's own death. Thus for years Pete had managed to feel invulnerable to death, secure behind the 'blockade' that he, like many of his fellow soldiers, had built around his anxiety (even the metaphors are grounded in his military world). It was only when Pete's mother was dying and his world fell apart that he was able, in therapy, to sit with his anxiety; he began to engage with the possibility of his own death and redefine his goals and priorities in life.

In *Being and Time*, Heidegger sees anxiety as a 'fundamental attunement'. Anxiety is 'disclosive': it faces Dasein with its mortality and thrownness – the fact that it has no control over its origin. (In a later lecture in 1995, Heidegger mentions other such 'fundamental attunements': joy, boredom[11] and despair.) For Pete, anxiety about his mortality also opened up possibilities and became a catalyst for change. 'Anxiety makes manifest in Dasein . . . its *being-free for* the freedom of choosing itself and taking hold of itself' (1962: 232; 188). How does that freedom manifest itself? Heidegger speaks of the silent 'call of conscience', which suddenly, 'out of nowhere', makes itself heard. He is not referring to conscience in the everyday moral sense of

14

what my conscience dictates: it is the '*the call of care*' (1962: 322; 277) in which I remind myself of what really matters to me. 'The call of conscience has the character of an appeal to Dasein by calling it to its ownmost potentiality-for-being-itself; and this is done by way of summoning it to its ownmost being-guilty' (1962: 314; 269). In 'being-guilty' Heidegger is playing on the different meanings that are subtly intertwined in *Schuldig*, the German word for guilty: *Schuld* is both 'guilt' and 'debt'. This guilt/debt is twofold. English can render one aspect of it with a similar metaphor: I am *schuldig*, 'guilty' in that I '*owe* it to myself' to make changes in my life. This realization, and the 'resolute' decision to put it into practice, may enable me to see possibilities that, until now, I was not prepared to contemplate. At the same time, by the very act of choosing a possibility, I am also, in a sense, 'guilty' of not fulfilling another. (Macquarrie's translations of '*Entschlossenheit*' as 'resoluteness' miss the connection with '*Erschlossenheit*', 'disclosedness' which is crucial for Heidegger; 'resolute disclosedness' [Besteigui 2005] is preferable and highlights the connection between authenticity and truth.)

I mentioned at the beginning that 'care' was an overarching description of ek-sistence as being-in-the-world, which could be illuminated from various angles. It should now be possible to demystify the following piece of 'Heideggerese', Heidegger's summary of 'care': 'ahead-of-itself-being-already-in-(the-world) as being-amidst beings encountered within-the-world' (1962: 237; 192). I am ahead-of-myself, since, in order to make sense of the world in which I live and take decisions, I am always 'projecting myself upon' meanings and possibilities. As 'thrown' and always 'attuned', I am already-in-(the-world). And I am amidst-the-world, in that being always involves being-with others and making use of things; also because, as 'fallen' most of the time, I fall in with the customs and opinions of others. 'Ahead-of-itself', 'already-in', 'amidst', by referring to future, past and present respectively, situate Dasein in relation to time. Hence: '*The primordial unity of the structure of care lies in temporality*' (1962: 375; 327).

On the whole, we live our day-to-day lives in the here and now, and consider the present to be guiding our lives: we may 'retain' past experiences, but we no longer question their significance and we only look to the future to daydream or make plans. Heidegger argues that, in moments of authenticity, Dasein can hold its existence together in one glance, both its 'thrown' past and its indefinite future. In that 'moment of vision',[12] it realizes that it lacks control over both its foundation and its ending – 'it *is* the null basis of its own nullity' (1962: 354; 307). Looking to the future with 'resolute openness', in full 'anticipation' of its death, ek-sistence can face the fact that although it has been 'thrown' and is a 'null basis', it 'has been released from its basis . . . *to* itself, so as to be *as this basis*' (1962: 330; 285). That is, it sees that it is responsible to and for itself. And reflecting on the past, by 'retrieving' it and 'going over' it (*wiederholen*) in a constructive way, Dasein can uncover as yet undiscovered possibilities. I would like to think that therapy offers many such 'moments of vision' in which: 'In one's coming back resolutely to one's thrownness, there is a handing down to oneself of the possibilities that have come down to one, but not necessarily, *as* having come down' (1962: 435; 383). It involves a revisiting and 'revision' of the past in the light of and for the sake of the future. Certainly, working with people who have been confronted with their mortality, I often sense these moments when, for a client: 'Anticipation reveals to Dasein its lostness in the they-self, and brings it face to face with the possibility of being itself ... in an impassioned **freedom towards death**' (1962: 311; 266). 'Freedom towards death', for Heidegger, far from meaning a desire for death, refers to a freedom for life: for an existence free from anxiously covering up its finitude – 'the possibility of the absolute impossibility of Dasein' (1962: 294; 250), for an 'impassioned freedom' to engage with any situation in which it is thrown and an 'unshakeable joy' in discovering its ownmost potentialities (1962: 358; 310).

This section has focused on some of Heidegger's main ideas in *Being and Time*, because of their concrete existential character and their influence on existential therapy. His later approaches to the question of being have received little attention in existential therapy in the UK and yet they too have much to offer us.

The quest in Heidegger's later work [13]

Heidegger regarded his *Introduction to Metaphysics* (2000) as an excellent introduction to his thought and complementary to *Being and Time* in its further elucidation of the question of being. Ironically, it is also a good introduction to the way in which Heidegger's originality as a thinker became perverted in political action. Heidegger here turns to Early Greek philosophy in his search for a more 'primordial' uncovering of being. Notwithstanding his often highly idiosyncratic and controversial etymologies and interpretations, Heidegger can illuminate these beautiful, tantalizing fragments and the words at their heart – *aletheia*, *logos*, *physis* and *harmonie*. He points out that in Indo-European languages the verb 'to be' uses three different roots: **bhu*, 'to emerge'; **es* 'to live' and **ves* 'to abide' – even English still bears traces of this (to *be*, he *is*, he *was*). How is it that these 'three initial and vividly definite meanings: emerging, living and abiding' (2000: 76) have died out? 'How are the three stems unified? What carries and leads the saga of being?' (2000: 76).

It is 'physis', which, for Heidegger, as the 'emerging-abiding sway' represents being in a fundamental and 'originary' way. However, 'being [emerging appearance][14] intrinsically inclines towards self-concealment' (2000: 121).[15] For Heidegger, the process of bringing being out of concealment is the essence of *aletheia* (truth) (cognate with *lanthanein* 'to conceal' and *Lethe*, the river of forgetfulness [Chantraine 1974: 618]). Heidegger's concept of truth as 'unconcealing', 'uncovering', is one that is thought provoking and to which we shall return; so is his claim that our very humanity is intimately linked with our capacity to apprehend that emergence of being (2000: 150). Heidegger argues that asking the question about the meaning of being is an essential, fundamental expression of ourselves as human beings. It is something that we need to do to live our lives in a rich and meaningful way – this need is not a moral obligation, but an 'urgency', *Not* (2000: 180). The question about being 'has its ground in a leap by which human beings leap away from all the previous safety of their Dasein, be it genuine or presumed' (2000: 6). This, he adds, is more likely to occur in moments of 'despair', 'boredom' or 'joy'. In traumatic situations, our clients ask: 'Why?' 'Why did it happen?' 'Why me?' Underlying these questions, though not phrased in those terms, is the 'broadest', 'deepest', 'most originary question' (2000: 2), the question of the meaning of being – of why things are at all, why they are as they are, of why I myself am, etc. This also challenges us, as therapists, to tear ourselves away from our complacency, to sit with that uncomfortable loss of safety and think about our relationship to being.

To conjugate the verb 'to be' involves, we saw, 'emerging', 'living' and 'dwelling'. Heidegger now asks us to attend to the way we 'dwell' in our world. He argues that we have become alienated from our world, no longer at home in it. In *Being and Time*, he had introduced the notion of the uncanny (*unheimlich*, literally 'not-at-home-like') for Dasein's experience of anxiety. He had shown how, in our attempt to allay this feeling, we try to feel at home by falling in with the 'they' or falling prey to the busy-ness of this world. Heidegger's focus has now shifted. He is referring to our lack of rootedness within the 'fourfold', *das Geviert*: we have lost the sense of belonging, as mortals, on this earth, beneath the sky, before 'the gods' (1971b). *Ereignis*, the 'happening of appropriation',[16] becomes the most important word in Heidegger's later thought: it represents that co-created space and event, within the fourfold, between beings and being, where/when human beings appropriate the truth of being as it unfolds. This requires a different, more 'reserved' way of being attuned to the world: the emphasis is less on 'resolute willing' and more on 'contemplative thinking' (*Besinnung*) – on being open to the 'mystery' of being, to its history of emerging and self-concealing; on *Gelassenheit*, 'letting be' (Heidegger 1966; see insert p. 145). He calls us to realize: 'The human being is not the lord of beings. The human being is the shepherd of being' (1998c: 260). Heidegger sees in the common phrase *es gibt*, 'there is' (literally 'it gives'), more than the 'givens' of existence in the sense encountered so far: it now represents for him a true expression of the mystery of being and the way 'it grants'. Being grants, being 'destines'. In his search for the meaning of being, Heidegger has come to see history as the truth of being as it unfolds – a constant struggle between unconcealment (i.e. truth) and concealment ('untruth' the mysterious ground, or rather *Ab-grund*, abyss from which truth arises; Heidegger 1998a, 1998b). He links *denken* and *danken*: to 'think' the question of being is to offer 'thanks' (in Stassen 2003:

84). Heidegger is turning more and more to poetry (Hölderlin in particular) and poetic language to voice his thought.

Heidegger understands the alienation of modern times as primarily due to an excess of 'unconcealment', leaving no room for its mysterious ground, in an urge for ever more 'presencing'.[17] Though counter-intuitive, this notion can be thought of more concretely, for example, as a hologram in which only one facet ever comes to the fore; or as music in which we could only hear tunes in major keys, missing their interplay with tunes in minor keys in which they were 'concealed', missing the unfolding of the truth of music. In therapy, when clients throw too much light on one story (issue, quality, fault, etc.), they can become blinded by it and miss its interplay with the other stories, within which it is imbedded. What is happening to us human beings within the constant drive to 'calculative thinking' and 'presencing' of things is Heidegger's main issue with technology. He is not against technological progress per se. He is opposed to its prevailing mindset, which he calls *Gestell*,[18] 'System': our prevailing way of 'revealing' has become one of 'Unlocking, transforming, storing, distributing' (2003b: 288). As masters of System, we seek to dominate our world. His image of Nature as 'standing in reserve' ready to be 'mobilized' is timely and powerful.[19] We have become caught up in the System. System prevails and, with it, our alienation from the fourfold. *Gestell* 'blocks the shining-forth and holding-sway of truth' (2003b: 297). Heidegger argues that art and poetry (which, like technology, were once also part of Ancient Greek *technē*), while revealing and illuminating what they depict, still retain an ambiguity: unlike technology today, they do not seek to wrest the earth of its secrets, they still shelter the mystery of being. Yet, Heidegger argues: 'when we once open ourselves expressly to the *essence* of technology, we find ourselves unexpectedly taken into a freeing claim' (2003b: 295). For we can reconnect with the struggle between concealment and unconcealment, with the truth of being. Therein lie technology's 'saving power' and our freedom. Here again Heidegger turns to Hölderlin:

> But where danger is, grows the saving power also.
>
> (cited 2003b: 297)

Language, we saw, possesses an age-old wisdom, e.g. above it revealed the lost meanings in the conjugation of the verb 'to be'. For Heidegger, 'Language is the house of being' (1971d: 135). It is the mode by which being lays claim on us, by which we may listen and respond. 'Everyday language is a forgotten and therefore used-up poem, from which there hardly resounds a call any longer' (1971c: 205). Yet, if we listen attentively to our clients' language, to the metaphors and slips[20] in the counselling room and the linguistic images of their dreams, it may let that call resound, for them and for us.

Heidegger dealt a fatal blow, by his political action, to his conception of history as the epochal unfolding of the truth of being, since he used that conception to exonerate Germany, and himself, for embracing National Socialism (see p. 21). I cannot follow Heidegger all the way on his more abstruse path. Yet a dialogue with his later thought – taking some steps down that path – can expand our questioning of ourselves in-the-world. In contemplation and questioning, beings 'open themselves up' differently to us at different times; it is the very essence of continuing personal development. And in the presence of our clients, it takes us further away from the tools and techniques of a trade to the mystery of an encounter.

The Heidegger controversy

Existential therapists whose practice is informed by Heidegger's thought have tended to underplay 'the Heidegger controversy' (with notable exceptions, Cohn 2002: 3–4; Stadlen 2005). As existential therapists, we have a responsibility to be aware of the facts. Only then may we choose to adhere to certain aspects of his thought for their therapeutic value.

- In 1919 to his fiancée Elfride and 1929 to Privy Counsellor Schwoerer, Heidegger speaks of the 'growing Jewish contamination' of the German universities (Faye 2005: 10, in Stassen 2003: 1).
- In his Rectoral Address in 1933: 'Spirit is . . . knowing resoluteness toward the essence of being. And the *spiritual world* of a people . . . is the power that most deeply preserves the people's strengths, which are tied to earth and blood' (Heidegger 2003a: 6).
- Autumn 1933, in the local *Freiburg Students Newspaper*: 'Do not let doctrines and ideas be the rules of your being. The Führer himself and he alone *is* the present and future German reality and its rule' (2003d: 28).
- February 1934, to newly enrolled student-workers: '*To the man of this unprecedented resolve, our Führer Adolf Hitler, let us give a three-fold "Heil!"*' (cited in Stassen 2003: 15).
- Postwar, 20 January 1948, Heidegger to his erstwhile student, the philosopher Marcuse: 'Concerning 1933: I expected from National Socialism a spiritual renewal of life in its entirety' (cited in Wolin 1993: 162).

The question is not whether Heidegger was ever a Nazi, the quotes (of which the above are a small selection) speak for themselves; the facts are there, plain and undeniable. He was not coerced; he was not half-hearted. He was a card-carrying member of the party until 1945 (Polt 1999: 113; Faye 2007). Heidegger himself denied being racist (Petzet 1993: 29ff). He could indeed have claimed 'some of my best *students* were Jews' – Hannah Arendt (with whom he had a five-year affair), Lévinas, Marcuse, Jonas, Löwith, etc. and shown that he had entertained warm relations with most of them. Yet after 1933 he prevented all Jewish doctoral students of his from gaining their doctorate (Wolin 2001: 11)[21] and forbad all Jewish students from 'ever' receiving bursaries (Faye 2007: 17). While there is no doubt that he was culturally anti-Semitic (that he felt Jews were contaminating German culture) and that biologically based racism was at odds with fundamental aspects of his philosophy, his lectures of the time can be variously interpreted. The German authorities of the time, Wolin (2001: 182) and Polt (1999: 114) see in them an ontologically based 'private National Socialism', while Faye (2007) sees clear biological racism. Nor is the question: how much credence should one give to Heidegger's postwar accounts of his own 'spiritual resistance' and 'persecution' (e.g. Petzet 1993: 45)? Not much according to Wolin (1993: 26–27) and Faye (2007, e.g. 699–709). His gripe is like that of a man with a pimple on his toe complaining to another whose limbs have all been amputated.

The crucial questions regard the possible link between Heidegger's philosophy and his allegiance to Nazism. The seeds of Heidegger's Nazism certainly can be found in his early work. However, the seeds of many other movements are also to be discovered in Heidegger's work: from Derrida's deconstruction and Marcuse's 'existential Marxism', to anti-capitalism, anti-communism, anti-globalization, anti-GM agriculture and ecology movements. Can Heidegger's philosophy be held accountable for every movement that is rooted in it? Crucially, the development of Heidegger's allegiance to Nazism can be seen throughout his work: in spirit, linguistically, conceptually, and later through his deceit and his attempts at evading responsibility.

Even before 1933, Heidegger saw in National Socialism the answer to his major concerns – the crisis of 'this moribund pseudocivilization'; science and academe divorced from their philosophical foundations; radical deconstruction of traditional metaphysics; the fate of the Germans, 'the metaphysical people' (2000: 41). Nazism was a 'new dawn' (2003d: 29). Heidegger's obscenely ridiculous, bombastic speeches reflect these concerns and hobbyhorses – and he was an influential and most charismatic teacher reputed for *verHeideggern* his students, 'bewitching them Heidegger-fashion'. His philosophy lectures of the 1930s are permeated with a vocabulary of *Volk* and *Kampf, Boden, Stamme und Blut* (people, struggle, soil, root and blood). In 1953, when the *Introduction to Metaphysics* was published, Heidegger did not see fit to expunge admiring references to Nazism from the text, e.g. 'the inner truth and greatness of this movement' (Heidegger 2000: 213), even though he was recommending this book as an appropriate introduction to his thought. Yet after the war Heidegger could also be deceitful, e.g. putting a more acceptable slant or altering what he had said earlier, while alleging that these alterations were part of the original texts (1998c: 257, 2003d: 35; Fried and Polt 2000: xv–xvii; etc.).

Heidegger's concepts of historicity, authenticity and truth are certainly compromised. Löwith reports saying to Heidegger in 1936: 'I was of the opinion that his partisanship for National Socialism lay in the essence of his philosophy. Heidegger agreed with me without reservation, and added

that his concept of "historicity" was the basis of his political "engagement" '
(cited Wolin 1993: 142).

The concept of 'authenticity' lacks any guiding ethical principle: 'Heidegger
thinks, feels in categories outside good and evil' (Steiner 1992: xxxiii). Thus
Hitler's decisions and Heidegger's own 'open and resolute' choice, as he
stared into the abyss of a world in crisis and followed his 'hero', are, according to the criteria of *Being and Time*, 'authentic' historical acts. (Interestingly, Heidegger's political writings emphatically contradict his view (1962)
that authenticity is not ontologically superior to inauthenticity.)

The traditional correspondence theory of truth[22] is based on a view of
man as 'rational animal'. Heidegger was looking for a definition of truth that
was grounded in Dasein as being-in-the-world, as disclosedness – being open
to the world and opening it up, in its historicity and within the historicity of
being. He was seeking the 'primordial' essence of truth, which underpinned
the traditional correspondence theory of truth. Tugendhat (1993) argues that,
in his quest, Heidegger moved almost imperceptibly from a definition of truth
as Dasein uncovering an entity 'just as it is in itself' to simply 'it uncovers the
entity'. Thus, while the first definition involves a reality check (but also an
ahistorical essence that Heidegger wanted to avoid), the last definition is
'overgeneralized' and has lost 'the very specificity of truth' (Tugendhat 1993:
257). That is how Heidegger could speak of the 'inner truth' of National
Socialism (2000: 213). And once it is being that unfolds as truth and 'destines', then Dasein is exonerated: Heidegger can try to elude his personal
guilt, claiming being has 'destined' this for Germany.

For Heidegger, fallen Dasein's covering up is just as much an existential
as Dasein's disclosedness (1962: 265; 222). Error is 'equiprimordial' with
truth. Instead of using this as a cautionary reminder that we cannot uncover
the whole truth, he uses it as a justification for the problems attached to
his choice: all truths are necessarily accompanied by untruths – so the
errors of National Socialism have accompanied the 'inner truth' of the
movement.

For many of Heidegger's loyal admirers, the most difficult of all was his
postwar silence, in particular his silence about the Shoah.[23] Some came to
visit him in his hut on Totnauberg; Marcuse wrote a moving account of his
own conflicting feelings (in Wolin 1993: 162–163). The poet Paul Celan – a
survivor of Auschwitz, with whom Heidegger had had strong affinities –
expressed in the poem 'Totnauberg' his 'soul-lacerating deception' (Steiner
1992: xxxii). What were they looking for? Could any apology have been sufficient? The silence was devastating. Heidegger himself speaks of not wanting
to be associated with the 'opportunism' of other former followers of Hitler
who denounced their allegiance. A plausible, but feeble reason. Heidegger
did refer to his *grosse Dummheit*, his 'great stupidity'. The expression has
shocked many, yet while it may appear trivializing, his adherence to Nazism
seems more a sign of stupidity, vanity and naivety than of blood-thirsty

Nazi extremism. Philosophically, how are we to view his silence? As his chosen mode of discourse to articulate his meaning – as golden? Or as inauthentic silence: as the antithesis to his belief that 'questioning is the piety of thought' (Heidegger 2003b: 303)? 'But how could he have [admitted to flaws in his thought] when it was a question of acknowledging – and self-acknowledgement – that the "thinker" had never been able to think the essential' (Bourdieu 1993: 267).

So, has Heidegger's work been fatally contaminated (Farias, Faye's view) or simply compromised (most Heidegger scholars' view)? This is a matter of opinion. What should be clear is that while we can follow Heidegger in his questioning, we cannot unquestioningly accept his answers (not that he would have wished anyone to do so). Personally, I regard his philosophically compromised concepts as also presenting problems for therapy.

Heidegger's concept of authenticity cannot escape, for me, the taint of its author's political, 'authentic' choice. I cannot agree with Guignon's claim that Heidegger's 'description of authenticity does provide a basis for being able to take a meaningful stand on whatever first-order moral commitments we make' (Guignon 2006: 285), since it does not rely on any moral criterion to invalidate certain life choices. Guignon stresses authentic Dasein's indebtedness to its historical heritage, as it ' "remembers" its rootedness in the wider unfolding of its culture (p. 287) and follows the 'authority' of its 'heroes'. Guignon offers Abraham Lincoln, Martin Luther King and Mother Teresa as such 'heroes' or 'cultural exemplars' – he seems to forget that Heidegger's own heroes were quite other! Interestingly, Heidegger's concept of *Schuld*, existential guilt and the 'unshakeable joy' that follows an authentic choice could offer a useful restriction on what constitutes authentic choice: my authentic choice would be guided by 'what I owe it to myself' to do, which will afford me a special, recognizable feeling of fundamental satisfaction. However beneficial this reading may be for therapy, it goes way beyond what Heidegger had in mind; it owes more to the thought of the French thinker and psychotherapist Paul Diel. For Diel, all forms of life are guided by a 'search for satisfaction' (e.g. even sunflowers turn towards the sun). He defines human satisfaction as the 'harmonization of our desires' (material, sexual, spiritual) and *la coulpe vitale*, 'existential guilt' occurs when we stray from this search for harmonization (Diel 1969, 1986, 1992, etc.). In Heideggerian terms, Dasein would have to have a 'pre-ontological' sense of his *Schuld*, of what he owes himself.

As therapists we speak of not imposing our own agendas. Yet, 'the aim of the therapeutic work is to help clients become more authentic' tops Mick Cooper's list of 'practices shared across the existential therapies' (Cooper 2003: 138). Surely the idea of 'authenticity', *Eigentlichkeit*, as a therapist's agenda for a client is itself rather paradoxical (*autos, eigen* = 'self', 'own').

For Heidegger, authenticity is intimately connected with anxiety in the face of one's mortality. While I believe that anxiety is, in all probability, an existential of human existence, as a therapist I do not assume death anxiety to be universal. However, I do believe that looking to our death, if done constructively and in 'sober anxiety' (1962: 358; 310) or without anxiety, can benefit our lives. Indeed, this emerges time and again in this book.

Although his politics raise major problems for me, I believe that Heidegger's work has a great deal to offer therapy, as the first section of this chapter shows. Above all, it is Heidegger's holistic conception of human existence that most informs my world-view and therapeutic practice: Dasein as being-in-the-world – the inseparability of its elements, ek-sistence as care, as always being-with, as 'always-already' thrown and attuned. Together with being-in-the-world, I value the importance of questioning and self-questioning and, as a therapist, of 'da-sein', 'being-there' in openness to the mystery of being.

Other existential philosophers

In planning this section I have felt a tension between the idea of personal dialogue which is at the heart of this book and the wish to offer an overview of the philosophical grounding of existential therapy. I have chosen the former. What follows, therefore, is a very idiosyncratic résumé of some other existential philosophers who inform my own therapeutic practice. For a more comprehensive survey of the various philosophical roots of existential therapies, I refer the reader to van Deurzen's *Everyday Mysteries* (1997) and Warnock's *Existentialism* (1996).

Søren Kierkegaard (1813–1855)

Kierkegaard is usually regarded as the 'father of existentialism' and a number of existential (and other) therapists have repeatedly acknowledged their debt to his philosophy (e.g. Binswanger, Laing, May, van Deurzen, Yalom). While I am fascinated by the acuity of Kierkegaard's psychological observations, he is not a philosopher to whom I tend to turn: for me, his brand of tortured Christian *Angst* often gets in the way. Still, his writings resonate with some of the values I hold and the questions I ask myself about therapy: the value placed on the passion and commitment of the 'existing, ethical individual' engaging with life's challenges and dilemmas and exercising his freedom of choice and responsibility; the potentially revitalizing power of despair; the dual role of anxiety, as both the 'weakness in which freedom faints' and a major catalyst for change, etc. It is, however, in Heidegger's secularized version that they speak to me – thus human existence as Dasein rather than as Kierkegaard's view of Christian *Existents*, the 'moment of vision' closer to Heidegger's *Augenblick* than to Kierkegaard's *Øieblik*. (For a secularized reflection on Kierkegaard's despair, see Chapter 7 by John Heaton.)

Friedrich Nietzsche (1844–1900)

The impact of Nietzsche's iconoclastic remarks imbued the spirit of the twentieth century and still reverberates today. His influence pervades psychoanalysis and psychotherapy from Freud and Jung to the American and British schools of existential therapy. While Nietzsche is not my existentialist philosopher of choice, he expresses what I see as some core aspects of existential therapy (though these do not, I stress, *define* existential therapy for me): existential therapy as iconoclastic, involving the 'revaluation of all values' – including values about the body (e.g. Nietzsche 1993), and the search for a 'why? to live for'.

The 'struggle against the morality of unselfing' (Nietzsche 1992: 67) and 'saying yes to life even in its most strange and intractable problems, the will to life' (Nietzsche 1997: 91) are common themes in an existential therapy with people who have been faced with their mortality. 'Whatever does not kill me makes me stronger' (Nietzsche 1997: 6) resonates with so many of my clients. And there are those who, towards the end of therapy, are almost prepared to 'redeem the past transforming every "It was" into an "I wanted it thus!" ' (Nietzsche 2006: 275). They feel that, in some way, what happened to them (the cancer, the near-fatal accident, etc.) turned out to be the best thing that could have happened to them. They have learnt to love their fate, 'Amor fati: let that be my love henceforth!' (Nietzsche 2006: 227).

Nietzsche's '*idea of eternal recurrence*, the highest formula of affirmation that can possibly be attained' (Nietzsche 1992: 69) has received many interpretations. When a client expresses the sense of going round in circles, of being 'back at square one', I am often inspired by Deleuze's (1965) interpretation of the eternal return. Though the client may feel back at the same point, things have shifted slightly – in effect, I visualize the eternal return not as a circle, but as a spiral.

Edmund Husserl (1859–1938)

For Edmund Husserl, father of phenomenology, 'transcendental phenomenology' is both a philosophy – exploring the essential structures of all conscious experiences and their intentional objects – and a specific method. Husserl was not an existential philosopher, but the phenomenological method he devised, with important modifications, became the method of choice for existential philosophers and therapists (see 'Phenomenological', p. 207). Personally, I have difficulties with both the aim and practice of Husserl's reductions (indeed, so did Heidegger 2003c), especially in the field of psychotherapy. However, Husserl's later concept of the lived world, *Lebenswelt*, speaks to me through Merleau-Ponty and anthropological and phenomenological research (e.g. Toombs 2001).

Paul Tillich (1886–1965)

For me, the very title of Paul Tillich's book *The Courage To Be* is inspirational and encapsulates an existential approach to life. Tillich argues that the courage to be requires taking on non-being, meaninglessness and condemnation into oneself, despite the anxiety they provoke, so as to affirm oneself as a person and live a meaningful life, with self-acceptance. His distinction between existential and 'neurotic' guilt, and the interplay between the two, is central in existential therapy. So is the importance he attaches to there being a person/therapist 'who can realize guilt, who can judge, and who can accept in spite of the judgement' (Tillich 1980: 166).

Jean-Paul Sartre (1905–1980)

I am most often reminded of Sartre's *Being and Nothingness* (1969) when I see clients who seek to lose themselves entirely in their roles and self-definitions – 'I am a doctor', 'a patient', 'a victim', a 'survivor', etc., so too clients who state firmly 'I am a person who always . . .'. According to Sartre, unlike objects who are through and through what they are (a jug is a jug through and through, it is what it is, it is 'in-itself' and not in relation to any other being or to itself), we as human beings always are *in relation to* ourselves. We can never 'coincide' completely with ourselves: we always stand slightly detached in relation to ourselves. That detachment is what allows us to be conscious of ourselves and of the world, and to make decisions. It is not a tangible distance, it is no thing, just 'nothingness'; yet it is where our freedom resides. However, Sartre argues, we are always trying, in vain, to fill that nothingness at our core and become a plenitude of being – to be through and through a doctor, a victim, a mother, etc. Although we seek this full self in vain, it is what gives value to our life (just as the full moon confers meaning to the crescent as moon crescent). It is the 'value' we pursue; it is our 'fundamental project'. For Sartre, existential psychoanalysis is the attempt to discover the client's original project as opposed to some original cause or theoretical construct of the therapist's creation. (For a Sartrean approach to therapy, see Cannon 1991.)

My relationship to Sartre is strongly polarized: the above is but one of many of Sartre's concepts which, I believe, illuminate therapy. Yet, for me, his work is contaminated by his own lifelong manipulative style of interpersonal relations, as witnessed in his nuclear family (Sartre 2003), in his relationship to women (Rowley 2007) and in his hypocritical attitude to freedom in politics. He used his own freedom of speech in the West to publicly support the Soviet Union, while remaining silent about the latter's violation of its people's most basic freedoms, although he was fully aware of the dire fate of dissidents there (Rowley 2007: e.g. 268, 281–282). This makes his conceptualization of being-for-others – in terms of a vain desire to capture the other in his freedom, a powerful evocation of his own, and other, dys-functional ways of relating. It certainly represents the antithesis of a thera-pist's ethical way of relating to a client. Sartre's *engagements*, both with Simone de Beauvoir and with politics, display either supreme bad faith, or the fatal flaw of this fundamental concept.

Maurice Merleau-Ponty (1907–1961)

Surprisingly, Merleau-Ponty has been more acknowledged in the field of phenomenological research, e.g. anthropology (Murphy 1990), sociology (Csordas 1994), philosophy (Toombs 2001), than in existential therapeutic practice. (Paul Smith-Pickard 2006 is a notable exception, see Chapter 8.) For Merleau-Ponty, it is our body, first and foremost, which grounds human exis-tence as being-in-the-world, not just physically, but in all ways – emotionally, socially, culturally. It is 'inseparable from a vision of the world' (1976: 445) and embodies that very vision (see 'The Body', pp. 87–88).

Gabriel Liceanu (1942–)

About Boundary by Liceanu (translator of Heidegger into Romanian) deserves to be known by existential therapists. 'A book born of passions and forgotten readings' (Liceanu 1997: 11), it owes much to Heidegger and Sartre, only to then turn the latter on his head, both in his description of loving relationships and in his credo, developed during years under the Ceaucescu regime, that freedom is a gift: 'Supreme responsibility consists in integrating freedom itself into my project . . . this means experiencing it fully as a gift, not as a burden' (Liceanu 1997: 144).

Influential dialogues in existential psychotherapy

The above summary of existential themes emerged from my own personal dial-ogue with existential philosophy. Existential therapies grow out of such per-sonal dialogues, which is why we cannot speak of 'existential psychotherapy' as such. However, a number of influential existential dialogues have pre-vailed and at present we can draw a map of existential therapies around five schools.

In the 1930s and 1940s, two Swiss psychiatrists, Ludwig Binswanger (1881–1966) and Medard Boss (1903–1990), independently encountered Heidegger's thought; it revolutionized their practice. Both were unhappy with the medical model of psychiatry and had become disillusioned with Freudian theory. Heidegger's concept of being-in-the-world enabled Bin-swanger to think of his patients' problems in terms of 'the *how* of being-*in*-the-world and the attitude *toward* world' (Binswanger 1994: 195). To facili-tate this study, Binswanger distinguished between a person's 'three worlds' –

his *Umwelt*, *Eigenwelt* and *Mitwelt* (physical, personal and social worlds respectively). He further described the *Mitwelt*, the social dimension, according to 'existential modes' – including the 'dual mode' of love, conspicuous by its absence in Heidegger. For this, Binswanger acknowledged his indebtedness to Buber's work (Agassi 1999: 187). Binswanger laid the foundations for what became the Daseinanalyse school of therapy, of which Boss later became president. Boss was totally *verheideggert*, 'under Heidegger's spell'; he was also interested in Eastern philosophy and hence possibly had greater affinity with Heidegger's later thought. Thus, under Boss, Daseinanalysis, while still holding on to a Freudian-influenced frame, focused on the importance of being open to what addresses us and on the obstacles to our openness (Boss 1994). Heidegger was scathing about Binswanger (Boss 2001: 203), but collaborated very closely with Boss (Boss 1979, 2001).

It was May, Ellenberger and Angel who, by editing *Existence* in 1958, introduced existential therapy in the USA; there it took on a life of its own. The early collaboration with humanistic therapists such as Maslow and Rogers was also an important influence and a mutual one (May 1961). Notwithstanding the popularity of May's books (1977, 1986, etc.), it is Irvin Yalom, with his case studies (1991), personal reflections (2002) and quasi-text books (1980, 1995) who has had the greatest influence on broadening the appeal of existential therapy in the UK. His focus on the 'ultimate concerns' of 'death', 'freedom', 'isolation' and 'meaninglessness' has offered an additional existential frame to therapists of various theoretical orientations (e.g. Melanie Lockett's Chapter 2).

Viktor Frankl (1905–1997) had to surrender the manuscript of his first logotherapy book on entering Auschwitz. Logotherapy was centred on his belief that 'the primary motivational force in man' is the '*will to meaning*' (Frankl 1964: 99). His vow to rewrite it reinforced his sentiment that 'He who has a *why* to live for can bear almost any *how*' (Nietzsche, cited in Frankl 1964: 106). From his experiences in the camp he derived the conviction that 'Life's meaning is an unconditional one for it even includes the potential meaning of suffering' (Frankl 1964: 116). Logotherapy still flourishes around the world, but does not exist as a school in the UK. Frankl's influence, however, can be perceived within the British existential tradition, which also 'dares to enter the spiritual dimension of human existence' (Frankl 1964: 103).

R.D. Laing's questioning of traditional psychiatry, his subsequent experience of psychoanalysis (British Object Relations school) and his extensive reading of existential philosophy underpinned his search for a more humane and human psychiatry. Laing (1927–1989), as psychiatrist and as therapist, was seeking to get away from an approach that does violence to the other,[24] whether through treatments, compulsory committal, or a power-based, objectifying relationship. Focusing on 'schizophrenia' as the paradigmatic 'mental illness', Laing and a number of colleagues sought to discover an alternative way of accounting for the diagnosed person's behaviour. They showed how it could be understood as that person's meaningful attempt to respond to an interpersonal situation which is experienced as intolerable (e.g. Laing and Esterson 1970; Esterson 1972). The concept of 'ontological insecurity', giving rise to a terror of engulfment, implosion and petrification, underlies Laing's understanding of 'schizophrenia' as a way of relating. Thus, the 'true self' (a Winnicottian concept) seeks to protect itself by entrenching itself, leaving only a 'false self' shell to deal with the outside world (Laing 1990). A critical evaluation of Laing's ideas, aspirations and practice has enabled the Philadelphia Association, which he co-founded, to prosper and his influence to live on (Heaton 2006).

Laing's influence can be felt in the British school of existential psychotherapy, which owes its existence to Emmy van Deurzen (1951–). She favours a non-pathologizing stance and sees the concept of 'ontological insecurity' as an integral aspect of the human condition (van Deurzen-Smith 1991). Van Deurzen's own personal dialogue with the whole range of existential philosophy has reinforced her conviction that 'it is the process of passionate overcoming that is life's paradoxical joy' (van Deurzen-Smith 1998: xiv) – a conviction that guides both her private and professional life (van Deurzen 2006). By introducing training in existential therapy in the UK, van Deurzen has offered a platform for other existential dialogues, most prominently those of Cohn (e.g. 1997, 2002) and Spinelli (e.g. 1989, 1996, 2006). Van Deurzen, Cohn, Spinelli and others' abhorrence of the 'certainties and dogmatism' so prevalent in psychotherapy (van Deurzen-Smith 1997: x) has given rise to a British school that can embrace divergence and thrives both despite and because of it.

Naturally, such a division into schools is but a generalization and there are important lone voices. For instance, Eugene Minkowski, though figured in the American existential therapy manifesto *Existence* (May *et al.* 1994), was such a voice in France. Minkowski (1885–1972) viewed the 'mental syndrome' as 'the expression of a profound and characteristic modification of the whole human personality' (Minkowski 1995: 211). This he sought to understand variously, for example, in terms of relations to time (disintegration of time into isolated elements, inability to project into the future, etc.), to space, or as an attempt to make sense of the 'various stones of the crumbling edifice' of the patient's disintegrating life (e.g. delusions).

In the UK, Anthony Stadlen (1940–), erstwhile student of Esterson's and world expert on Freud's case histories, straddles a number of those schools in his 'ethical, existential, phenomenological search for truth in psychotherapy' (e.g. Stadlen 2005), while calling them and us into question by means of erudite criticism.

Existential philosophy and psychiatry

Frances, Chairman of the *DSM-IV* Task Force warns us: 'It is important not to reify our diagnostic system and its mental disorders' (Frances 1994: ix). Yet clients often refer to 'the depression' which they 'got' at a time of crisis – as one gets the flu or measles. The concept of 'mental illness' pervades modern Western culture in a most confusing way. Not surprisingly, for '*DSM-IV* is a manual of mental disorders, but it is by no means clear just what is a mental disorder' (Frances 1994: vii).

From anti-psychiatry to postpsychiatry, a number of psychiatrists, influenced by existential philosophy, have sought to shift psychiatry away from trying to *classify, explain and cure* 'symptoms' – i.e. forms of perception, ideation, feelings and behaviour that deviate from a norm. Instead they seek a better *understanding* of patients. Their intention has been to make psychiatry a more humane and ethical enterprise. Already in the introduction to his *General Psychopathology* (first published in 1913), Karl Jaspers (1883–1969), psychiatrist and existential philosopher, speaks of the 'philosophical', 'theoretical', 'somatic', 'psychologizing and intellectualizing' prejudices hampering the work of psychiatry (Jaspers 1963: 16–20). Following the 'false analogy' of a medicine for the psyche, these prejudices create the illusion of a scientific discipline that can provide causal explanations for the phenomena which it objectively observes, based on an often value-laden, top-down theoretical system. Instead, he argues, these prejudices contribute to the sterility and concealing effect of psychiatric diagnoses: 'Completely dispassionate observation misses the essence of things' (Jaspers 1963: 22).

Yet, in his *General Psychopathology*, Jaspers falls into his own trap: he separates the content (narrative, meaning, values) from the form of 'phenomena of experience'. The second, existential part of the book concerns 'Meaningful Psychic Connections (the Psychology of Meaning)'; but it is the first part, in which Jaspers applies Husserlian phenomenology as a scientific tool to seek out the universal form of symptoms, that has unfortunately proved more influential in psychiatry (Bracken 2002; Bracken and Thomas 2006; for a scathing review, see Laing 1964).

Anti-psychiatry is usually mistakenly associated with Laing and Szasz. Cooper coined the term and first put 'anti-psychiatry' into practice in the 'Villa 21' unit which he ran at Shenley hospital (Cooper 1967). With Laing, Esterson and Briskin he was a co-founder of the Philadelphia Association (Ticktin 1986; Heaton 2006: 181). The questioning and demystifying attitude of psychiatrists such as Laing, Cooper and Esterson has created in the UK, even among those existential therapists that do not follow them wholeheartedly, a healthy scepticism towards psychiatric diagnoses.

The debate which Thomas Szasz' *Myth of Mental Illness* instigated in 1961 still continues today. It tends to focus on Szasz' point that, unless used metaphorically, 'disease can only predicate the body' (cited in Stadlen 2003: 223);

this has led to claims that he is being dualistic (which he denies).[25] Behind the formal aspect of the argument lie the important moral questions he raises about agency and personal responsibility concerning both those who have been diagnosed with a 'mental illness' and those who use these diagnoses. Furthermore, these questions have social and economic implications – a whole pharmaceutical industry and 'pharmacracy', he argues, are based on a lack of distinction between the brain and the mind (e.g. Szasz 1974, 2001).

The Postpsychiatry of Patrick Bracken and Philip Thomas is grounded in Heidegger's holistic concept of being-in-the-world and his method of hermeneutic phenomenology with its focus on meaning. They seek to 'destabilise the assumption that psychiatry has solid scientific foundations that protect it from critique' (Bracken and Thomas 2006: 6) and 'open up spaces in which other, alternative, understandings of madness can assume a validity denied them by psychiatry' (Bracken 2002: 223). They stress that they are 'not anti-science, but anti-dogma' (Bracken and Thomas 2006: 6). A postpsychiatry approach focuses first on understanding the patient's context – social, cultural, temporal and bodily, through a joint 'hermeneutic exploration of (i) meaning; (ii) significance; and (iii) value' (Bracken and Thomas 2005: 133). Such an exploration, they argue, should come before causal, biological explanations. They also challenge psychiatry's right to coercion and enjoin us to 'disconnect medical care from control' (Bracken and Thomas 2006: 7).

The debate regarding post-traumatic stress disorder

The development of the diagnosis of post-traumatic stress disorder (PTSD) has been described as 'the soul of psychiatry' (van der Kolk *et al.* 1996: 4) and carries important therapeutic, moral, political, financial and legal implications (e.g. problems of financial compensation; export of Western psychiatric PTSD diagnosis and treatment to other cultures, etc.). Although PTSD as a diagnosis is philosophically at odds with existential thought and only passing reference is ever made to it within these pages, I feel it is worth highlighting the nature of the debate and the importance of existential thought and therapeutic practice as an alternative perspective, since many among the client groups encountered in this book would fit a diagnosis of acute stress disorder (ASD) or PTSD.

The diagnosis of PTSD first appeared in embryonic form in *DSM-III* in 1980 and has since developed steadily. PTSD is almost unique in the nosology of 'mental disorders' in being defined by its cause – the experiencing or witnessing of a traumatic event. PTSD can be 'acute' or 'chronic' (according to whether the symptoms last less or more than three months) or it can occur 'with delayed onset' – many years even after the event (*DSM IV-TR* 2000: 463–438). ASD is diagnosed instead of PTSD when symptoms occur 'within 4 weeks of the traumatic event' and last for between two days and four weeks

(*DSM IV-TR* 2000: 469). Since *DSM IV-TR* it can even 'have a heritable component' (2000: 466). The core symptoms of PTSD are usually summarized as symptoms of 'intrusion' (including nightmares; 'flashbacks'), 'avoidance' (of anything that reminds one of the event; 'psychic numbing') and 'hyperarousal/hypervigilance'; but PTSD can, it is claimed, give rise to a broad range of other symptoms (p. 463). Opinions about PTSD as a diagnosis are strongly polarized; it is:

> a language that is at once faithful to the traditions of accurate psychological observation and to the moral demands of traumatized people.
>
> (Herman 2001: 122)

> a pseudo-condition, a label that not only pathologises but may dehumanise survivors by stripping them of the complexity of their living realities and associations.
>
> (Summerfield 1998: 31)

Young offers a less emotional formulation than Summerfield's for the problem with PTSD:

> The generally accepted picture of PTSD . . . is mistaken. The disorder is not timeless, nor does it possess an intrinsic unity. Rather, it is glued together by the practice, technologies, and narratives with which it is diagnosed, studied, treated, and represented and by the various interests, institutions, and moral arguments that mobilized these efforts and resources.
>
> (Young 1995: 5)

Yet, he argues, PTSD has acquired a reality for the sufferers and for society; but that reality does not correspond to the truth of what is going on for the person. That Herman and Summerfield, both coming from a strong moral position, can hold such divergent views equally passionately can be understood in terms of the history of the diagnosis and the use to which it has been put. Both sides agree that PTSD as a diagnosis could only have been created and developed within a specific political and ideological climate (post-Vietnam anti-war; feminism).[26]

Herman, and others within the PTSD field, draw parallels with 'shell shock' in the First World War, nineteenth-century 'railway spine', hysteria, etc. to argue that PTSD is a new name for an age-old illness (Herman 2001). Young, however, points out that the symptoms of 'shell shock', 'railway spine' and 'hysteria' (paralysis, seizures, blindness, muteness, etc.) were of a different type to those of modern PTSD and included none of its characteristic intrusion/avoidance features. Over the years, different orders of explanations

– psychological, neuropsychological, neurochemical, neuroanatomical (e.g. van der Kolk *et al.* 1996; Levine and Frederick 1997; Hagh-Shenas *et al.* 1999; etc.) – have been put forward to account for PTSD. Young matches them with counterarguments from these same fields to support his view that PTSD is a modern construct (Young 1995).

One of the most influential models for understanding PTSD in the last 15 years has been Ronnie Janoff-Bulmann's. She starts from the premise: 'All knowledge and experience is packaged in schemas. Schemas are the ghost in the machine, the intelligence that guides information as it flows through the mind' (Goleman, cited in Janoff-Bullman 1992: 28). She then argues that there are certain schemata that are central to the way we relate to the world: these are our 'grandest schemas, our most abstract, generalized knowledge structures' (p. 29) and, as such, most resistant to change. She proposes three such 'fundamental assumptions': 'The world is benevolent, the world is meaningful, the self is worthy'. In the face of trauma, 'this known universe is suddenly and powerfully threatened' (p. 45). We come to see our funda-mental beliefs about the world and ourselves as mere illusions; this fills us with 'terror' and leaves us 'disillusioned'. 'The result is cognitive disintegra-tion which, according to James Averill, is the defining characterisitic of anxiety' (p. 65).

For existential therapy, on the other hand, anxiety is not a 'form of cogni-tive disintegration' but a fundamental mood of human existence, always there, but which we seek to evade. Trauma only highlights it and propels it into the foreground. Janoff-Bulman says that anxiety as a mood makes us feel uncomfortable; Heidegger calls it *unheimlich* ('unsettled', literally not-at-home-like). Yet, he argues, anxiety is a 'disclosive' mood – disclosing to us both the world and ourselves. These two different conceptualizations of anxiety give rise to two different attitudes to therapy.

For Janoff-Bulman, the work of therapy consists in helping individuals to reappraise their schemata and transform the negativity of victimization into a 'positivity' of survival: 'By engaging in interpretations and evaluations that focus on benefits and lessons learned, survivors emphasize benevolence over malevolence, meaningfulness over randomness, and self-worth over self-abasement' (Janoff-Bulman 1992: 133). (This cognitive method is often inte-grated with desensitization techniques, some elements of psychoanalysis,[27] testimony writing, individual and group psychotherapy [e.g. Marmar and Horowitz 1988; van der Veer 1998; Yule 1999; for a particularly sensitive account see Herman 2001].)

While existential therapy may lead to reappraisal, that reappraisal would not be simply cognitive: it would be a new embodied way of apprehending the world and being addressed by it, a new way of being-in-the-world physically-emotionally-cognitively-spiritually. Existential therapy involves helping clients sit with their anxiety for a while and reflect upon the possibi-lity of the 'randomness' of our world and its occasional 'malevolence'. This may unsettle clients to the core, but in so doing it may take them beyond the horizon of their world: in their experience of anxiety, they may discover a hidden vitality, a richer existence.

Another fundamental philosophical difference between the existential and PTSD discourses is that the latter depends on a linear view of time and causality: i.e. a person experiences an event as traumatic and later develops symptoms in reaction to it, caused by the event. From the viewpoint of existential thought and therapy, past and present are influenced by our view of the future that comes to meet us – and this also applies to our reactions to trauma. In the following example, can we say that the symptoms of intrusion and avoidance are a direct reaction to the traumatic event, or rather, are they not also due to the sort of life this person was leading before the event and that which he saw lying ahead of him in the future?

> J was doing well after his time in ITU; indeed, in his weakened state he had recovered a will to fight and live 'after all that the nurses had done for him'. (He had lost interest in life after the death of his wife three years previously.) He showed much determination, forcing himself to eat and do his physiotherapy exercises and was able to walk again and go back to his house to independent living. After two months at home, things took a turn for the worse and he began to get flashbacks of his ITU dreams, and numbing; he decided to come for counselling.

At first glance, this looks like a classic situation of delayed onset PTSD. Exploring the situation together, it became clear that the greater trauma was related to his return home, to his lonely life, which he experienced as being empty and leading nowhere except to the grave. The numbing and dissociation (e.g. getting lost on the way to therapy) referred to his present anxiety in relation to his life (past, present and future) and the flashbacks reconnected him to a time in ITU in which he had sufficiently valued his life to fight for it. As therapy progressed, he was able to discover within these flashbacks a source of meaning, purpose and renewed vigour. This would seem to illustrate Young's view that 'the sense of time that is now firmly attached to PTSD does not emerge spontaneously from the facts' (Young 1995: 116).

DSM IV-TR has added transgenerational PTSD; this further conflicts with existential thought. I do not deny that children of victims of trauma may well be traumatized in relation to their parents' trauma – Wardi harrowingly bears witness to this (1992). However, existentially speaking, the relation to that trauma cannot be that of a simple linear causality. So how are we to understand such second or third generation trauma? Does it have to come from the handing down of 'traumatic memory' or can it not arise from growing up with the emotions (guilt, pain, etc.) that imbued the survivors' lives, their stories or indeed their silence?[28]

Objecting to PTSD as a diagnosis is not denying that trauma can have an enduring impact. From an existential perspective, however, this impact need not be harmful in the long term, indeed it can be life enhancing: that is a major theme of this book.

Notes

1 *Abbau, Destruktion*. The word 'deconstruction' was made famous/infamous in the 1960s by Derrida who was much indebted to Heidegger. It has now passed into everyday English. However, in doing so, its original composite meaning of 'taking critically apart to reconstruct' has been lost.
2 The view that we are made up of a mind, a 'thinking substance', and an 'extended substance', the body. The mind, or the 'subject', then represents the 'objects' out there to itself. Descartes' position has dominated both Western philosophy and everyday common thinking.
3 That is, without viewing them as simply partaking of or standing for some ideal entity (Plato, Kant); and regardless of whether the phenomenon exists or not (e.g. a unicorn).
4 His idiosyncratic translation of Heraclitus's *Physis kruptesthai philei*, commonly translated 'nature loves to hide'.
5 Whereas German (like French) can make nouns out of both the present participle of a verb and its infinitive, English cannot do so with infinitives. This means that the fundamental distinction between *das Seiende*, beings (lit. 'the being'; French *l'étant*) and *das Sein* (lit. 'the to be', French *l'être*) is totally lost in an English translation. Many translators and authors use a capital letter for 'Being' and small case for 'beings'. (All nouns start with a capital letter in German.) My view is that 'Being' can introduce religious connotations, so I have kept to small case 'b' for both (as indeed do a number of scholars including Dreyfus (1991), McNeill (1988), Farrell Krell, Sallis). I have amended translations in my own chapters accordingly, but have not imposed my choice on contributors.
6 In his departure from the dominant philosophical traditions of his day, Heidegger has felt the need to develop a vocabulary of his own, forging new words, hyphenated expressions and altering the meaning of some common terms.
7 In *Being and Time*, Heidegger argues that our primary relationship to beings is governed by our involvement with them as 'ready-to-hand' equipment; thus, he regards science's supposedly neutral observation of phenomena as secondary.
8 In Zollikon Seminars, Heidegger links *Lichtung* with *leicht* – lightened of its trees (Boss 2001: 13).
9 I agree with Dreyfus that, as a translation of *das Man*, the 'one' is preferable to the 'they' as the latter appears to exclude Dasein. There are, however, difficulties: One with a capital has religious connotations and 'the "one"-self' for *das Man-selbst* would be too ambiguous. I have therefore kept to conventional usage. I have, however, used Dreyfus' 'amidst the world' for *sein-bei*, rather than 'alongside' which seems to imply that Dasein is separate from beings in the world.
10 Wordplay: eigens 'expressly, on purpose', eigentlich 'authentic'.
11 Heidegger's lectures on boredom were very popular: four times a week, he would fill the largest lecture hall and enthusiastic students would meet in the evenings to debate the lectures (Petzet 1993: 13). For an illustration of the disclosive character of boredom, see Chapter 4, pp. 80–1.
12 The English translation plays on the two meanings of *Augenblick* : 'moment' and literally 'eye-glance'.

13 Opinion is still divided as to a possible 'turn' in Heidegger's thought after *Being and Time*: the focus does move away from Dasein to being itself and Heidegger himself uses the word *Kehre*, 'turn'. It would seem that, unlike the English 'doing a U-turn' and 'going back on', *Kehre* does not necessarily imply renouncing what was previously stated. The following passage would seem to corroborate this. The context is a discussion on language between a Japanese scholar of German and an 'Inquirer' viz. Heidegger:

> *J:* You are said to have changed your standpoint.
> *I:* I have left an earlier standpoint, not in order to exchange it for another one . . . And ways of thinking hold within them that mysterious quality that we can walk them forward and backward, and that indeed only the way back will lead us forward.
>
> (Heidegger 1971e: 12)

The later Heidegger is working backwards from being itself to Dasein. It is also worth noting that in the late Zollikon Seminars Heidegger returns to many themes from *Being and Time*.

14 In parenthesis in the 1953 edition.

15 See note 4.

16 *Ereignis* usually means 'event' in German. Heidegger is playing on the false etymological connection with *eigen* (own), hence the various translations – 'the propriative event', 'appropriation', etc.

17 And he sees this as the culmination of Western metaphysics – metaphysics of presencing.

18 Usually translated as 'enframing'. Besteigui's translation 'System' is both readily understandable and ingenious: using Greek roots (*sun-* together and *ste-* to place) it represents an exact etymological rendering of the German.

19 This defensible view lies behind this oft-cited, deeply shocking passage: 'Agriculture is today a motorized food industry, in essence the same as the manufacture of corpses in gas chambers and extermination camps, the same as the blockade and starvation of countries . . ., the same as the manufacture of atomic bombs' (cited in Wolin 1993: 290–291).

20 For a Heideggerian exploration of slips and a further illustration of how 'language speaks' with reference to questioning 'schizophrenia', see Stadlen (2007a: 127–137).

21 Although the policy was a national one, Heidegger was ' "plus royaliste que le roi": his political compromises were earlier and more radical than anything the regime demanded' (Wolin, 9 October 2007).

22 *Veritas est adaequatio rei et intellectus* refers to the correspondence, which can be verified beyond doubt, between an assertion or belief and an entity/state of affairs, e.g. this is a book.

23 I have followed the French custom in using the Hebrew word to draw attention to the inappropriate connotation of 'sacrificial offering' in 'Holocaust'.

24 Anthony Stadlen points out that Laing, and Bracken and Thomas below, unlike Szasz, are not as radically opposed to coercive psychiatry as they claim to be (8 July 2007).

25 For example, the debate: Stadlen (2003); Szasz (2003); Wolf (2002, 2003).

26 Through the growth of feminism, an ever more powerful women's voice was able to draw attention to the gender bias that characterized assumptions underpinning the classification of 'mental illnesses' and to the devaluation of the traumas more commonly suffered by women – childhood sexual abuse, rape and domestic violence (see Russell 1994: 247; Herman 2001).

27 Early psychodynamic work with Shoah survivors had given psychoanalysis a privileged place in the trauma field. However, as 'clinicians found it difficult to face the
painful issues presented by survivors ... instead [they] attached a pathological
diagnostic label to post-traumatic phenomena' (Klein-Parker 1988: 195). Yael
Danieli gives a blood-chilling example of such a theory-driven therapy:

> In supervision, a therapist described a patient, Mr S., whose presenting
> problem was compulsive showering and scrubbing ... The therapist
> worked under the assumption that Mr S's symptomatology was a
> manifestation of an anal fixation and kept probing into his childhood.
> An old intake report stated: 'In Aushwitz Mr S. worked for 10–12
> hours a day' without mention of the nature of his work. Following
> the supervisor's suggestion to explore the nature of the patient's 'work
> detail', the therapist learned that Mr S. removed corpses from the
> crematorium.
>
> (Danieli 1988: 225)

28 For an existential understanding of such a process see Conclusion, pp. 220–1.

Further reading

On Heidegger

Richard Polt (1999): this introduction is a model of its kind.
Hans Cohn (2002): A clear and concise book that relates specifically to existential
therapy.
Reading Heidegger's own work requires, at first, a great deal of perseverance. Stassen
(2003) offers an excellent selection of texts (though starting with the political
texts might well put the reader off completely).

On existential therapies

Mick Cooper (2003) and Emmy van Deurzen-Smith (1997) are very accessible and
offer a useful overview.

References

Dates in square brackets refer to the original edition.

American Psychiatric Association (APA, 2005 [1994]) *Diagnostic and Statistical
Manual of Mental Disorders, DSM IV-TR*, 4th edn, Washington DC: American
Psychiatric Association.
Agassi, J. Buber (1999) *Martin Buber on Psychology and Psychotherapy, Essays, Letters
and Dialogues*, Syracuse NY: Syracuse University Press.
Besteigui, M. de (2005) *The New Heidegger*, London: Continuum.
Binswanger, L. (1994 [1958]) The Existential Analysis School of Thought, trans.
Angel, E., in May, R., Angel, E. and Ellenberger, H.F. (eds) *Existence*, Northvale:
Jason Aronson.

Boss, M. (1979 [1970]) *Existential Foundations of Medicine and Psychology*, trans. Conway, S. and Cleaves, A., Northvale: Jason Aronson.

—— (ed.) (2001 [1987]) *Heidegger, M. Zollikon Seminars, Seminars, Protocol, Conversations*, trans. Mayr, F. and Askay, R., Evanston: Northwestern University Press.

Bourdieu, P. (1993 [1988]) Back to History: An Interview, trans. Wolin, R., in Wolin, R. (ed.) (1993 [1991]) *The Heidegger Controversy*, Cambridge MA: MIT Press.

Bracken, P.J. (2002) *Trauma: Culture, Meaning and Philosophy*, London: Whurr.

Bracken, P. and Thomas, P. (2005) *Post-Psychiatry: Mental Health in a Postmodern World*, Oxford: Oxford University Press.

—— (2006) Post-psychiatry – A Manifesto, in *Openmind*, 138: 6–7.

Cannon, B. (1991) *Sartre and Psychoanalysis: An Existentialist Challenge to Clinical Metatheory*, Lawrence KS: University Press of Kansas.

Chantraine, P. (1968–1977) terminé par Masson,O., Perpillou, J.L., and Taillardat, J. (1980) *Dictionnaire Etymologique de la Langue Grecque*, Paris: Klincksieck.

Cohn, H.W. (1997) *Existential Thought and Therapeutic Practice*, London: Sage.

—— (1999) Why Heidegger?, in *Journal of the Society for Existential Analysis*, July, 10.2: 2–9.

—— (2002) *Heidegger and the Roots of Existential Therapy*, London: Continuum.

Cooper, D. (1967) *Psychiatry and Anti-Psychiatry*, London: Tavistock.

Cooper, M. (2003) *Existential Therapies*, London: Sage.

Csordas, T. (1994) *Embodiment and Experience: The Existential Ground of Culture and Self*, Cambridge: Cambridge University Press.

Danieli, Y. (1988) Confronting the Unimaginable: Psychotherapists' Reactions to Victims of the Nazi Holocaust, in Wilson, J.P., Harel, Z. and Kahana, B. (eds) *Human Adaptation to Extreme Stress, from the Holocaust to Vietnam*, New York: Plenum Press.

Deleuze, G. (1965) *Nietzsche*, Paris: Presses Universitaires de France.

Diel, P. (1969) *La Psychologie de la Motivation*, 3rd edn, Paris: Presses Universitaires de France. (First edn 1947.)

—— (1986 [1971]) *The God Symbol, its History and Significance*, trans. from 3rd edn Marans, N., San Francisco: Harper and Row. (First edn 1950.)

—— (1992 [1968]) *La Peur et l'Angoisse, Phénomène Central de l'évolution du Psychisme*, 2nd edition, Paris: Petite Bibliothèque Payot. (First edn 1956.)

Dreyfus, H.L. (1991) *Being-in-the-World, A Commentary on Heidegger's Being and Time*, Cambridge MA: MIT Press.

Esterson, A. (1972 [1970]) *The Leaves of Spring: Schizophrenia, Family and Sacrifice*, Harmondsworth: Penguin.

Faye, E. (2007 [2005]) *Heidegger, l'introduction du nazisme dans la philosophie: Autour des séminaires inédits de 1933–1935*, 2nd edn, Paris: Albin Michel. Livre de Poche.

Frances, A.J. (1994) Foreword, in Sadler, J.Z., Wiggins, O.P. and Schwartz, M.A. (eds) (1994) *Philosophical Perspectives on Psychiatric Diagnostic Classification*, Baltimore and London: Johns Hopkins University Press.

Frankl, V. (1964 [1962]) *Man's Search for Meaning*, trans. Lash, I., London: Hodder and Stoughton. (First edn 1946.)

Fried, G. and Polt, R. (eds) (2000) Translators' Introduction, in Heidegger, M. *Introduction to Metaphysics*, New Haven: Yale University Press.

Guignon, C.B. (ed.) (2006) *The Cambridge Companion to Heidegger*, 2nd edn, Cambridge: Cambridge University Press.

Hagh-Shenas, H., Goldstein, L. and Yule, W. (1999) Psychobiology of Post-Traumatic Stress Disorder, in Yule, W. (ed.) *Post-Traumatic Stress Disorders: Concepts and Therapy*, Chichester: Wiley.

Heaton, J. (2006) The Early History and Ideas of the Philadelphia Association, in *Journal of the Society for Existential Analysis*, 17.1: 181–191.

Heidegger, M. (1962 [1927]) *Being and Time*, trans. Macquarrie, J.R. and Robinson, E., Oxford: Blackwell.

—— (1966 [1959]) *Discourse on Thinking*, trans. Anderson, J.M. and Freund, E.H., New York: Harper and Row.

—— (1971a) *Poetry, Language and Thought*, Hofstadter, A. (ed.), New York: Perennial Classics.

—— (1971b [1954]) Building, Dwelling, Thinking (lecture delivered August 1951), trans. Hofstadter, A., in Hofstadter, A. (ed.) *Poetry, Language and Thought*, New York: Perennial Classics.

—— (1971c [1959]) Language (lecture delivered 7 October 1950), trans. Hofstadter, A., in Hofstadter, A. (ed.) *Poetry, Language and Thought*, New York: Perennial Classics.

—— (1971d [1959]) *On the Way to Language*, trans. Hertz, P.D., San Francisco: Harper and Row.

—— (1971e [1959]) A Dialogue on Language, in *On the Way to Language* (conversation took place 1953/4), trans. Hertz, P.D., San Francisco: Harper and Row.

—— (1995 [1983]) *The Fundamental Concepts of Metaphysics, World, Finitude, Solitude* (lecture delivered 1929–30), trans. McNeill, W. and Walker, N., Bloomington: Indiana University Press.

—— (1998a [1929]) What is Metaphysics?, trans. Farrell-Krell, D. (1993), in Heidegger, M. (1998 [1976 2nd edn, revised and expanded]) *Pathmarks*, McNeill, W. (ed.), Cambridge: Cambridge University Press.

—— (1998b [1930]) On the Essence of Truth, trans. Sallis, J. (1993) in Heidegger, M. (1998 [1976 2nd edn, revised and expanded]) *Pathmarks*, McNeill, W. (ed.), Cambridge: Cambridge University Press.

—— (1998c [1947]) Letter on Humanism, trans. Capuzzi, F. (1967) in Heidegger, M. (1998 [1976 2nd edn, revised and expanded]) *Pathmarks*, McNeill, W. (ed.), Cambridge: Cambridge University Press.

—— (2000 [1953]) *Introduction to Metaphysics* (lecture delivered 1935), trans. Fried, G. and Polt, R., New Haven: Yale University Press.

—— (2003a [1933]) The Self-assertion of the German University, trans. Harries, K. (1985), in Stassen, M. (ed.) (2003) *Martin Heidegger, Philosophical and Political Writings*, New York: Continuum.

—— (2003b [1949]) The Question Concerning Technology, trans. Lovitt, W. (1977), in Stassen, M. (ed.) (2003) *Martin Heidegger, Philosophical and Political Writings*, New York: Continuum.

—— (2003c [1963]) My Way to Phenomenology, from On Time and Being, trans. Stambaugh, J. (1972), in Stassen, M. (ed.) (2003) *Martin Heidegger, Philosophical and Political Writings*, New York: Continuum.

—— (2003d [1966]) Only a God Can Save Us: Der Spiegel Interview, trans. Alter, M. and Caputo, J.D., in Stassen, M. (ed.) (2003) *Martin Heidegger, Philosophical and Political Writings*, New York: Continuum.

—— (2006 [1927]) *Sein und Zeit*, Neunzehnte Auflage, Tübingen: Max Niemeyer Verlag.

Herman, J. (2001) *Trauma and Recovery, from Domestic Violence to Political Terror*, 2nd edn, London: Pandora. (First edn 1992.)

Janoff-Bullman, R. (1992) *Shattered Assumptions: Towards a New Psychology of Trauma*, New York: Free Press.

Jaspers, K. (1963 [1959]) *General Psychopathology*, translation of 7th revised edn, Hoenig, J. and Hamilton, M. (eds), Manchester: Manchester University Press. (First edn 1913.)

Klein-Parker, F. (1988) Dominant Attitudes of Adult Children of the Holocaust Survivors towards their Parents, in Wilson, J.P., Harel, Z. and Kahana, B. (1988) *Human Adaptation to Extreme Stress: From the Holocaust to Vietnam*, New York: Plenum Press.

Laing, R.D. (1964) Review of 'General Psychopathology. By Karl Jaspers', In *International Journal of Psychoanalysis*, 44: 590–593.

—— (1990 [1960]) *The Divided Self*, Harmondsworth: Penguin.

Laing, R. D. and Esterson, A. (1970 [1964]) *Sanity, Madness and the Family: Families of Schizophrenics*, Harmondsworth: Penguin.

Levine, P.A. and Frederick, A. (1997) *Waking the Tiger*, Berkeley CA: North Atlantic Books.

Liceanu, G. (1997 [1994]) *De la Limite, petit ouvrage à l'usage des orgueilleux*, trans. Laignel-Lavastine, A., Paris: Editions Michalon.

McNeill, W. (ed.) (1988) *Martin Heidegger Pathmarks*, Cambridge: Cambridge University Press.

Marmar, C.R. and Horowitz, M. (1988) Diagnosis and Phase-Oriented Treatment of Post-Traumatic Disorder, in Wilson, J., Harel, Z. and Kahana, B. (eds) *Human Adaptation to Extreme Stress, from the Holocaust to Vietnam*, New York: Plenum Press.

May, R. (ed.) (1961) *Existential Psychology*, New York: Random House.

—— (1977 [1950]) *The Meaning of Anxiety*, New York: Norton.

—— (1986 [1983]), *The Discovery of Being: Writings in Existential Psychology*, New York: Norton.

May, R., Angel, E. and Ellenberger, H.F. (eds) (1994 [1958]) *Existence*, Northvale: Jason Aronson.

Merleau-Ponty, M. (1976 [1945]) *Phénoménologie de la Perception*, Paris: Gallimard.

Minkowski, E. (1995 [1933]) *Le temps vécu*, Paris: Presses Universitaires de France, Quadrige.

Murphy, R. (1990 [1987]) *The Body Silent*, New York: Norton.

Nietzsche, F. (1992 [1888]) *Ecce Homo*, trans. Hollingdale, R.J. (1979), Harmondsworth: Penguin.

Nietzsche, F. (1993 [1883–5]) *Thus Spake Zarathustra*, trans. Common, T., revised with introduction and notes Birx, H.J., New York: Prometheus Books.

Nietzsche, F. (1997 [1889]) *The Twilight of the Idols, Or, How to Philosophize with the Hammer*, trans. Polt, R., Indianapolis: Hackett.

Nietzsche, F. (2006) *The Nietzsche Reader*, Pearson, K.A. and Large, D. (eds), Oxford: Blackwell.

Petzet, H.W. (1993 [1983]) *Encounters and Dialogues with Martin Heidegger 1929–1976*, trans. Emad, P. and Maly, K., Chicago: University of Chicago Press.

Polt, R. (1999) *Heidegger: An Introduction*, London: UCL Press.

Rowley, H. (2007 [2006]) *Tête-à-Tête, The Lives and Loves of Simone de Beauvoir and Jean-Paul Sartre*, London: Vintage.

Russell, D. (1994) Psychiatric Diagnosis and the Interests of Women, in Sadler, J.Z., Wiggins, O.P. and Schwartz, M.A. (eds) *Philosophical Perspectives on Psychiatric Diagnostic Classification*, Baltimore and London: Johns Hopkins University Press.

Sartre, J.P. (1969 [1943]) *Being and Nothingness*, trans. Barnes, H.E., London: Routledge.

—— (2003 [1964]) *Les Mots*, Paris: Edition Gallimard.

Smith-Pickard, P. (2006) Merleau-Ponty's Husserlian Heresy, in *Journal of the Society for Existential Analysis*, January, 17.1: 55–70.

Spinelli, E. (1989) *The Interpreted World: An Introduction to Phenomenological Psychology*, London: Sage.

—— (1996 [1994]) *Demystifying Therapy*, London: Constable.

—— (2006 [1997]) *Tales of Un-knowing: Therapeutic Encounters from an Existential Perspective*, Ross-on-Wye: PCCS Books.

Stadlen, A. (2003) A poor model for those in training, in *Journal of the Society for Existential Analysis*, 14.2: 213–244.

—— (2005) Inner Circle Seminar, on *Gelassenheit*, 30 October 2005.

—— (2007a) The Madhouse of Being, in *Journal of the Society for Existential Analysis*, 18.1: 117–154.

—— (2007b) Re: chapter, email 8 July 2007.

Stassen, M. (ed.) (2003) *Martin Heidegger: Philosophical and Political Writings*, New York: Continuum.

Steiner, G. (1992) *Heidegger*, 2nd edn, London: Fontana Press. (First edn 1978.)

Summerfield, D. (1998) The Social Experience of War and some Issues for the Humanitarian Field, in Bracken, P.J. and Petty, C. (eds) *Rethinking the Trauma of War*, London: Free Association Books.

Szasz, T. (1974 [1961]) *The Myth of Mental Illness: Foundations of a Theory of Personal Conduct*, New York: Harper and Row.

—— (2001 [1999]) *Is Mental Illness a Disease?* Thomasz S. Szasz, M. D. Cybercenter for Liberty and Responsibility.

—— (2003) The Secular Cure of Souls, 'Analysis' or Dialogue?, in *Journal of the Society for Existential Analysis*, 14.2: 203–212.

Ticktin, S. (1986) Brother Beast: A Personal Memoir of David Cooper, in *Asylum Magazine for Democratic Psychiatry*, 1, 3, reprinted, Colloquia, in person. http://laingsociety.org/colloquia/inperson/davidcooper/brotherbeast1.html.

Tillich, P. (1980 [1952]) *The Courage To Be*, New Haven CT: Yale University Press.

Toombs, S.K. (2001) *Phenomenology and Medicine*, Dordrecht: Kluwer.

Tugendhat, E. (1993 [1984]) Heidegger's Idea of Truth, trans. Wolin, R., in Wolin, R.(ed.) (1993 [1991]) *The Heidegger Controversy*, Cambridge MA: MIT Press.

van der Kolk, B.A., McFarlane, A.C. and Weisaeth, L. (eds) (1996) *Traumatic Stress: The Effects of Overwhelming Experience on Mind, Body and Society*, New York: Guilford Press.

van Deurzen, E. (2006) New School of Psychotherapy and Counselling, 10th Anniversary Conference, London.

van Deurzen-Smith, E. (1991) Ontological Insecurity Revisited, in *Journal of the Society for Existential Analysis*, 2: 38–48.

—— (1997) *Everyday Mysteries: Existential Dimensions of Psychotherapy*, London: Routledge.

—— (1998) *Paradox and Passion in Psychotherapy: An Existential Approach to Therapy and Counselling*, Chichester: Wiley.

Veer, G. van der (1998) *Counselling and Therapy with Refugees and Victims of Trauma: Psychological Problems of Victims of War, Torture and Repression*, 2nd edn, Chichester: Wiley. (First edn 1992.)

Wardi, D. (1992) *Memorial Candles: Children of the Holocaust*, London: Brunner-Routledge.

Warnock, M. (1996) *Existentialism*, Oxford: Oxford University Press. (First edn 1970.)

Wolf, D. (2003) The Absurd and the Embarrassing, Adopting the Szasz Position with Dr Stadlen, in *Journal of the Society for Existential Analysis*, 14.2: 245–250.

Wolf, D.J. (2002) Nietzsche's Psychopathology, in *Journal of the Society for Existential Analysis*, 13: 297–308.

Wolin, R. (ed.) (1993 [1991]) *The Heidegger Controversy*, Cambridge MA: MIT Press.

—— (2001) *Heidegger's Children*, Princeton NJ: Princeton University Press.

—— (2007) re: Heidegger and his doctoral students, email (9 October 2007).

Yalom, I. (1980) *Existential Psychotherapy*, New York: Basic Books.

—— (1991 [1989]) *Love's Executioner and Other Tales of Psychotherapy*, Harmondsworth: Penguin.

—— (1995) *The Theory and Practice of Group Psychotherapy*, 4th edn, New York: Basic Books.

—— (2002) *The Gift of Therapy, Reflections on Being a Therapist*, London: Piatkus Books.

Young, A. (1995) *The Harmony of Illusions: Inventing Post-Traumatic Stress Disorder*, Princeton NJ: Princeton University Press.

Yule, W. (ed.) (1999) *Post-Traumatic Stress Disorders: Concepts and Therapy*, Chichester: Wiley.

BEING-IN-THE-WORLD

'Being-in-the-world' does not mean the same thing as 'being in the world': the hyphens make all the difference. The hyphens express the fact that all the elements of the expression are significant, that they all belong together and that none can be understood in isolation. Being-in-the-world is Heidegger's description of human existence (*Dasein* or *ek-sistence*): *-in-* does not denote a container (we are not in the world like apples are *in* a fruit bowl), *-in-* stands for dwelling within a web of interconnected meanings (rather like being *in* fashion, *in* limbo).

Human existence is always in a shared world, the world of the particular era, country, culture, family, etc. in which we are born, with all its traditions, customs and beliefs. But at the same time it is always a private world: it represents the way I myself relate and exist, it is my world and it matters to me.

We bring understanding and meaning to our perception of the world, without having to think about it: we do not have to think 'this is a chair' before sitting in one; or 'this is sad' before crying. We have an embodied, emotional, practical understanding of the world and relation to it. Our moods and the way we are tuned into the world at any given moment affect our take on it. (Our detached conceptual and scientific understanding is secondary.)

When clients have a major life crisis, they often have the sense that their world has been 'turned upside down'. And indeed it has: one thing may have changed and their whole being-in-the-world has been altered, for all its aspects are interconnected. It may affect the way they see and define themselves and hence the way they relate to others and others to them. It may affect their experience of time and space, for we do not measure space geometrically, nor time by the clock: we have a lived experience of space and time. After serious illness, distances may seem longer, objects may go out of reach, time may feel more precious, or drag to a standstill; for the bereaved, a loss that occurred ten years ago may feel like yesterday.

2

REFLECTIONS ON
CANCER COUNSELLING

Melanie Lockett

Introduction

I, the counsellor, am in an oncology clinic. I am listening to a doctor and he is talking to me: 'Melanie I think I am looking at cancer. Can you see how your blood supply has been rerouted to the tumour?' I am still. I hear the voices of the many women I have worked with describing this moment. I am in the room. I feel the nurse's hand holding mine. I am out of the room. I am in shock.

In this moment I move from cancer counsellor to cancer patient. Some 18 months on I still straddle these two identities. I invite you to join me, by sharing this experience. It is impossible now for me to hang on to the illusion that I am separate, safe and immortal. I too face the questions, physical sensations and emotions that my clients described to me. My identity is altered. I am no longer just an empathic observer. I am a participant in learning to live with a life-threatening illness.

A colleague showed me a new poster in the hospital where I am a cancer patient, group facilitator and cancer counselling supervisor. It was of a woman receiving chemotherapy. I felt a jolt through my body. I was aware of nothing except the needle in her arm. I was back in the chemo suite. I could feel the needle, taste the chemicals streaming through my veins. I stood there, reshocked. Once again I felt the bewilderment and disorientation that engulfed me at the beginning of chemotherapy. I had stepped into someone else's life. It was unreal, unbelievable.

My diagnosis, subsequent treatment and recovery helped me to know that I am not special or different from other people who get cancer. I too can no longer deny that life is finite. The knowledge I had gained over the years about cancer, its treatment and the psychological effects did not help me much. I was in turmoil with little sense of me or of the life I had previously been living. I knew that my world was changed and that I could control very little. I did not know how I would cope. I felt scared and vulnerable. I was going through what many of my clients had experienced before me, shock and disbelief followed by a rollercoaster of emotions as treatment began.

This chapter is about how my own cancer experience has increased my understanding of what it means to be a cancer counsellor. When I first agreed to write this, I had not had cancer. Then, it would have been a different chapter based on my work with many clients. Now I write it as a result of deep personal reflection of a different quality. What does it mean for me now to be human? What does it mean to me to have my life threatened by cancer? What are the implications for my work as a cancer counsellor? I also include quotes from my clients, to illustrate both the universality and the individuality of being human in the face of a life-threatening illness and the possible helpful responses that might be made by a cancer counsellor.

Cancer counsellor and cancer patient

Although my initial training was integrative, it is Yalom's approach to existential psychotherapy that has mostly informed my work with people affected by cancer. Effective cancer counselling can be based on the four existential concerns of death, freedom, isolation and meaninglessness (Yalom 1998). I believe that cancer counsellors need to explore their own issues about dying and their existential anxieties to enable them to work more effectively with cancer patients. Counsellors need to provide reassurance that they are prepared to listen to the client's existential concerns without taking flight into cliché or unrealistic hopefulness. Besides facing the knowledge that we will one day die, doing so can free us to live a less fearful life. Only then can we really meet those who are facing the threat of a shortened life.

I returned to work after a break of eight months. Much that I had known about myself both personally and professionally was altered. Cancer had attacked my identity. Who was I now? Was I anything more than a patient? It had attacked my sexuality. Where had my sexual energy gone? Where was my life energy? Would I die from this disease? It had attacked my physicality. I had one breast, was scarred, numb, bald and very tired. I had closed down. I was just trying to survive.

In my client work I was already familiar with the four existential concerns identified by Irvin Yalom. However, after my diagnosis, I noticed myself shift from an understanding of these to a recognition that they were now more directly to do with my life. I was concerned with what I wanted to do with my life now, where I wanted to live and the kind of life I wanted. I needed to connect deeply with myself, the world and people. I needed to let go of friends and places that no longer had meaning for me.

My motivation for working in this field had partly been about learning from my clients how to live, rather than how to die. As a counsellor I strive to reach my potential to be aware, accessible and vulnerable and to reach a level of subtle connectedness which includes acceptance, understanding and curiosity that I might describe as 'love'. It is from this place and by offering the core conditions (Rogers 1967) that clients can heal.

Some years ago I was standing on a beach in Dorset beneath the midday sun looking out to the horizon. It was early summer. Light was everywhere, dancing on the rippling surface of the sea, and the pebbles on the beach were hot underfoot. I felt a moment of intense joy. I was filled with the conviction that cancer counselling was absolutely right for me, but that I had yet to reach the depths in myself that were needed for this work. Since that day, I have directed my work to opening myself up further to what it means to be alive and to have that life threatened. Many clients have taught me much about both. Since my diagnosis of cancer I have become clearer. I have had an opportunity to face in a real way the possibility of my death and to express some of my dread and anxiety about dying. My anxiety is focused on how I might die and knowing that I will. I live with the knowledge that it might be sooner than I would want and from breast cancer. This is compounded by my belief that only nothingness follows death. I will not know before I die what it is like to be dead and I have no control over when or how this will happen. The more I explore this, the calmer I mostly feel.

Counsellors who are open, engaged, fearless and courageous enough to explore their existential concerns and motives for doing this work may develop a more genuine presence with clients affected by cancer. Yalom does not think a counsellor can effectively work with a client by making a dichotomy between 'us', the living therapists, and 'them', the dying patients. Group therapists, he says, lead effectively when they appreciate that it is 'we' who face death: the leaders are members who must share in the group's anxiety.

The therapeutic relationship is unlike any other relationship the client may have. A counsellor creates a safe and certain space in which thoughts and feelings can be expressed about being diagnosed, undergoing treatment and the likely prognosis. Through this process, clients may begin to adjust to life with or after cancer.

My experience and growth as a counsellor in 'sharing' in the client's anxiety happened for me when I returned to work. I was questioned by clients who were all living with advanced disease – at my request they had been told of my diagnosis – about whether I was up to the task. I believe that these clients were expressing their underlying concern that I might not be robust enough to listen, respond and contain their concerns and fears. I had to think deeply about this. I wanted to be able to contain them, but knew it could not be in the same way as before my diagnosis. I didn't know if I was up to the job, I lost confidence and suddenly I felt like a novice counsellor. However, with the help of my partner, counsellor, supervisor and some good friends I began to talk openly about my anxieties and concerns and to face the possibility of my death. As a result of this, I could reassure my clients that I actually felt more open and willing to share in their anxiety than before. I could be a container, but now I had a different shape, a shape that more closely resembled theirs and yet was also different.

Some of my supervisees felt unsure about whether they could bring issues about death and dying to me now that I had had cancer. As a clinical supervisor I endeavour to create a safe but challenging space for my supervisees to explore their work. They were telling me this space was no longer safe. I found myself on the receiving end of all sorts of projections about their own existential vulnerability. I was angry. It became clear that by getting cancer I had broken the unspoken rule that those of us who work in the field are somehow immune from the disease and even perhaps death. Might they be able to protect themselves from their own very difficult feelings if they could avoid talking to me about clients who are dying? This challenge could have been an isolating experience for me. Are we not all human and therefore all going to die? Was my new status of cancer patient going to eject me from their world? Although I felt angry and rejected I also recognized that my anger protected me from my fears about my change in identity and my increased fragility.

The heart of therapeutic work

Most of us live life in a state of death denial. Keeping busy, not stopping, filling every moment can help us to believe that we are special and immortal. We may try to order our universe by seeking to control ourselves and others to prevent our world view from being challenged. For if we do stop, reflect and connect with ourselves, we run the risk of glimpsing that we are insignificant and transient. We might see that our lives are without purpose or meaning and that we are alone.

Clients diagnosed with cancer are often confronted with this uncomfortable reality. Counselling may help them uncover thoughts and feelings that might otherwise remain unsaid and cause considerable distress, anxiety and confusion. This may block fruitful communication with those closest to them, as well as with the medical professionals involved in their care. Existential anxieties will always be in the field of the work between client and counsellor, whether spoken about directly or not. It is the job of the counsellor to facilitate their expression and avoid collusion.

I have often heard clients say, even those who are living with a terminal diagnosis, that the experience of cancer has led them to a more 'lived' life. Through therapy, clients may take stock of their situation and question, with the counsellor's help, the values, beliefs and assumptions that have governed their lives so far and re-examine their relationships with significant others. They may come to live more in the present and develop more loving relationships.

Yalom's four 'existential concerns', from a client's perspective

Clients may deny the seriousness of their illness. This is usually a temporary defence against the existential concerns and a natural part of the adjustment to a changed life and the grief that it brings. Some clients may bring up issues that are apparently unrelated to cancer. They may talk about other traumatic events or speak of regrets or wrongdoings and will rarely refer to their illness. Yet in my experience clients are actually addressing some of their ultimate concerns, however obliquely, because a diagnosis of cancer provokes questions about being alive and the meaning of mortality.

Counsellors, including myself, can find it very hard to sit with their clients' existential concerns. They are not exempt from denying the inevitability of their own deaths. Some counsellors can be unaware that such issues are even present in their sessions with clients. Or if they do hear them, they worry about making an already vulnerable client suffer more by speaking openly and directly about such difficult material. Despite my own fragility, I have appreciated talking about my fears and continue to welcome the curiosity and care of others. It has helped me to feel less alone, stronger and to live my life more fully. I believe that by helping clients to connect with their deepest anxieties, they will actually gain deeper insight, more control and a greater calm. From this place, they can prioritize what is important now and become more of who they are. I asked Gloria, aged 38, to write about what it was like for her living with a shortened life:

> Being told you may die soon is now not the end of the road, but the beginning of a very powerful, emotional, traumatic and beautiful journey (if you let it). It's a unique and often lonely and isolating experience but I am trying to make the most of it . . . I want to get through the chemotherapy, wear all the clothes and shoes in my wardrobe, pass my experience and knowledge on to those who have yet to be where I am, to try and do things that make me happy, improve on the love I give to my family and friends.

Gloria valued those who could sit with her distress and their own and give her the attention she needed to face the end of her life. With their help, she was able to make plans, stay connected by participating in various 'cancer' events and become closer to her family.

Dying

I am sitting with a 58-year-old woman who is very ill. Mary is a feisty, prickly individual, who was difficult to get to know. She has been very angry about her diagnosis and directed much of this anger at the medical profession:

> They have told me I only have a few weeks left, I hope to make that a few more. I'm going to a hospice but only for a few days and then home.

I don't want to be there if it is full of very ill people. I'm well looked after in hospital, I know I'm dying although I feel too well [she actually looked very poorly], so it doesn't feel very real. Is this what it is like because it feels allright? Melanie how are you coping with your diagnosis?

I deliberately brought myself into the present, adjusted my posture so that I could relax, breathe and bring the whole of myself to this conversation. She was talking to me about holding the tension of knowing she was dying and yet wanting to go on. She wanted to make sense of the process of dying. She wanted protection and care and yet still to be a part of and in control of her life at home. She asked me how I was and I told her that I was still very shocked at my own diagnosis. She agreed that it is shocking, but went on to say that we all cope and we all die. She made death ordinary. I was moved by encountering this more open part of Mary. She was letting me and others see her. I responded to what she had said by telling her I felt sad about losing her and that it was good to have this time with her. I said I would miss her when she died. By both of us being authentic, direct and heartfelt we really met each other. I sat with her, encouraged and strengthened by her adjustment to what was happening. She had let me into her world. I was a fellow human who was also living with a risk of cancer returning. She made the thought of death more normal. The ingredient that makes this kind of encounter possible is not to be found in counselling texts. It is about allowing oneself to feel vulnerable and mortal. Mary died three weeks later and I miss her.

I asked Joe, a 78-year-old man with prostate cancer that had spread, to describe what he felt about having been told he had a terminal illness:

This time scale also sets a limit for one's life and planning for the future, the proverbial 'sword' hanging over one. Being a Celt, well 50 per cent, I can get emotional and the zoladex implants don't help. Sitting in the sun lounge on a glorious summer's day, would I see many more? A choir singing my favourite carol, 'In the Bleak Midwinter', can bring a tear; my daughter planning a long-term holiday, will I still be there? How will I cope in extremis, with the likely severe physical side effects of the advanced stages of the prostate cancer, the pain, the difficulty in controlling the basic functions: will I be strong enough to voluntarily leave my beloved home for hospital?

Joe has raised many crucial issues. He ponders on how to plan for the future. He grieves for his life and expresses concerns about what he might expect towards the end of his life.

Discussing such issues with clients is important. Clients may be ready to do this at different times during their illness and may need to come and go from the topic. It is essential to be direct about preparing for death, as much may be lost if it is not spoken about. Within this context, clients have the freedom to raise many issues. These can include making practical decisions, saying goodbye, dealing with unfinished business and choosing where to die. They may express concerns such as feeling a burden and not feeling in control. They are then better prepared to make decisions with other professionals about their treatment, for example, about pain and symptom control, and then to make choices about how to live the time that they have. A counsellor can encourage clients to explore their options and make some decisions.

Freedom

> The individual is entirely responsible for – that is, is the author of – his or her own world, life design, choices and actions. 'Freedom' in this sense, has a terrifying implication: it means that beneath us there is no ground – nothing, a void, an abyss.
>
> (Yalom 1980: 9)

We base our identity on how we see ourselves and how others see us, and on the basis of that we make choices about how to live our lives and create for ourselves a sense of being in control. We develop roles and responsibilities that support this construction. The dread we feel is an acknowledgement that, despite our efforts to build structure in our lives, underneath there is a yawning abyss. Cancer can be an attack on our bodies, identity, sense of self-worth, invulnerability, security and our belief and spiritual systems.

We long for certainty in an uncertain world. My experience of this abyss was, and still is, an endless emptiness where nothing is familiar. It began when I had to close my practice. I lost the relationship with my clients, routine and structure. Suddenly there were hospital appointments, financial concerns and even the relationships with friends and family were changed. Now there are no landmarks and I feel less safe. At the heart of it is fear. I am frightened of this difficult place and of being in touch with such bleakness. Yet I believe it is from here that I can allow new structures to emerge which will give meaning to my life and return me to a better sense of who I am becoming.

Although I have 'picked up' various roles since the end of my treatment, I am aware of and continue to struggle with my groundlessness, my void. Here there lie many uncertainties and dark places that I am determined to embrace so that, in time, I may create real change in my life.

Spiegel and Classen (2000) describe how cancer can challenge what we have constructed and how our clients will often need to reconstruct a sense of self and of how they want to live their lives now. Clients may be expressing the existential concern of freedom to the counsellor when they say: 'Who am I now?' 'What is normal now?' 'How can I still be useful?' These questions are linked to the roles that we have adopted in life, those of being a lover, parent, daughter, son, sister, brother, worker, homemaker and friend. If these roles are altered or taken away, many of us struggle to define ourselves and yet it is underneath these roles that our essence of self – our qualities, values, beliefs, experiences, desires and fears – can be uncovered.

Cancer disturbs our identity. Clients will have suffered a variety of attacks on their identity and, either because of a loss of stamina or the side effects of treatment or the progression of the disease, they may be unable to continue to work, do jobs in the house, fully parent children. They may be prevented from doing the things that gave them pleasure and contributed to how they defined themselves. The counsellor may be supporting a client who needs to reconstruct or transform an identity which is now changed or lost. They can help their clients to begin to rebuild a sense of self and make realistic choices within the context of their cancer diagnosis. Working with clients in the here and now can help them to connect and express their darkest thoughts and desires. With new insight gained by staying with their most distressing feelings, they can make choices about what they really want, like Rose aged 44 years:

> I have such regrets that I haven't made more of my life but I want to make 'now' count. I know that I have spent my life pleasing others and not being myself. I have always been afraid of my mother's disapproval so it was better to do nothing.

Rose was able to explore her regrets and understand how difficult it had been for her to be the 'author of her world'. It transpired that she had always lived life feeling fearful and this had stopped her from properly living. In due course, by allowing her to voice these fears and explore her courage in living with cancer, she became less fearful and more proactive. She allowed herself to do more and embarked on a relationship, life became more meaningful and she felt less alone.

Exploring how 'now' can be meaningful may reduce a client's sense of isolation. It can increase their ability to take control once again, feel less helpless and begin to 'live' in the time they have left. Being able to communicate what matters, to feel useful and connected to others can increase, in all of us, a sense of being alive.

By helping clients into the here and now, counsellors can enable them to express painful feelings and, in doing so, find some peace. I was reminded of the power of being only in the present by Jean who was living with advanced disease. Here, she is recounting her recent memories of a holiday from which she had just returned: 'For us, sitting out on our balcony watching the sun come up or go down was so incredibly relaxing.' Jean was only aware of the rhythm of the sun. She would absorb herself in those sunrises and sunsets and, feeling alive and relaxed, let go of her fears about her future. Jean died a few months later.

Isolation

A diagnosis of cancer tends to throw most people out of the world they know. This is disorientating, confusing and frightening. What clients might have assumed they could rely on is replaced by increased uncertainty about almost everything. They may feel very isolated while being reliant on the care of others. Providing the right kind of help is not easy. Counsellors who protect themselves against their own existential anxieties, blocked by fear, may notice that they adopt a protective role. They want to rescue their clients from their distress or perhaps distance themselves by disengaging at times during the sessions. By being protective we can unwittingly erode an individual's sense of self or resourcefulness. When we adopt this role we are actually protecting ourselves from what we feel and from our own vulnerabilities. When we notice we feel distant and not engaged, there is usually something powerful and unspoken going on. The need to protect or distance ourselves from a client can close the door on being able to talk about what it is really like for them. The client may feel increasingly isolated with a diminishing sense of who they are. For some, the role of cancer patient may begin to dominate.

The experience of isolation can occur at any time. I remember my own radiotherapy treatment being a time when I felt the existential tension of both knowing I was on my own with my cancer, but desperately needing the contact and care of others. When I had chemotherapy, I always had someone with me. However, I was not prepared for radiotherapy which, I had been told, was 'a breeze' after chemo and I therefore did not give it much thought. Although, given the treatment, I expected to be alone in the room, I found that when I was lying on the radiotherapy table for the first time, I truly felt I was the only person left in the universe. I was in this large chilly room, my one remaining breast exposed, my head bald, while a large machine swung round me, zapping me. I felt absolutely on my own. This was my cancer. To comfort myself, I remembered all those cards, emails and flowers that I had been sent – a flow of love from the people who had had the courage to write to me and had been so frank about their feelings for me. I became part of the outside world.

A counsellor can offer a deep empathic understanding of their clients' experience and help them to tap into their own resourcefulness. This can reduce a client's sense of isolation and help them to choose how they want to be in the world, without denying the universal truth that we are all here on our own. They can ensure that their clients remain in touch with who they are, even though this will have been altered by the shock of the diagnosis and the invasive nature of treatment. They can help clients to continue to feel useful and in-the-world. Counsellors may also encourage clients to review their support system and help them create friendships. They may let go of those that no longer work, while maintaining or building relationships with health professionals.

Meaninglessness

We all strive to make sense of our world. We have a set of beliefs, values and assumptions to guide us in how to live our lives. One of the many difficulties about cancer is that often there is no proven reason why some people get it and others do not (there are exceptions to this). Its random nature means that there is no answer to 'why me?', which is a plea for control and a desire to feel less helpless in the face of a cancer diagnosis. If we knew why we got cancer, then we could possibly stop it returning or spreading. I have worked with many clients who have struggled to let go of the search for an explanation for their illness. 'Is it stress?' they ask, 'a divorce or bereavement, a time of immense change? Or was it that I did something, ate the wrong things, and didn't look after myself?' When they can accept that no one knows and that it seems random, they can begin to accept the chaotic nature of the world over which they have no control. By making this adjustment, clients are often more able and willing to focus on what responsibility they can take in their lives.

An experience that helped me to deepen my understanding of meaninglessness occurred during my treatment: I would stand on my back doorstep and look at the night sky. I would gaze at the planets and stars and sense the vastness of our little understood universe. I found in these moments that I could feel and accept my insignificance, my meaninglessness and transience. This experience made me feel very calm and, as a result, more accepting of what I was going through. It became easier for me to find meaning and purpose in my life at this difficult time.

Clients who can be helped to accept the 'lottery' of cancer, the underlying chaos of the world, their inability to control what happens, may discover what has meaning in their lives, what is trivial and what they want more of. This may mean reprioritizing goals, enjoying small day-to-day events and valuing the pleasures and accomplishments of the here and now. Clients who are living with the knowledge that their cancer may return can benefit from seeing what is really important and discuss ways of making some changes. For David, a man aged 56, this meant taking some decisions for his life ahead:

> I decided to take medical retirement and leave my job. I didn't want to waste my time in something I wasn't enjoying. I don't know if my cancer

will come back, but I want to go and see my family in Australia. I have also volunteered at the local cancer centre where I got some help. I can help others who are going through this and show them there is life after cancer.

Not all clients will make changes following their diagnosis, but they are often changed because of it. Some, on the other hand, may feel stuck, depressed, their lives without meaning. This 69-year-old woman was diagnosed two years previously:

My day is good if I can make a meal and then do a little shopping; then I'm usually too tired to do anything else and I don't want to go out, I feel worthless and ugly.

She can do very little, her voice is quiet and flat, her self-esteem very low. She may just be grieving for the life that is gone and this is natural, but if her low mood persists and she shows other signs of depression, sleeplessness, anxiety and inability to function or care for herself, she may need to be encouraged to visit her GP. With the help of antidepressants she may be more able to make use of counselling support and regain her sense of self and her life.

Another client, aged 36, was less clear about her life now:

I know that cancer has changed how I see life. What was 'normal' before has gone, but I don't yet know what my new 'normal' is.

This client was encouraged to take some small steps towards rejoining life. Despite fatigue, she looked after her friend's allotment and set herself modest achievable goals each day. She became more satisfied and engaged with her life. Within a few weeks, she reported that she felt more herself, her stamina was improving and she was clearer about what was now important to her. She still didn't know what 'normal' was, but was discovering that she enjoyed a new spontaneity in her life. She had begun to live again.

Conclusion

Counsellors can help clients uncover what it means to be human by talking directly about difficult topics. Cancer patients are often in touch with the inevitable anxieties about being alive. Anxieties and tensions exist between knowing that 'I am going to die' and the desire to go on living; knowing that there is no solid ground, even as we attempt to put structures into place; feeling isolated, 'nobody understands', 'I'm alone with this cancer', while needing contact, protection and to be part of a larger whole. Clients seek meaning – 'Why me?' 'What caused my cancer?' – in an essentially meaninglessness, random universe (Yalom 1998). Counsellors who are able to help clients confront these tensions may help them to acquire clarity about how they want to live their lives and thereby gain more control at a time of extreme uncertainty.

I am walking on the Sussex Downs on a winter's day. The sea is grey-blue, the cliffs white. This is a favourite place for me, beautiful and vast. I am alive and in-the-world. I now live a life that better reflects what I want and who I am. I am not without fear, but I am not fearful. I am vulnerable, but less controlling. I do not walk on solid ground, but I feel safer, I know that I am transient and one day will die. It is from this greater sense of me and my knowledge of my mortality that I now meet my clients.

Acknowledgements

My grateful thanks to Laura Barnett, Rosemary Burch, Caroline Doherty, Maggie Fisher, Lesley Thomson, and all the clients I have known.

References

Rogers, C. (1967) *On Becoming a Person*, London: Constable.
Spiegel, D. and Classen, C. (2000) *Group Therapy for Cancer Patients*, New York: Basic Books.
Yalom, I. (1980) *Existential Psychotherapy*, New York: Basic Books.
—— (1998) *The Yalom Reader*, New York: Basic Books.

FREEDOM

From my earliest childhood in France, I was taught about 'Liberté, Egalité, Fraternité'. Yet, it was not until I started training as an existential therapist that freedom lost its abstraction and entered into my understanding of everyday life. Freedom is about the choices we have, the decisions we make and the actions we take. Freedom is about our values, beliefs and priorities: it is about the meaning we choose to attach to people, to nature, to situations and to things. And the way we exercise that freedom will have an impact on our world: we are responsible for the way we use our freedom. This is why Viktor Frankl suggested that a Statue of Responsibility face the Statue of Liberty.

Sartre famously said that 'we are condemned to be free': freedom involves thinking about life, death and the meaning of our existence; it therefore brings us dilemmas and makes us realize that we are, in fact, responsible for our lives. But we can also assume freedom and responsibility as gifts, albeit onerous ones at times. Freedom is sometimes about seeing a dark cloud's silver lining, about turning adversity into enrichment. Freedom goes with hope. It can also be about giving in or giving up. It can go with hopelessness and despair.

For some of our clients, choices have become extremely restricted through injury or illness, etc.; they may have become totally dependent on others for their basic needs; they may only have a few weeks to live. Yet they still have the freedom to choose how to relate to their carers, how to live certain aspects of their last weeks.

3

HIV AS A MIRROR TO LIFE

David Horne

For over a quarter of a century we have lived with the presence of HIV. The challenge of HIV, a 'dread' disease, has raised many questions as to what the process of adjustment, integration and adaptation to such suffering means. We probably need a whole compendium of definitions to help clarify all the ramifications of this particular virus' arrival. Having a relatively new virus that may not seem to affect an individual overtly, but has the potential to be life threatening, is difficult to assimilate. In addition, the fact that in 2006 a 47-year-old man became the first gay British male to be convicted for deliberately infecting his partner with HIV shows that we are navigating uncharted territory. The advent of HIV has had a profound effect on the gay male community, and the history of how HIV is perceived has, in turn, been strongly affected by its link to homosexuality. In the early 1980s, the 30 diagnoses per month in San Francisco alone resulted in palpable shock waves of fear that led to the questioning of life as it had been.

As the subject is vast, I shall be focusing on the following questions:

- How does this virus affect the way we see sex and life itself?
- Does HIV highlight issues that were already present in a person's life history?
- Has the distinction between an HIV positive and negative status created a barrier that conceals an existential commonality between the two?

Since I first encountered HIV when living in California in 1982, I have felt that there is a whole cultural, political and social background to HIV, which cannot be overlooked when considering HIV in a psychotherapeutic context. In the West, the wide use of anti-retroviral drugs has resulted in people now living much longer with HIV; indeed, the terminal nature of HIV is increasingly uncertain. This, and the greater prevalence of HIV throughout the entire community, has resulted in a radically different picture: we can no longer accept the original stereotyping of HIV+/AIDS as a 'homosexuals' illness'. Our attitude to HIV in our lives has to evolve with the virus, its demographic distribution and its treatment. The impact and development of

HIV in Africa, where universal access to highly active anti-retroviral therapy (HAART) remains elusive, is dramatically different. Human consequences of HIV echo, therefore, the diversity of cultural values, public policy, society, religion and economics.

In June 1981, the first cases of unusual immune system failures were medically identified in the USA. These were mainly among gay men and intravenous drug users. By the following year, acquired immunodeficiency syndrome (AIDS) was defined for the first time. Although recognised then, it is likely that this virus had been around much longer, due to the sometimes lengthy and variable period between infection and the onset of symptoms. Earliest evidence of the human form of the virus dates from 1959 in the Democratic Republic of the Congo. In 1983 Dr Luc Montagnier working in France isolated lymphadenopathy-associated virus (LAV), which was later renamed as human immunodeficiency virus or HIV. In the same year in Central Africa, a heterosexual AIDS epidemic was becoming evident. Then in 1984 Dr Robert Gallo in the USA identified HIV as the cause of AIDS.

Four years on from the first cases, HIV was being reported on every continent and, at the same time, HIV antibody tests were becoming available. Yet it would take another 11 years before evidence of the effectiveness of HAART was revealed. In the developed world, this was to revolutionize treatment as we know it. Indeed, long-term side effects of HAART have now become a greater concern among those infected with HIV than the illness caused by HIV itself. The focus for treating HIV has shifted from efficacy, to potency, to issues such as long-term resistance and tolerability. However, there is no room for complacency, with 25 million deaths and an estimated 40 million infections worldwide (WHO 2006). We still do not have a cure or vaccine and many scientists doubt that either is imminent. Furthermore, misinformation about HIV treatment and the false assumption that HIV is no longer fatal have contributed to the increase in diagnoses. Despite growing numbers of people infected with HIV, an Ipsos MORI poll, commissioned by the National AIDS Trust (2006) found that people in the UK were generally less aware of how HIV is transmitted than they were five years ago.

We are all exposed to the existence of HIV in our society. In this chapter, I shall be looking at an HIV positive (HIV+) diagnosis as an existential crisis or trauma, exploring phenomenologically what it means for that person, without pathologizing that experience. I shall focus on the non-biological, non-medical aspects of this phenomenon to highlight the existential issues that are central concerns for individuals infected with HIV, showing how an existential–phenomenological approach can assist in understanding that person's experience. I want to view the HIV+ predicament in relation to existential themes such as the meaning of life and death, 'ontological insecurity'[1] and our state of being temporal. I also want to consider whether or not the most obvious of the ontological[2] aspects of existence, namely the phenomenon of death, really is the archenemy.

Death certainly presents us with a conflict – that of striving to construct our being with the inevitability of non-being. 'What is the point?' one may well ask – and indeed some of our clients do. The significance of our mortality as recognized existentially is that it may foster an attitude of authenticity and thus contribute to reducing fear and anxiety, allowing growth, renewal and vitality for life. I shall introduce three clients, Lyle, Helena and Celine, to help illustrate existential thinking within my practice. Most importantly I do not define them exclusively in terms of being HIV+. In each of these case histories, the client is fundamentally concerned with death (although I want to stress that HIV, here in the West, does not automatically bring the assumption of a hastened death any more). I shall show instances of how the existential recognition of the significance of being-toward-death may offer a positive contribution to life and that the transcendence of fear, anxiety and struggle may accompany this process.

As an existential psychotherapist, if I am to work with integrity and be useful in my practice, I must maintain my own sense of uncertainty. For me, 'the vitality of our death' (Koestenbaum 1971) and nothingness – vitality, in the sense that the acceptance of our mortality may enable us to approach limits and vicissitudes in life with greater resourcefulness and clarity – lies in the ability to hold the tension in this uncertain certainty: we know that we shall die, but know not when.

I work from the assumption that perspective-changing therapy is brought about by the client and therapist's joint exploration of the client's world. Clients bring to the therapeutic relationship their whole being-in-the-world – their meaningful perceptions, feelings, thoughts, relations to others, apprehensions, fantasies and dreams. It is their private engagement with the world, but it is not defined once and for all. It is ever changing, even if only subtly; the process of therapy, however, may accelerate that change. By challenging clients from within their own spheres of reference, by highlighting discrepancies, paradoxes and contradictions, I seek to question their assumptions – including the assumption that they can see the world objectively. As the therapist, I know that I too have my own my take on the world. However, I need to develop a stance of 'un-knowing' – questioning my assumptions and theories, treating 'the seemingly familiar ... as novel, unfixed in meaning' (Spinelli 2006: 6). I affirm the 'unknowability' of human response and my respect for the human individual and the uniqueness of the human condition.

Although a person with an HIV+ diagnosis confronts many of the same existential issues as others who suffer from a potentially life-threatening disease, there are particular issues for a person with HIV. These arise because of the relationship between HIV and sexuality: the impact of HIV on the person's way of being sexually-in-the-world, the fact that HIV is primarily a sexually transmitted virus and the way it was, and still is, perceived by many as a homosexual man's disease. The fact that HIV is associated with drug users and with immigrants from the African continent further compounds the stigma. Perhaps one of the elements that makes HIV so complex to grasp is that it concerns areas of experience generally considered to be deeply personal. Western society offers us conflicting messages about sexuality: while it is always of great public curiosity and interest, it is also something private and not an area for public discussion. Yet, sexuality is an intrinsic aspect of our existence (Cohn 1997). It is 'an intentionality which follows the general flow of existence and yields to its movement . . . in his sexuality is projected [man's] manner of being towards time and other men' (Merleau-Ponty 1962: 157–158).

Merleau-Ponty speaks of sexuality as being present at all times 'like an atmosphere'; similarly, the potential threat of HIV+ pervades, 'like an atmosphere', a person's existence as being-sexually-in-the-world. I therefore must be mindful to focus on all aspects of my client's existence, including the impact of HIV on their body and their physical sensations. Through our bodies and our sexuality we become open to the world and realize our existence. 'Our own body is in the world as the heart is in the organism' (Merleau-Ponty 1962: 203).

Yalom (1980) posits the concept of the ultimate rescuer, a benign force or omnipotent higher being that human beings fantasize, to feel watched over and protected. It is interesting to note that, in our secular age in the West, the 'ultimate rescuer' has become abstracted into the belief that drugs may cure all our diseases. Medical advances throughout the last century have left society today with the implicit assumption that we have a future. HIV can shatter this for some and it can highlight the existential aloneness of the individual. There may be considerable solace in the idea of the ultimate rescuer. Indeed, I have encountered many clients who, after a diagnosis of HIV+, have presented with the need or desire to merge with a partner, to be rescued by love and intimacy. I have also worked with clients who have become sexually compulsive as a result of an HIV diagnosis. It has triggered their death anxiety and, it would seem, their need to merge. Attempting to sleep one's way out of an emotional quagmire is a familiar story. Yet it rarely works, as the desire to merge or to hold on to a sense of self through sex can overwhelm any attempt at reflecting on the situation and making beneficial choices. Paradoxically, other clients have become impotent through fear of death, and, as they see it, loss of self during sex. The clients' symptoms can be understood as a way of establishing a sense of security and certainty in response to the threat of HIV and basic existential, 'ontological insecurity'.

Lyle referred himself to therapy because he felt 'deadlocked'. At 40, he realized that he needed people, but couldn't connect and felt he couldn't go on as he was. He had become extremely isolated and unsupported, yet was aware that he never let people get close to him. He was deeply involved in his work as a freelance writer and felt that HIV had been the trigger to recognizing how alone he was and how concerned he was about being HIV+ and dying. He was now reviewing how he had spent the last 20 years and looking ahead, worrying about the future. Lyle revealed his pattern, since the age of 16, of countless sexual encounters and a never ending cycle of relationships that only lasted between three and 12 months. It seemed that Lyle had related to others mainly through his body.

Lyle said he intellectualized feelings and was aware in therapy of having to find a way to bring his emotions into the room in order to try and process them. This was consistent with Lyle's ease of talking about HIV in sessions by remaining distant from deep and difficult feelings. He rationalized about HIV and death – 'everyone dies' – rather than connecting with his own feelings on these matters. He didn't want to believe the test result, saying 'They must have mixed me up with someone else.' Paradoxically, HIV and all its ramifications had freed him from the life that he found so dissatisfying. At the same time, he was sad about being alone and feared dying alone. (In my experience as a therapist, the anxiety of HIV is infinitely greater in those who feel alone and unfulfilled.) Lyle explored the meaning he ascribed to the advent of HIV. Everything for Lyle was now revolving around HIV, but with the focus very much on life and how best to live it. HIV had highlighted his choices about lifestyle and he now wanted to address his relationships to others. It no longer seemed an option for him to pursue one night stands or to 'exit' relationships without confronting difficulties. He found it difficult to communicate and believed that anyone who was HIV negative could not really understand what it was like to be positive.

There are many aspects of our sense of being alive which remind us of our finitude. Yet, our Western culture's preoccupation with youth and an idealized body and its obsession with denying the process of ageing seem to mirror a denial of death. In my practice as a therapist, I have witnessed how an HIV+ diagnosis can cause profound shock and disillusionment when clients realize death or disease will attack or alter their body. To be in the world is to be a body, fleshly and sexual. It is through our bodies and sexuality that we interact with others in the world. We need to appreciate that we are firmly welded to this physical self and cannot be free from its material limitations: our body is our 'I-ness' – we 'are' body. It is our mode of participation in the world. Through attacks on the body we become aware of our mortality. HIV can therefore alter the focus from which we survey the territory of our life and world, and organize our spatial and temporal awareness and presence. We are body and have a body; the intimation of decay, ageing and death threaten our worldview and our whole world in all its dimensions.

Our response to HIV stems from often deep and dividing forces in our culture and experience. It is the relationship between experience and meaning that needs to be considered in the light of an HIV+ diagnosis, as this is central to how an individual processes such a trauma as HIV. Working existentially, I see each person as having to construct his or her own meaning in a world that lacks intrinsic meaning. Awareness of the ontological givens of existence is closely linked to a person's degree of self-reflection, self-questioning and connection to their experience. HIV, as opposed to other life-threatening illnesses such as cancer, also raises personal dilemmas about morality and truth. The afflicted are wrapped in a plethora of powerful emotions, the threat of untimely death, the guilt of a 'self-infected' illness and sometimes overwhelming anxiety of contagion. The glamourized images of sexuality and drugs, with which our commercialized culture had surrounded them, have now been transformed from desires to risks.

There is a correlation between the meaning that clients attribute to their diagnosis and the way they engage with their lives – that is the focus of much of our work. As an existentially informed therapist, it is crucial for me to attempt to understand and appreciate the various stances which each client adopts towards themselves and the world. This presents me with a challenge, as I have to abandon any notion that I know what is best for my clients. Human beings process crises differently and over variable lengths of time and this will be dependent on a person's psychological and physical constitution, past experiences, age, relationship to self and surrounding support. As a therapist, I have to maintain an awareness of how different issues can be central to the process of adjustment to HIV and to recognize these as they come to life in the therapeutic encounter.

Helena came to see me after the discovery of her positive diagnosis. In the 12 months between her diagnosis and the commencement of our sessions, Helena had felt out of control and in trouble: she was drinking heavily and waking up next to men that she did not even recall meeting. Also, she was driving recklessly. Helena, an Oxbridge graduate, had a senior position in corporate development within a recognized public company. She worked extremely hard and long hours. Her life, it seemed, was full: she was constantly busy. Helena had always enjoyed her body sexually. It was a crucial part of her existence and contributed highly to her recreational pleasure.

When I started seeing her, she was full of anger and blamed the man who had infected her, although she was unsure who this was. Becoming HIV+ had knocked her off course. At 36 years of age, this was the 'first hiccup' in her life. Now her confidence had been knocked too. In Helena's worldview, life was a continuous straight line: one grew up, had a career, married, had children and lived happily ever after. It was a world without pain or obstacles to stop one from pursuing these goals. She needed and created tremendous order in her life. However, now that there was, she felt, 'disorder' in her life, she kept asking herself: 'Who would want me now?' HIV for Helena had formed a background against which all other concerns had lessened in importance.

Helena's view of life did not encompass that we cease to exist and no longer play a part in the events of the world. An existential perspective would suggest that life and death are interdependent and that an acceptance of our temporality and own mortality may lead to a more authentic mode of being-in-the-world. Helena had brought to therapy the assumption that the process of therapy was to translate intentions into actuality, so that she could have the life she wanted. Her assumption was misguided, in that it did not take account of the fact that life may throw obstacles in our way, which limit our choices. Yet it implied an awareness of her own freedom of choice and of her capacity to bring about changes. This awareness and her capacity to apply herself, which she had demonstrated in her life so far, offered the hope that she would find a way of accepting and integrating her experience of HIV. The emotional energy it released led her to question her views on life. Initially, her concern centred on how she was to cope now that she 'was the virus', as this was all she could perceive of herself. She felt reminded of this on a daily basis at the point of taking HAART. I felt she was living as though she was about to die. Paradoxically, the medication maintaining her life was also the very thing that highlighted her mortality. The alcohol misuse helped to divert her away from a deeper emotional process, from recognizing that she was not realizing her potential: her life was 'full', but not fulfilling.

An HIV+ diagnosis offers an opportunity to reassess one's way of living and to bring about change by questioning one's view of life. We can choose our response to HIV as we do to any life event or indeed to life itself. In *Being and Time*, Heidegger (1962) stresses the uniqueness of *Dasein*,[3] human existence: 'Dasein is an entity for which, in its Being, that Being is an issue' (Heidegger 1962: 236). We are the only beings that can enquire into our own Being, reflect upon our own way of experiencing life and explore different possibilities of existence. It implies that we can have a sense and understanding of our relationship to life itself. We may choose, for instance, to question whether we are living life autonomously, according to our own beliefs and priorities, or whether we are being guided in our decisions by the expectations and values of others. The difference between these two approaches to life is fundamental to Heidegger in *Being and Time*. He argues that most of the time we follow the latter path, for it is a basic trait, an 'existential' of human existence, that we 'fall' in with the norms of the family and society within which we live. To a certain extent this is necessary, for we depend on shared norms, understanding and language to live and communicate with others. However, we also tend to fall in with others (the 'they') so as not to have to think for ourselves: 'For the most part *I myself* am not the "who" of Dasein; the *they-self* is its "who" ' (Heidegger 1962: 312).

Norms make day-to-day living comfortable and easy. Falling with the 'they' is, for Heidegger, the path of 'inauthenticity'. Conversely, authenticity involves reassessing one's values, beliefs and choices for oneself and owning them. The real test, for Heidegger, comes in the face of our mortality. Most of the time, we are prepared to think 'we shall all die', without taking the next step of saying 'I too shall die and it could be any day'. In the first, general statement, we are 'tranquillized' and lulled into forgetting our finitude; death has lost its sting – it is without potency. Heidegger suggests that by embracing our thrownness, temporality and death – by holding in our sight, even for a moment, both the groundlessness of our existence and our finitude – we can choose authentically which of our potentialities we shall seek to fulfil. A confrontation with our mortality can lead us towards a more authentic way of being.

> Celine was 42 years of age, widowed at 35 with three children under ten and became HIV+ two years ago, having begun dating again for the first time since her husband's death. She was completely devastated by her diagnosis; during our contract she was not on HAART. Celine had not adjusted to her status and prayed that a cure would be found, as she did not want to leave her children without their only parent. Celine was hyperconscious of her health and viewed every ailment or pain as a symptom of HIV. When she was well, the impact of HIV was reduced, but when she was ill, it was overwhelming. She was equally afraid of death and of being incapacitated by illness and felt she had no control over the future. Her expectations about the way she might die had also changed. Celine found long-term planning too difficult, as she felt that HIV would curtail her future.

Celine had only told one sibling and one friend about her diagnosis; she lived in fear of her ageing parents or others finding out about her condition. Her shame, guilt and anger were inextricably linked with the virus being sexually transmitted and she felt responsible for becoming infected. This was compounded by feeling 'a fool, as HIV has been around for so long'. Celine's diagnosis changed the way she thought about herself and made her hateful to herself. Everything was now altered by HIV for Celine: things that once seemed so important now appeared trivial to her, while others that she had once taken for granted mattered so much more than before. Her consciousness about time had been heightened and she realized how full she made each day; this revolved around her role as a mother. She felt she would never be able to socialize again. Through the counselling process, she also came to realize that her symptoms of anxiety and her behaviour were common reactions to an extreme situation and were not signs of, for example, her own intrinsic weakness.

A diagnosis of HIV can reveal our common existential concerns: it confronts us with the universal aspects of human existence, like a mirror to life. Life sets us many challenges from which we may learn and grow. HIV encompasses everything, it is very much about living and how to ascribe meaning to that living, and as such does not present anything unique to the human condition. In that sense, HIV can be seen as no more or less of a catastrophe than life itself; it is but another phenomenon of life. Heidegger does not assume that death is what Plato and Christians take it to be: the separation of the mortal body from the immortal soul. Death in *Being and Time* is the absolute end and drop into nothingness. As human beings, we are 'thrown' into a world that existed before us, one without any purpose or meaning, and in the act of being thrown one is also given over to death. By acknowledging our 'thrownness' and finitude, we are able to create our own response to the world in which we live: we can create meaning. In death we face a fundamental boundary to freedom. Freedom does not imply unlimited choices but exists within the boundaries inherent in human existence. Freedom with its concomitant anxiety is inextricably linked with responsibility and choices.

Lyle, Helena and Celine chose to explore the meaning they ascribed to their diagnosis of HIV. This, they felt, deepened their understanding of themselves by clarifying, for instance, which possibilities in life were theirs rather than the expectations and received opinions of others. They also had to acknowledge that some aspects of their lives would remain only as possibilities, as projects never to be fulfilled. In all three cases I can see a reflection of my dilemmas and struggles. My work heightens my awareness of the intrinsic fragility, uncertainty and limitations of my existence. I am profoundly yet differently affected by my work. Being continually confronted with psychologically demanding HIV client situations, I have found that I need to pay attention to the way my emotions can easily fluctuate from empathy, compassion and admiration for the client to anxiety, helplessness and inadequacy.

When working with HIV+ clients I feel it is important to accept the clients' account of what happened and what they are experiencing, as these are essential elements of the relationship. However, because of the shame and stigma attached to HIV, I listen out for the possible selectivity of the material presented and of the way I might be receiving it.

As therapists working with this client group, we may be at risk from the phenomenon of vicarious traumatization (VT), which is the impact on the therapist of repeated exposure to traumatic client material. By attempting to enter into the client's worldview, our own worldview comes into sharp focus and this is either validated or challenged. It is therefore extremely important that we remain aware of our own vulnerabilities and stress reactions and be attentive to what our HIV+ clients may trigger in us. I have supervised therapists who have become inhibited and intimidated sexually, as well as demoralized and depressed due to the emotional stress of working with HIV. We also need to be able to create a balance between work and our personal lives. Furthermore, with the changing face of HIV and with treatment strategies continuing to evolve, it is imperative not to become complacent, but to integrate and adapt knowledge into therapeutic practice and evolve as therapists. As HIV evolves and changes, so must we.

The focus on VT in the psychological literature of the last decade rests on the underlying assumption that VT has a negative effect on therapists – it may profoundly disrupt their frame of reference, affecting their basic identity, worldview and spirituality. Although this may be true, at the same time there is potentially much to be gained for us therapists from this challenge and disruption to our worldviews.

Conclusion

HIV is an illness that has become an icon of our times and a constraint on the human spirit of our day. We can liken the history of HIV to that of leprosy, as it too confronts us with loss and menace, and has the capacity to spoil, hurt and burden human experience. Indeed, in parts of our society today, attitudes to HIV are still reminiscent of biblical times: 'All the days wherein the plague shall be in him he shall be defiled; he is unclean: he shall dwell alone' (Leviticus 13: 46). The means of transmission of HIV have played a part in this ostracism. On the other hand, the early focus on transmission through homosexual sex has also helped us become more critically aware of sexual norms. While certain sexual proclivities are accepted, others still remain taboo and, by and large, there is within societies a shared understanding about this. The norms by which we live our lives help us to build a picture of how the world is to us and ultimately about the sort of people we believe ourselves to be. Norms, however, encourage an insensitivity and intolerance to differences. Human societal norms can also act as a kind of shelter from repeated exposure to death, pain, loss and failure. Much of my work with clients involves an exploration of their sexuality as an expression of our relatedness to the world, with all its implications. The act of sex may be seen as one of our most vital, powerful and life-affirming activities as human beings, yet it can become risky and possibly life threatening. Such a paradox distinguishes HIV from other viruses. Thus, HIV may face clients with strong moral dilemmas, as they endeavour to balance desire with responsibility.

Individuals' feelings about HIV and their experiences of it influence their satisfactions and frustrations and the tone of their lives. The person with HIV is often responding to the threat of being fragile and the possibility of death at any time. It is frequently the minor physical complaints and symptoms, as we have seen with Celine, which herald the greater terror and anguish and awaken in clients the consciousness of their finitude. I do not see such anxiety as a symptom to be relieved but rather as a reality to be confronted and to be lived with constructively: it is an illusion for anyone to believe that they can change the unchangeable.

Kierkegaard regarded human existence as absurd and ambiguous; Heidegger as 'the null basis of its own nullity' (Heidegger 1962: 354; 306). Yet, they both argued, life should be lived with total commitment, and, this commitment should be a personal commitment. By confronting clients with their finitude, an HIV+ diagnosis can lead them to re-evaluate the values, beliefs and assumptions by which they live their lives; it can provide a call to be more authentic, to open up to new possibilities and realize a sense of wholeness. Therein lies the vitality of death. It is a choice we have to make: we can choose to explore or ignore our relation to our personal existence; to accept or refuse to engage with existential questions.

Heidegger reminds us that human existence is bound by certain existential givens, including our 'thrownness'. Each of us is rooted to a specific time and place, with a specific body, as which we live and as which we shall die. Ten years ago, when life expectancy after a diagnosis of HIV was estimated at eight to 15 years, few people thought about old age. Since 1995 and the advent of HAART, chances of survival are better than ever. Still, an HIV+ diagnosis throws individuals into the maelstrom of their confrontation with mortality and their response to it. Yet, if we can attempt to face the worst that life can throw at us, we can, paradoxically, begin to live. If we, as therapists and onlookers, learn to let go of our prejudices and assumptions and allow understanding to grow, we may discover that we are able to identify with many aspects of the HIV predicament as being common to each and every one of us. This faces us with the element of uncertainty in our lives and may also bring us a 'wake-up call' to re-evaluate our priorities. For all of us the question then becomes 'I know that I shall die, but how am I going to live my life?'

Notes

1 Insecurity about one's sense of being. See Chapter 1, p. 28.
2 Heidegger distinguishes between an ontological and an ontic investigation of human existence. An ontological investigation reveals the fundamental givens that are inherent in human existence. These 'existentials' include being-in-the-world, mortality, temporality, mood, freedom, choice and facticity (thrownness). Ontical enquiry, on the other hand, focuses on particular concrete ways in which we live out these existentials, e.g. our anxieties, our sexuality, the choices we make, etc. The case studies represent three such ontic explorations, illustrating three ways in which being HIV+ can colour our whole way of being-in-the-world.
3 Dasein – Heidegger refers to human existence as *Dasein*. Literally translated – 'being there' or 'the there of Being' (Cohn 1997: 12).

References

Cohn, H.W. (1997) *Existential Thought and Therapeutic Practice: An Introduction to Existential Psychotherapy*, London: Sage.

Heidegger, M. (1962 [1927]) *Being and Time*, trans. Macquarrie, J.R. and Robinson, E., Oxford: Blackwell.

Ipsos MORI (2006) *Public Attitudes Towards HIV*, London: Ipsos MORI.

Koestenbaum, P. (1971) *The Vitality of Death: Essays in Existential Psychology and Philosophy*, Westport CT: Greenwood.

Merleau-Ponty, M. (1962 [1945]) *Phenomenology of Perception*, trans. Smith, C., London: Routledge & Kegan Paul.

Spinelli, E. (2006 [1997]) *Tales of Un-knowing, Therapeutic Encounters from an Existential Perspective*, Ross-on-Wye: PCCS Books.

Yalom, I. (1980) *Existential Psychotherapy*, New York: Basic Books.

TIME

Time occupies a privileged place in existential philosophy and there are two aspects of the existential view of time that have had a profound impact upon existential therapies.

When we consider 'time', we tend to think in terms of minutes, hours, days, months – time as measured by the clock or the calendar. For existential philosophy and existential therapies, however, that is not time in its basic form: time is such as we *experience* it, *lived time* in relation to the world. It is well illustrated by what I call 'the bad after dinner speech syndrome': the speaker speaks for 12 minutes as measured by the clock, the speaker experiences it as three minutes and to the audience it feels like 40. This can help us understand, for instance, how the grief of clients who open up to their unmourned loss after 15 years can feel so raw, as if it had happened only yesterday. Time is 'time for', time for what we choose to do: it is the 'what' and the 'how' we live (and in that sense, being is time).

Second, existential philosophy privileges the future: our plans and the way we see the future have a major influence on the way we live the present and view the past. For example, clients whose possibilities have become severely restricted by ill health may suddenly view the successful career they once valued in terms of wasted opportunities. We think of time as being linear and continuous, going from the past, via the present, to the future. That is 'common sense'. And when we see time as a straight line, it is easy to assume that what came before caused what came after – that the past trauma caused the present issues. If time is no longer viewed as unfolding in a straight line from past to future, if it is more of a web where present, future and past interconnect, we can no longer explain the present by the past: one can never say that a client is as he is *because* of what happened in the past. It is *how* we deal with the trauma (the diagnosis of cancer, the loss, etc.) and how we see it in the context of our whole life, past, present and future, that counts. An implication of the existential view of time is that existential therapies are fundamentally non-deterministic.

Existential therapy is often thought of as a therapy of 'the here and now', yet it gives equal importance to all three dimensions of time: the choices

71

and possibilities before us, the way we colour the future; our past, our story so far – and how it may be helpful to see it and understand it differently; and how we carry both our projects for the future and our past into the present moment.

4

SURVIVING INTENSIVE CARE

Laura Barnett

Until the 1990s there was little awareness of the possible psychological 'fall-out' of Intensive Care (ITU, Intensive Therapy Unit). A number of doctors, nurses and psychologists have now turned their attention to the problem. The research is generally within the medical model, using the psychiatric paradigm of acute and post-traumatic stress disorder (ASD, PTSD; see p. 30ff.) and delirium, and focuses on what might be *causing* distress to Intensive Care patients (Ridley 2005).[1] The incidence of PTSD among post-ITU patients has been found to average over 9 per cent (Jones *et al.* 2007), i.e. three times as high as that of victims of assault or of non-injured war veterans. This gives some idea of the intensity of the problem. This chapter offers an alternative, existential perspective on what I have called 'the whole ITU event' – namely the person's lead-up and admission to ITU, their stay in ITU, discharge from ITU on to a ward and discharge from hospital (Barnett 2006a, 2006b).

My description of what it can mean for people to survive ITU is based on my work with hundreds of patients whom I have encountered through a psychological aftercare service for ITU patients, which I set up some years ago at Mayday Hospital in Croydon. The service offers a routine bedside session and a follow-up questionnaire a few months after discharge from hospital. Patients may also access counselling with me at any stage after ITU. I use the word 'patient' rather than 'client', because being a patient is an important aspect of their being-in-the-world (see p. 43) and hence very much part of our work together; besides, in its original sense of 'one who endures/suffers', the term is an apt one.

The ITU patient group is heterogeneous in age, gender, ethnicity, cause of admission – accidents, illness, post-operative complications, suicide attempts, etc. Intensive Care patients are most commonly dependent on machines for up to four of their vital organ functions (lungs, kidneys, heart and liver), as they drift in and out of consciousness, often heavily sedated. The reality of the situation is that without these machines and round-the-clock one-to-one nursing and medical care most patients would be unlikely to survive; indeed many die on the unit or soon after discharge to a ward. Three characteristic themes tend to emerge for patients who have been in ITU: survival, lost time and vivid dreams/hallucinations.

Various situations in life confront us with our mortality: with the realization that death does not just 'come to us all one day', it will come to me personally and it may be sooner than I thought. Patients who have been in ITU have come very close to death. Indeed, some feel that they have experienced dying or death itself: they speak variously of the white light at the end of the tunnel, of flying over white clouds with deceased loved ones, of being in pastures green, etc. Then something happens, e.g. the dead parent may take them back, and they conclude 'it was not my time'.

> It was only after months of working together that Emily was able to broach her beliefs about death and then only very tentatively: 'I feel really bad about this, I don't want to destroy your illusions but . . . when I was dying, I remember, there was nothing; death is . . . "nothing".

Emily felt immense gratitude at being alive. However, her experience of death, as she understood it, created a chilling dread that lay in a corner of her being. I assured her that I felt all right listening to experiences of death, that she was not responsible for their possible impact on me and my beliefs, whatever these might be. We explored her experience and assumptions about its meaning. Maybe she was right and death was that 'nothing' which she remembered. But alternatively maybe her experience was inconclusive and, heavily medicated and sedated, she simply had not remembered anything – rightly or wrongly, this is how most patients understood it. The question was: what role was she going to allow that chilling dread to play? She felt that it could either become her key to a fuller engagement with life or her excuse for backing out.

There are two sides to survival: there is survival *from* death and survival *for* life. Therefore working with survival is working with feelings and thoughts about death within the context of life, and with life within the framework of its finitude.

When I first met patients who had been in Intensive Care, I was struck by the impact of their lack of recollection of ITU. They often experienced this as a sense that, somehow, time had got 'lost':

> Malcolm had been admitted to ITU two days before Valentine's day and had regained consciousness in mid-March. He could not believe that he had 'lost' over a month, could not fathom how Valentine's day could have just come and gone, while he was here, yet not here.

I was reminded of Heidegger's concept of existential time and how our personal sense of time is developed through our involvement with the world, with the things and people that are meaningful to us. For ITU patients, it is not so much a matter of a few lost hours or days, as measured by the clock or calendar, rather it is a loss of time as viewed in the context of their lives: life-time as being-in-the-world (see 'Time', pp. 71–2). For some, it is also a feeling of losing a bit of life, just when, in their confrontation with death, time has become more precious. Lost time creates a sense of discontinuity that can persist over the months and even years to come:

> As I came onto a ward one day, I saw Joan with whom I had worked four years previously, following her stay in ITU. I went to say hello.
>
> 'I am so worried, please tell me, I know you'll tell me the truth, do you think I've got dementia? I just can't remember things no more. Yesterday they were talking on the telly about the anniversary of 9/11. I've heard of 9/11 of course, but I don't remember it.'

Joan did not show any sign of dementia. Simply, a few years previously, one of the major events of the century had passed her by as she lay unconscious in ITU. While she knew of it, she had no experience of it. She would never be able to answer in any personally meaningful way the question 'Remember what you were doing, when 9/11 happened?'

At first one thing puzzled me: almost every patient used to say to me 'I don't know what happened.' Had they not been told, I wondered. I asked the nurses, who assured me that the patient had been given the facts. Maybe they had been told too soon, when they were not receptive. It was not until J began to express his desire to see his medical notes and 'find out what happened' that I realized I had misunderstood my clients' concerns on this matter; for J, I knew, had a clear knowledge of the facts of his admission to ITU and his stay there. What he was trying to find out was what had happened to him – to piece together his own story, not what the nurses had done, nor what his relatives and friends had observed, nor, as he came to realize, what the doctors may have written in his medical notes. Other people's thoughts and observations represented their experience of him in ITU, not his own. Yet he did not know what his own experience of ITU had been. All he could recall was the occasional sensation of being wired up to machines and strange, incredibly vivid dreams. He felt the need to fill the gap in his memory, to bridge the discontinuity between the person he had been prior to ITU and the person he now was. (Not every patient wishes to have a detailed story of what happened. Some feel safer with the briefest of summaries, such as 'I collapsed at home and came to ITU, but now I'm much better.')

It is clear that dreams in ITU have a vividness which is unlike that of any dream in ordinary life. They feel so real that it is often the first thing that patients talk about to their relatives on regaining consciousness, much to their relatives' concern and distress:

When Ivor asked his wife how she had managed to get him out of the clutches of his interrogators in Mongolia, she thought he must have suffered brain damage and, from her reaction, he himself feared for his sanity.

Dreams and hallucinations[2] are one of the major causes of distress for patients who have been in ITU:

> In understanding hallucinations, one must not start with the distinction between 'real' and 'unreal', but rather with an inquiry into the character of the relationship to the world in which the patient is involved at any given time.
>
> (Heidegger, in Boss 2001: 152)

As for dreams, existential therapy approaches them as another form of being-in-the-world, in which the dreamer responds to what addresses him. We need to 'let the dreams themselves tell their own stories by what they say and reveal about their orientation toward the world' (Boss 2001: 245). In the following examples, three patients recount their dreams, in reply to one of my routine post-ITU questions: 'Did you have any vivid dreams or hallucinations when you were in ITU?'

Sean: I was lying there and there were all these silly little figures on the ceiling. [*cringes*]

L: Do you remember how you felt as you lay there?

Sean: I was shit scared. They were coming at me and I was trying to fight them off.

L: Those silly little figures?

Sean: Yes.

L: And what did they look like, could you describe them?

Sean: They were like hooded grim reapers.

Philip: I know this is going to sound mad to you, and I'm ashamed when I think of all they were doing for me, but I thought the nurses were trying to kill me. My wife tells me that I kept trying to remove the tubes and get out of bed, I even punched my nurse in the stomach. It's really not like me.

Denis: I was lying in bed with my family around me – I could see they were really scared. I know it sounds stupid, but there was a sphinx asking us questions.

L: What sort of questions?

>   *Denis:* I don't remember . . . They were life and death questions. My brothers were terrified, because without the correct answers I wasn't going to survive. But I knew that I was the only one with the answers.

While I am sure that I can let these dreams and hallucinations speak to you for themselves, most patients are so caught up in their feeling of fear or panic that they cannot see beyond it. In fact, they tend to belittle the image of their dream ('silly', 'stupid') which renders their own emotions even more incomprehensible, mad or shameful. Giving clients the opportunity to speak about their ITU dreams, acknowledging and validating their feelings and helping them draw out the themes is, in my experience, one of the most beneficial parts of routine post-ITU sessions with patients. It enables them to hear their dream, to see what was going on for them and what they were trying to do, albeit in their dream. In the above dreams, instead of experiencing fear and panic, they can now appreciate their fighting spirit. (Intriguingly, I have never met anyone who had been overcome in their ITU fights or had stopped trying to escape; is it possible that they are the ones who do not survive?) From nightmares these dreams may become for post-ITU patients a testimony to their own resources. What is more, they can help patients give meaning to their ITU experience – something significant did happen in that 'lost time' – and integrate it within the context of their lives. A number of patients, Denis included, recount having the feeling, at the time, that their dream was a turning point in their recovery. However, it is not until they have explored it with me that they come to see that this makes sense.

When patients have not reached a satisfactory understanding of their dreams, these may become repetitive and distressingly intrusive. Occasionally, I meet clients who were in ITU at another hospital a few months or years previously and still complain of getting flashbacks of their dreams; some are too terrified to close their eyes because of them.[3] When dreams have become so distressing and intrusive, it may be necessary to 'resource' clients (see Chapter 5) before starting on the dream. 'The dreamworld cannot be separated as an object domain unto itself, but rather it belongs in a certain way to the continuity of being-in-the-world' (Heidegger, in Boss 2001: 229). For the ITU patient, this is a life and death situation and it is reflected in the dreams: dreams of fighting and escape (the most common); meaning dreams (like Denis's); 'inspirational' dreams; dreams of engaging fully with life (e.g. intensely sexual; giving birth); dreams of a world beyond; dreams of safe havens:

>   *Vera:* Promise you won't laugh.
>   *L:* OK.
>   *Vera:* Well, there was Frank Sinatra sitting on my bed. I can still see

him as clearly as I see you now. He was sitting on my bed and singing, just for me.

Marcia dreamt she was swimming with dolphins as in that memorable time when she had felt safe as never before.

John: I thought I'd been flown to a hospital in Sweden – they have all the latest equipment in those countries.

Past personal history also permeates ITU dreams: fighting and escaping can be from prisoner of war camps, interrogations or drug pushers.

For Terry, work-hard-play-hard, 'one of the lads', his battle took place on the Isle of Man [sic!], where two discos were battling each other as to which would be the loudest and most successful – the other would sink into the sea.

While these dreams throw a powerful light upon patients' experiences of ITU, they also present us with challenging questions. For instance, where does the awareness, which these dreams display about the dreamers' situation, stem from? Is it gleaned in the dreamers' moments of consciousness or do the dreamers have a pre-reflective, bodily awareness of their situation? Also, in the light of the resourcefulness that these dreams tend to manifest, is it the case that 'preventing ICU patients having these experiences at all must always be our ultimate aim' (Skirrow 2002: 30)?

The whole ITU event faces patients with many questions. 'What happened?' 'Why?' and 'Why me?' are the commonest; they all voice different attempts at making sense of the experience. The first of these questions, as we saw, tends to be an attempt to regain ownership of the experience of ITU. The second is a search for a cause and the third throws open the patient's whole system of beliefs. For patients who have been in ITU 'Why?' often turns into a need to apportion blame, whether to others (GP, family, hospital) or to oneself (lifestyle, not paying sufficient attention to warning signs, etc.). With some post-ITU clients, much of the early work can centre around taking responsibility for their lifestyle (e.g. excessive drinking), without sinking into self-accusatory self-loathing, shame and depression. With others, it may involve acknowledging and validating their justified anger at the surgeon, the negligent GP, the careless driver, without getting stuck in fantasies of revenge or feelings that their life is now irremediably ruined forever. In existential terms, the accident has become a given of their existence and they are free to choose how they are going to react to it. Or as Terry succinctly put it: 'It wasn't fucking my fault, but I'm not going to be a fucking victim for the rest of my life.' Sometimes clients' accusations are unjustified or impossible to ascertain – e.g. was the GP negligent? Did the security guard abuse his position after that violent episode of 'ITU syndrome',[4] or was the patient still being paranoid? We have to work together with the fact that we shall never know for certain.

Wanting to find a 'cause' for what happened in ITU is a common reaction. We are brought up in a world of linear causality: there is no smoke without fire; everything is the effect of a cause that precedes it. Life, however, is not that simple. From an existential perspective, there are two problems with such a worldview. First, it assumes a linear view of time that goes from past to future, where the past determines the future, which is not applicable to human existence (see 'Time', p. 71–2). Second, it assumes that we can 'explain' human beings the way we can explain events in the physical world. But, one could object, surely illness and injury are physical events? From an existential viewpoint, to be 'ill' is a way of being-in-the-world: it is a different way of being attuned to the world (Svenaius 2001). It cannot be divorced from the world and from the whole suffering person as being-in-the-world. For that reason, the patient's condition cannot be fully 'explained'. There is no simple answer to the question 'Why?'

'Why?' and the search for a 'cause' can also be an attempt at regaining control over the world and oneself, when everything feels out of control. Uncertainty lies at the core of our lives and our work. Will this happen again (e.g. serious epileptic fit, asthma attack, diabetic coma)? How quickly will my condition deteriorate (e.g. cancer, degenerative illness)? What is round the corner for me? 'Why?' seeks an answer for the unfathomable:

> Jasmine was walking alone at night when a car drove straight at her, two people got out, beat her up, ran her over and left her for dead. They did not sexually assault her, nor steal anything from her.

How was Jasmine to comprehend such senseless violence? What sense could she make of 'being at the wrong place at the wrong time'? Questions such as these, like the question 'Why me?', challenge our whole system of values and beliefs: beliefs about good and evil, right and wrong, the existence of God – a God of mercy or a vengeful God? Like so many patients who ask 'Why me?' Jasmine added 'I'm not a bad person', expressing an assumption that life is fundamentally fair. Sometimes underlying 'Why me?', though not phrased in those terms, is what Heidegger called the 'broadest', 'deepest', 'most origi-nary' question, the question of the 'meaning of being'. The question of why things are at all, why they are as they are, of why I am: why was I born, why have I turned out as I have, what lies ahead for me?

In existential terms, in their confrontation with their mortality, these patients have also been faced with their 'thrownness' or 'facticity': with the fact that there are 'givens' in their life which it is not in their power to change – from their birth, over which they had no control, to the present traumatic event. Heidegger argues that, in our anxiety, we tend to run away from this realization into the busy-ness/business of the world (see 'inauthenticity', 'falling', pp. 13–14, p. 117). Alternatively, he adds, I can in 'sober anxiety', hold in my sight my whole life from birth to death, realize that I am responsible for the way I live it and decide what I want to make of it (the 'authentic' 'moment of vision'). In such moments, 'resoluteness constitutes the loyalty of existence to its own self' (Heidegger 1962: 443; 391). 'Resoluteness' expresses both a sense of resolve and an openness to myself, the world, my past and what may lie ahead for me. It is a call to live my life according to my own values and beliefs, as opposed to simply following (or rebelling against) what others (my peers, my parents, the Church, society, etc., the 'they') suggest or ask of me.

'Why me?' can send us into the busy whirlwind of daily life: it can keep us stuck in a sense of victimization, depression or despair; it can be a catalyst for taking stock, for changing. I have survived but what have I survived *for*?

> *Bernadette:* The doctors called my family twice in the night, they thought they were going to lose me. I know I've been given a second chance. He must have saved me for a purpose.

> Sonia had taken an overdose of paracetamol. It had only been a cry for help – her life, she felt, was spiralling out of control, but this too had spiralled out of control. Sonia decided: 'It is time I sorted myself out.'

While they remain on a hospital ward, it is difficult for patients to look to the future and make realistic choices: for many it is too soon; others, protected from temptation in the hospital environment, forget how different it might be once they return home.

> Rory, 33, had been admitted to Intensive Care with burst oesophageal varices and a diseased liver. When we first met, he did not express any sense of responsibility or even concern about the drinking, just mentioned he should give up smoking. Rory complained that it was 'so fucking boring here, all I can do here is think and it won't get me nowhere'.

Profound boredom is for Heidegger a 'fundamental mood' akin to anxiety, for the expansion of time 'oppresses [human existence] and thus includes in itself a peculiar indication of its shortness' (Heidegger 1995: 153; 229). Boredom, like anxiety, has the ability to 'disclose' human existence to itself, in its fragility – its mortality and thrownness, and in its freedom. Heidegger distinguishes three forms of boredom; what they all have in common is that in boredom we are being '*left empty*' and '*held in limbo by time*' (Heidegger 1995: 100; 151). Lying in hospital is a very good example of the first simple form of boredom. In 'the second case what is distinctive is a *not wanting to listen*' (Heidegger 1995: 136). I am often reminded of this second form of boredom when I hear people like Rory, with life-threatening, alcohol-related health problems, talk about 'having a laugh at the pub with their mates over a few pints'. In these 'few pints', bolstered by his mates, Rory was losing as much count of himself as of the pints he was drinking. 'Losing itself in the publicness and the idle talk of "the they", it [*Dasein*, human existence] *fails to hear* ... its own self in listening to the they-self' (Heidegger 1962: 315; 271). In the third, 'profound' form of boredom, this underlying unease is 'disclosed' and we are made to listen to it, 'compelled in the sense of that kind of compelling force which ... is related to Dasein's *innermost freedom*' (Heidegger 1995: 136).

The freedom to open ourselves to our possibilities is a major focus of work with people who decide to come for therapy months after their discharge from hospital. It involves an exploration of all that is meaningful to the client – their worldview, values, priorities, relationships, dreams, etc., and making responsible choices. Some have experienced particularly tragic and traumatic losses:

> Leila was looking forward to the birth of her child and awoke a few days later in ITU to the news of a still birth and a hysterectomy.

> Patrick walked into hospital, collapsed in Accident & Emergency and regained consciousness in ITU with an amputated leg.

Clearly, for them, life suddenly has been transformed. But even for patients who regain health and return to apparent pre-ITU 'normality', the confrontation with mortality has coloured the world differently. It has altered their relationship to time,[5] space, the world around them, to family, friends and strangers. It changes the way they see themselves and others see them. It changes the way they 'tune into' the world:

> *Terry:* The accident was like an explosion that threw the bits every-
> where; then, me mum and dad's love, me family, me girlfriend,
> me work are like the colours added to it to make a picture.

The experience of ITU is one of discontinuity, disruption and disorientation in time.[6] Time has also changed in quality, it may have become permeated with anxiety, anger, despair, wonder and joy, etc. It is the time remaining, the time I was almost cheated of, the grim future ahead, the lack of future ('what's the point?'), the bonus ('my second chance').

Lying in a hospital bed, bored and frustrated, time does not 'behave' as it used to: the 'here and now' may drag interminably, past and future may feel very distant and 'shrunken'; time is distorted. Clock and calendar have become poor measures of time for these endless days that tend to blend into one. The cycle of painkillers – awaited, taking effect, wearing off – measures the hours. The change from having to use a bedpan, to being able to transfer to a commode, then walking first aided and later unaided to the toilet has become a far more meaningful measure of days and weeks. When patients are discharged home, they may find the time they allow themselves to perform familiar everyday tasks conflicts with 'the personal time' which they carry 'embedded' in their body and its movements in the world (Brough 2001: 42). Getting washed and dressed, a familiar 20-minute routine, now takes half the morning. And as one gets slower, so, it seems, the world around one is moving faster. For patients who have been in ITU, this distortion of time is added to their sense of 'lost' time in ITU:

> *Joan:* The boys are talking about Christmas, but I can't think about Christmas, I'm still waiting for spring and summer.

Just as our attunement to the world alters our sense of time, so it affects our relationship to space: in tiredness, helplessness and despair the world may feel distant and out of reach; while in anxiety it may close in on us. The changes in our body also affect our sense of space: shelves have become too high; the bottom of the garden too far; toenails are now out of reach for cutting; bodily changes affect the way we 'feel' the world – the mild incline feels steep, plates feel heavy, everything is effortful. German has two words for body: *Leib* (lived body) and *Körper* (body as object). That distinction is fundamental to existential philosophers and therapists. It distinguishes between the 'body which I am' versus 'the body which I have' (see 'The body', p. 87). In illness and pain, the body makes its presence felt, it obtrudes as an object; for doctors it is nothing but an object. At the same time, my 'lived body' embodies my particular take on the world: it gives me my bearings in space and time, and also in my relations to myself and to others, even to society and its values. Through changes in the body, everyday life (the pub, church, gym, etc.) may now be out of bounds. Robert Murphy describes how when 'Words and acts that took place on the second floor, in the basement, or outside were beyond my range', this led to an 'estrangement from family life' (Murphy 1990: 212).

After their confrontation with their own mortality, some patients open themselves more to the world, while others withdraw. Some, feeling blessed, experience everything with awe and wonder; for others, the world has become cold and grim. Patients commonly oscillate between conflicting emotions. The work of therapy needs to acknowledge that altered being-in-the-world. 'I want to get back to normal' is a common refrain. Yet while clients can regain some normality, it will never be 'like before' and they themselves will never be their old selves. This does not mean that it will necessarily be worse. For many, it will mean mourning lost possibilities, exploring what possibilities now remain within the givens of their present existence, developing a new self-definition and changing the focus for their self-esteem. Yet, some are surprised to discover in their worsened physical state a greater zest for and engagement with life.

I realize that, with my ITU clients, I have something of an agenda – not a closed agenda, but simply the hope that at least something good might come of 'the whole ITU event'. This often fits with what has drawn the client to come to therapy. From a Heideggerian perspective, one could say that their confrontation with mortality has brought to the fore their 'existential guilt', their sense of what they 'owe' themselves.

I have focused on patients who have had 'a stay' in Intensive Care. Some conditions, however, may necessitate repeat admissions to ITU. Caroline D (who asked to retain her identity) emailed me after reading my articles (Barnett 2006a, 2006b) and expressed her relief at finally feeling heard:

> The scariest thing about being a repeat offender! is the knowledge that every time I am there someone will die there and it is merely a matter of time before that someone is me! . . . The reality is I will be admitted to ITU again this coming year, I have not yet had 1 year of my life where I haven't but what is more of a scary thought is the lack of change . . . I wish I had said something before now but didn't feel anyone would believe what I felt or my interpretation of what I felt had been happening.
>
> (Caroline D's email, 13 February 2007)

Death has always had an important presence in my life, one that is not particularly anxiety provoking (I am far more anxious about serious ill health); this aids me in my work in this field. At the same time, I am aware that I am, as I write, a healthy woman with no first-hand experience of what my clients have gone through. I am conscious of the total otherness of their experience. I have come to realize the importance of building a basic therapeutic relationship very swiftly in this work and of creating a safe enough place despite the setting (often by the bedside behind curtains). I have learnt to treat every initial session as if it might be the only one. 'Normalizing the experience' is an essential part of my routine post-ITU assessment sessions and I have to take care not to carry that didactic attitude into my general therapy work.

Discovering the plight of post-ITU patients has opened my eyes to aspects of existence which I never knew existed. For this and much else – witnessing courage, resilience, trust, despair – I feel privileged. Once again the poetic Terry:

It was a rebirth, no, not a rebirth, more like turning round on a different axis. How I see it, it's like: after the accident I went into a cocoon, then I became a caterpillar – I learnt to walk again, now I've got wings, I'm like a butterfly, I can fly.

I have kept my favourite 'inspirational dream' for last – I have named this category of ITU dreams 'inspirational' after this dreamer's reply to my consent letter asking her for permission to quote it. She thanked me for my 'inspirational' letter; my letter was bland, only her dream was 'inspirational'. It was inspirational for her, as it has been for me – in my work and my life it fills me with wonder about the human spirit:

L: When you were in ITU did you have any vivid dreams or hallucinations?

Gloria: Yes . . . [*thinking*] . . . Yes . . . beautiful, beautiful dreams. Flowers, flowers everywhere, like a wallpaper of flowers. Yes . . . [*thinking*] . . . there were petals, can I draw them for you? [*starts drawing five petals, looks rather like a hand*]; and behind each petal there was a diamond . . . and on the three petals in the middle, it said: 'I want to live', 'I want to live', 'I want to live'.

Notes

1 Granberg *et al.*'s (1998) phenomenological study is a rare exception.
2 Patients use both 'dreams' and 'hallucinations' to describe their experience. Sean's (p. 76) started as a dream and recurred as a hallucination. The ITU literature tends to use the expression 'delusional memories', which to my mind is pathologizing for patients.
   Within the PTSD paradigm, the incidence of ASD/PTSD has been found to be highest among people whose only recollection of ITU are their dreams (Jones *et al.* 2007: 979).
3 Anecdotal evidence (follow-up meetings and self-assessment questionnaires) would suggest that this very seldom happens for my Mayday patients. To be researched.
4 Also known as 'delirium'. An ill-defined and ill-understood psychotic condition of short duration which affects many ITU patients (Jones *et al.* 2007).
5 Toombs (1990, 1995).
6 In Christopher Wearing's (2005) extreme experience of time disruption, the immediate past simply dropped out and every moment was for him *the* awakening out of his coma.

References

Barnett, L. (2006a) A Neglected Client Group: Patients Who Have Been in Intensive Care, in *Therapy Today*, 17.4: 19–21.
—— (2006b) Working with Patients Who Have Been in Intensive Care, An Existential Perspective, in *Therapy Today*, 17.5: 33–35.

Boss, M. (ed.) (2001 [1987]) *Heidegger, M. Zollikon Seminars, Seminars, Protocols, Conversations*, trans. Mayr, F. and Askay, R., Evanston: Northwestern University Press.

Brough, J.B. (2001) Temporality and Illness: A Phenomenological Perspective, in Toombs, S.K. (ed.) (2001) *Phenomenology and Medicine*, Dordrecht: Kluwer.

Granberg, A., Bergbom Engberg, I. and Lundberg, D. (1998) Patients' Experiences of Being Critically Ill or Severely Injured and Cared For in an Intensive Care Unit in Relation to the ICU Syndrome. Part I, in *Intensive and Critical Care Nursing*, 14: 294–307.

Heidegger, M. (1962 [1927]) *Being and Time*, trans. Macquarrie, J.R. and Robinson, E., Oxford: Blackwell.

—— (1995 [1983]) *The Fundamental Concepts of Metaphysics, World, Finitude, Solitude* (lecture delivered 1929–30), trans. McNeill, W. and Walker, N., Bloomington: Indiana University Press.

Jones, C., Bäckman, C., Capuzzo, M., Flaatten, H., Rylander, C. and Griffiths, R.D. (2007) Precipitants of Post-traumatic Stress Disorder Following Intensive Care: A Hypothesis Generating Study of Diversity in Care, in *Intensive Care Medicine*, 33.6: 978–985.

Murphy, R.E. (1990 [1987]) *The Body Silent*, New York: Norton.

Ridley, S. (2005) *Critical Care Focus 12: Psychological Challenges of Intensive Care*, Oxford: Blackwell.

Skirrow, P. (2002) Delusional Memories of ITU, in Griffiths, R.D. and Jones, C. *Intensive Care Aftercare*, Oxford: Butterworth-Heinemann.

Svenaius, F. (2001) *The Phenomenology of Health and Illness*, in Toombs, S.K. *Phenomenology and Medicine*, Dordrecht: Kluwer.

Toombs, S.K. (1990) The Temporality of Illness: Four Levels of Experience, in *Theoretical Medicine*, 11: 227–241.

—— (1995) The Lived Experience of Disability, in *Human Studies*, 18: 9–23.

Wearing, D. (2005) *Forever Today, A Memoir of Love and Amnesia*, London: Doubleday.

THE BODY

It is still 'common sense' in the Western world to view the body and the mind as two separate entities. This is usually referred to as 'Cartesian dualism' or the 'Cartesian split' after Descartes, who enshrined this mind–body split in philosophical terms (*res cogitans* and *res extensa*). This separation of mind and body dates back to antiquity and goes hand in hand with a devaluing of the human body. The body was viewed as the soul's tomb (Plato), and often as 'sinful', 'dirty', shameful. Over the centuries, the Church has reinforced this attitude, especially where women are concerned.

Existential philosophers from Nietzsche onwards have fought against this 'centaur' view of the human being (human head and animal body). They have sought to give the body the valued place it deserves. They have challenged the mind–body dualism. Among existential philosophers, it is Merleau-Ponty who most developed the concept of embodied existence.

Merleau-Ponty distinguishes between the body as object, the 'body that I have', and the body as subject, 'the body which I am'. The body as object is the body I scrutinize in the mirror or wash in the bath; it is the body with which the doctors are concerned. On the other hand, 'the body which I am', my 'lived body' is my gateway to the world – and the doctors may not realize that sufficiently. My lived body understands its world: it knows its physical, relational, cultural environment from a lifetime's experience of it. It is 'this habitual knowledge of the world' that is disturbed by serious accident or illness (see Chapter 4). Changes to the body may affect the sense of time and distances; social life, perceptions of oneself and others, and relationships are altered. Thus for a woman who has had a mastectomy, it is not only a matter of body image, but also of reorientating herself in her new embodied experience of the world. Merleau-Ponty's philosophy underpins a therapeutic practice that is mindful of the client's body as a 'knot of living meanings' and of 'insertion in a human world'. Refugees, for instance, have to learn how to 'read' their host countrymen's body language, together with new ways of bearing themselves.

So many of our clients present with a sense of being split in countless ways: head–body, above the belt–below the belt, left–right, etc. Existential therapy offers a holistic approach to human existence: a 'psychosomatic' symptom is not viewed as the physical emergence of repressed psychical content, but as a whole person's reaction to a situation (Heidegger's example of blushing is a good one). Nothing is simply 'in the mind' or simply physiological. In my experience, epileptic or severely asthmatic clients find it helpful and empowering to see how their attacks vary in character, by plotting each of them along a continuum that goes from almost purely physiological to almost purely psychological.

5

CREATING SAFETY FOR THE CLIENT

The London 7/7 bombings

Sanja Oakley

In this chapter I argue that trauma therapy is a specialized form of psycho-therapy with some directive components. In most situations, the best place from which to meet clients' dramatically changed experience of themselves is through their body, via an embodied encounter. I shall illustrate this with reference to the therapeutic work I carried out in the immediate aftermath of the London 'July bombings', as part of a team of therapists at Transport for London (TfL).

On 7 July 2005, in London, 51 people were killed and a further 700 needed hospital treatment as bombs exploded in the Underground and on a bus. TfL staff had begun the rescue operation some 20 minutes before ambulance, police and fire professionals turned up. Unsure whether the attack had finished, they stayed underground and proceeded with the rescue, distinguishing the dead from the wounded, triaging the injured and escorting the able bodied to safety, out from the tunnel. They were involved in the situation before they could fully appreciate the nature or implications of the terrorist event. Margaret Mitchell (1991), who studied the stress effects on police officers following the Lockerbie disaster, noted how this increased the risk of traumatic reaction. The immediate purpose of our interventions was to ease the impact of the traumatic shock on TfL staff by 'normalizing' their reactions. We also had to look out for those who were more vulnerable and deemed to be more likely to develop longer-lasting trauma stress symptoms.

The underground is a violent place for Transport for London operational staff at the best of times and, on the whole, they feel it is part of their professionalism to cultivate robustness against the effects of death's appearance. However, the extreme violence of the terrorist suicide bomb attacks of 7/7 shook everyone's sense of how the world 'works' and many staff members involved in the rescue felt they had lost mastery over themselves.

As a therapist with an existential training informed by Heidegger, I see living with an awareness of the limitations of existence, including dying, as a valuable attitude to life. Despite the now thriving body of research covering potential for transformation after trauma under the name of post-traumatic growth (Tedeschi *et al.* 1998; Calhoun and Tedeschi 1999), the 'existential' perspective is sometimes foreign to trauma therapy. In my experience, when trauma therapists engage with the paradox of life and death, their clients are more likely to experience traumatic events as a 'gift', a fast lane to a more energized lifestyle and a more self-aware way of being. There is, however, a time and a place for exploring such existential issues and, if the client is suffering from traumatic shock, the immediate aftermath of trauma is neither.

When the client arrives, if he is being assaulted by images of carnage, overwhelmed by anxiety and unable to make sense of the event or the world, I should not start by asking him what happened, or by exploring his anxiety and his understanding of the world. Creating a safe environment is the first requisite: before he can begin to tell his story, he will need to learn to calm himself down or 'put on the brakes' (Rothschild 2000). Control over the 'arousal' level can be attained if clients are encouraged to be mindful of their embodied experience.

Trauma 'first aid'

I will now outline the key elements of the trauma 'first aid' I used after 7/7. I apply this approach in the initial stages of all trauma work, regardless of the nature of the traumatic event, its duration, when it started to affect the person, their trauma history or how resilient the person appears to be.

Do not ask 'What happened?' but 'What have you been experiencing?'

Traumatic incidents can easily arouse counsellors' curiosity, especially when they are public events of the magnitude of 7/7. I could have been tempted to invite the 7/7 clients to tell me a story of the traumatic event. This is not only unnecessary, but potentially retraumatizing to the client and traumatizing to the therapist.[1]

> Brian chooses the seat near the window (emergency exit!) and lowers himself into it. I take the other available chair. It is 14 July 2005. The sirens outside are so loud it is hard to hear your own thoughts. We go into a spontaneous 30 seconds silence. As we come out of it we both shake our heads signifying our inability to comprehend what is happening to us, to London, and to the world.
>
> 'What has it been like for you since?' I ask. Brian looks relieved. Maybe,

like many other clients, he thought the counsellor was going to make him recount the event.

'Awful. I can't sleep. Jittery . . . But I can't do anything: just sit indoors whole day. Can't use the tube. The firm got me a cab to you. I have to say they are being decent . . . but this has ruined my life.'

Jusuf says: 'I can't talk to anyone . . . Nobody would understand. And I don't want to upset my wife and kids. The scary film keeps playing in my head. And the smell! I think I'm going mad. I'm going to be sick.'

'Have you noticed any changes in your body since the incident?' I ask Paul. He puts a hand on his tummy. 'I'm having to go all the time. You know, when you have butterflies in your stomach. Like I'm constantly panicking. My hands are clammy. What's happening to me?'

Reconstructing a narrative of the event has an important place in trauma counselling (Herman 1992), but this needs to be undertaken in a safe way and with an understanding (from both parties) of how traumatic shock occurs. In the days following 7/7, I acknowledged the intense feelings people were reporting, but focused the initial exploration on bodily sensations. This was welcomed by clients as they were preoccupied by this changed sense of embodied self.

Most felt they were the only ones going through this turmoil and were seriously considering the possibility they may have 'gone mad'. The sense of isolation from others and the world at large is a common trauma phenomenon. This is often compounded by the fact that survivors tend to overprotect loved ones and hence don't share their preoccupations with them. My trauma 'first aid' aimed to normalize their fear-laden experience of traumatic shock. In response to clients' recounting of their changed experience of themselves/with others/in-the-world, I explain the phenomenology of traumatic stress to them. The overwhelming symptoms are a normal reaction to an extraordinary, life-threatening situation. In my experience, it is not uncommon for this reaction (symptoms) to take up to eight weeks to subside, but I usually refrain from divulging this fact, as any divergence from the time scale may add to clients' already present sense of failure.

In the weeks following the event, TfL staff felt in a constant state of agitation, unable to sleep, irritable, explosive and frequently lost in memories of traumatic scenes which could be triggered by sights, smells or sounds with minimal resemblance to the originals. Others felt numb. All felt cut off from the 'normal' world and only able to connect to their colleagues who were with them during the event. These very different states of being from their usual ways, were not pathological – nor did they need management, to be suppressed or adjusted to. In fact they were a 'result of a natural process gone awry', as Peter Levine assures in *Waking the Tiger* (1997).

In this simple yet revolutionary text, which stimulated the development of a number of somatically oriented trauma therapies, Levine reminds us of our shared physiology with other animals when he describes the chase between a predator and its prey. As the cheetah jumps from its cover to attack a herd of grazing impala, the impala try to escape ('flight response'). One trips, then recovers, but in the process loses precious time and this gives the cheetah an advantage. Just before the cheetah catches up, the impala falls to the ground, surrendering to death. It has entered an altered state of consciousness, a state all mammals involuntarily go into, when they cannot fight or flee from death. The freeze is a gift from nature; it anesthetizes the pain when we are being eaten alive or (feel) we are trapped in an engagement with death from which there is no escape. If and when the danger passes, the prey shakes its body out of its frozen state. When humans do not experience this 'resetting', according to Levine (1997, 2006), trauma ensues. In an ideal situation there is a successful activation and completion of fight or flight action. If this is followed by a moment of reconnection with another human (experiencing safety) in which a release (including shaking) is experienced, it is reasonable not to expect the development of chronic trauma symptoms.[2]

I briefly explain to clients our shared heritage with animals, illustrated by the theory of the 'triune brain', hypothesized by Paul MacLean (1990). While this theory is an oversimplification, it provides a very useful representation for different neural functions. MacLean (1990) suggests our brain consists of three interdependent layers: the 'reptilian' part which controls the body's involuntary functions, readying it for fight, flight or freeze; the mammalian which regulates emotions; and the 'human' neocortex, involving thought processes.[3] I do not go into any of the physiological and neurological detail with clients. However, most feel 'understood' when I describe how their responses derive from a primal, instinctual mechanism. '*That's how I felt* ... like I was stuck to the wall ... that third thing you said: frozen!' This could be the first time that anything has made sense since the incident, and they connect to these facts and to me. 'I am feeling so much better now,' they tell me with a deep breath out (relaxing, letting go). A number of activities are enacted during this process. By putting together an explanation for how they have felt since the incident, clients are beginning to make some sense of their experience, thus regaining a certain feeling of control (neurologically, they are engaging their neocortex, structurally, the latest addition to the triune brain). They also start to reconnect to the world by learning they are not alone in their predicament. All of this seems to serve as assurance that they are not going mad.

Modulating arousal

In *Trauma and Recovery*, Herman, along with others, recommends starting the process of re-establishing safety by 'focusing on control of the body' (1992: 160). Clients and I jointly experiment with various strategies for reaching a sufficient level of calmness from which to engage in the work of therapy. This can be done in various ways.[4] A calm but 'tuned in' therapist's presence will further foster safety. The idea behind 'arousal management' is twofold: (a) success will give the client control over their symptoms; (b) the client will be protected from retraumatizing himself by constantly revisiting the traumatic memory.

'Resourcing' is my favourite way of 'putting on the brakes' (Rothschild 2000, 2003). It is best explained by Turner and Diebschlag (2001) in their chapter on resourcing the trauma client. In short, the client is asked to recall an experience, activity, person, object, etc. which brings them calmness or, as Turner says 'puts a smile on their face' (2007).

Paul: I used to like cooking but haven't done it since the incident . . . Just can't be bothered.

Me: Do you remember the last time you cooked and enjoyed it?

Paul [*pauses for a while to remember*]:   Yes, I often experiment with food. I made a pie a few months ago for some friends and it came out nice.

It doesn't matter in which direction I pursue my enquiry. I'm looking at his face waiting for it to be lit up by a resourceful state: joy, confidence, calmness, a memory of working in 'the zone', as he recalls an aspect of his cooking which has that effect on him. I could ask him what ingredients he used for his pie; how he kneads his dough; whether he prefers to use butter or margarine in his pastry; if he likes acidity in his sauces and how he achieves it; how his kitchen is organized and what the work surfaces are like. My aim is to help him to connect with the pleasure of the experience, through all his senses:

Me: When you remember kneading the dough on your marble surface and how nice and puffy it was turning out, does that feel nice? [*I'm being suggestive by giving words to the good feeling which I have previously read from his face and body. My intervention is designed to amplify the sensation.*]

Paul [*smiling broadly now*]:   Yes, it's as if I'm doing it now.

Me: Where in your body does it feel nice?

Paul [*tunes in now to give me an accurate answer. He's become mindful of his body and puts a hand on his tummy*]:   It's all nice and calm here. No butterflies. I can breathe more easily. My chest feels open.

Me: How's your tongue now? [*It was dry earlier in the session when he was anxious.*]

Paul: My mouth is not dry any longer. I can swallow.

Me: And your legs? [*They were heavy, a result of the trauma-induced numbness.*]

Paul: Much lighter. I feel I can move the legs. They are strong like when I'm cooking.

Having asked him to track this good feeling through his body, I teach Paul how to get in and out of this resourceful state at will. He is now using his imagination to bring about a pleasant state, gaining control over his body and modulating arousal.

I usually encourage the client to search for a resource which 'makes him feel connected to the whole universe'. I often deliver this invitation while spreading my arms, as if to encompass the whole world. Walkers often choose walking; those who once 'swam with dolphins' accurately remember an embodied experience of well-being which seems to go with this adventure. Clients who pray almost immediately get into a calm state by remembering their praying ritual; others still feel calmed by the memory of a grandchild on their lap. Despite their highly anxious state, trauma clients seem to respond to the reminder of their connectedness with the rest of the world. They are engaging, in a felt sense, with the environment, with the physical ground of their existence, and even with the spiritual dimension of their life. They may not have that feeling of connectedness at that moment in time, but can remember having felt a part of the larger picture. Together we establish a system which enables us to prevent the client from retraumatization. We can then more usefully start dealing with painful emotions and meanings.

Trauma emotions

In the weeks and months following the disaster, TfL staff were overwhelmed by the most uncomfortable emotions: shame, guilt, fear, horror, helplessness, hatred and anger. The 7/7 workers who came forward for counselling invariably felt like failures. Those who suffered most were the men and women who handled the dying and seriously injured, and were exposed to the most gruesome sights of human frailty. Underground staff are not professional disaster workers. Although many had previously been involved in aftermaths of train suicides ('one-unders'), they did not have a procedure which would prepare them for the action they undertook when they volunteered that day.[5] They were challenged by sights, sounds and smells of human suffering and death, which cause deep disgust and distress (Ursano and McCarrol 1990). They were faced with their own limitations when they couldn't get everybody to safety:

She died in my arms. There was nothing I could do. I put her head on my lap and talked to her.

(Lisa)

Emergency services took so long to get down there. What were they doing? And what were we supposed to do with the few stretchers we had? Only some of us had first aid training. Now everybody is singing their praises. What a joke!

(Bill)

The desperate wailing of the man who was missing half of his body is still in my head. I can hear it all the time.

(Paul)

As I listen to my clients' stories I tune in to their embodied experience. I pick up clues about their arousal by the colour and dampness of their skin, the way they hold their large muscles, the sound of their voice, the movement of their body when they breathe and their breath's rhythm. My attention is oriented towards them and also inwards to my embodied experience of being with them. I resonate with Paul's breathing pattern as he tells me about the unbearable cry of the dying man and I notice that I'm running out of breath and feel a slight pressure on my heart. I wonder whether Paul is going into hyperarousal? Is he getting lost in the flashback?

Me [*gently and calmly*]: It's all finished now Paul. It's not happening any longer. Tell me, what goes on in your body as you are telling me this?

Paul: I feel heavy here [*touching his chest*]. It's hard to breathe.

Me: We'll go back to your story, I really want to hear it, but it might be useful for us to just remember the pie you made the other day. You said you particularly liked making the pastry on your new marble kitchen surface. Can you remember doing it now?

Paul [*having recalled the good experience*]: Yes. The marble is shiny and cool. It only takes a moment to make good dough.

We talk about his resourcing experience until I sense his arousal levels are down again. Then I ask him about his body. Paul says, 'My chest feels open again. The pressure lifted a bit.'

We go back to the story that troubles him. Eventually, having considered the situation, Paul comes to terms with his limitations:

Paul: There was nothing I could do for him. I couldn't leave the woman I was carrying and attend to him. I took her to ground level and

> returned for him. He was dead. I feel so bad I left him, but what
> could I have done?

Later, as arousal levels went down, the distressing emotions of our 7/7 clients became modulated by pride, love for their colleagues, tender feelings towards the dead, the rescued and their families, and competitiveness with other 7/7 participants who may have been better recognized for what they have (or have not) done.

Respecting the trauma survivor's encounter with mortality

The above describes directive components of trauma therapy. These should not mislead the reader to believe the trauma therapist to be the only 'teacher' in the relationship. My 7/7 clients (and many other trauma clients) have had a good long look at death itself. For them, it is not just an idea. They have felt it in their hearts and through their bodies, as passengers died in their arms. The memory of the smell and taste of death stays with them for a long time after the encounter. 'The problem is,' as I said to one client, 'you know something about life that the rest of us try to lie to ourselves about. You cannot lie to yourself that you are not going to die, like you could before this happened and like I still can and do. What must that be like?'

My previous experience of working with people who had faced traumatic experiences such as train suicide, traffic accident, assault, rape, long-term abuse, or sudden death of a loved one taught me to expect to hear some very strong existential themes. I was ready to listen to people as they struggled with existential guilt and anxiety, and I expected to hear them ask themselves: 'What am I doing with my life?' 'How am I choosing to live?' As Heidegger points out, the death of another can confront us with our limitations, vulnerability and mortality (1962: 282; H. 239); it may make us anxious not about our own death per se, but about our life and the way we live it in the light of our mortality (van Deurzen 1997). I expected many of my clients to change the way they had been living, leave their 'underground' careers, start new relationships, embark on new studies and travel the world. This did not happen, or at least those themes never came up in our conversations. All but two employees involved in the incident, both near retirement, eventually went back to their duties. Although their lives did not take a different direction, the experience changed them in most profound ways: they started to relate to one another and to others in a different way. From the very first moment during the morning of 7/7, when staff on duty realized the 'code red' alert signified a major danger, they pulled together and placed the needs of others before their own. The dying and the injured passengers, their colleagues and their staff all became precious fellow humans, worthy of my clients' concern and care. Each told me of their struggle to call their loved ones that morning. They will forever remember the encounters they had with the dead, dying and injured. They were moved by the kinship they felt with the colleagues alongside whom they had worked. In each of the five sites, once station control had been handed over to the police, staff gathered in the local pub. This is when they first remember 'relaxing a little', and experiencing an atmosphere of community. Next, they recall how the manager organized a taxi home and the welcoming safety of the loved one who opened the house door. They felt a strong connection with all London Transport workers (including Muslim colleagues) and a connection with all Londoners. At times I felt they experienced me as 'one of them' too.

The spirit of comradeship and community that helped TfL staff work together on the day, carried over, it would appear, into later months. Binswanger, inspired by Heidegger's concept of being-in-the-world (see p. 43), refers to three dimensions of human existence: the physical world or *Umwelt*; the personal world or *Eigenwelt*; and the social or *Mitwelt* (to which van Deurzen has added the spiritual dimension or *Überwelt*). Binswanger challenges Heidegger for ignoring, in his analysis of human existence in *Being and Time*, the positive aspects of the *Mitwelt*, the social dimension, preferring to focus on the problem with 'falling' in with others and falling prey to public opinion (see pp. 13–14 and 'authenticity' p. 117). He argues that Heidegger's ontology disregards 'the role of human relationships in the achievement of self-realization' (Frie 1997: 87). To be authentic, for Heidegger, is to 'comprehend and accept the parameters of human living, including the fact that one has one's own life to lead and that death is an inevitable part of the human condition' (van Deurzen and Kenward 2005: 11). Heidegger is dismissive of Binswanger, claiming that the latter had misunderstood him and his fundamental distinction between ontic and ontological (see p. 10; Heidegger 2001: 228). Much has been written about Binswanger's misunderstanding of Heidegger's ontology and Heidegger's more individualistic position and inadequate treatment of the intersubjective (e.g. Sadler 1969; Habermas 1985; van Deurzen-Smith 1997; Frie 1997; van Deurzen and Kenward 2005). A comprehensive review of those arguments is, regrettably, beyond the scope of this chapter. However, the concept of the social dimension of human existence is very relevant to a discussion of the impact of 7/7 on the rescue staff involved.

In Binswanger and van Deurzen's language (van Deurzen-Smith 1997), the existential explorations and learning for my clients after 7/7 were in the domain of the *Mitwelt*, or being with others in the world. As I listened to what my 7/7 clients learnt from the aftermath of the terrorist attack, I noticed that the event had dramatically changed their experience of themselves in and through relation. Buber has special words for this different way of relating:

> On the far side of the subjective, on this side of the objective, on
> the narrow edge where *I* and *Thou* meet, there is the realm of the

between. This reality, whose disclosure has begun in our time, shows the way, leading beyond individualism and collectivism, for the life decision of future generations. Here the genuine third alternative is indicated, the knowledge of which will help to bring about the genuine person again and to establish genuine community.

(Buber 2002: 243)

I and Thou, in which Buber develops the idea of 'dialogical principle', proposes concrete meetings between people as the most important aspect of being human. Moreover, the reciprocal essential relationship between two beings signifies a primal opportunity of 'being' (Buber 1996: 209). Unlike Heidegger, Buber proposes that we become ourselves through mutual, confirming and open contact with others. This, I would argue, accounts for my clients' changed experience of themselves:

> I learnt to rely on my colleagues more. I know there's nothing they wouldn't do for me now . . . When I was feeling bad in July and August, they'd call every day to see how I'm doing and told my missus to be patient with me. It's like they understood me better than I understood myself.
>
> (Mike)

> I didn't think I was going to be strong enough to bounce back from that . . . But *I am* strong! You were important in that . . . the way you were always there and I could just call you whenever I started to get wobbly again.
>
> (Olifujawa)

They (we) made ourselves available and *attended to* each other. Gabriel Marcel gives the concept of availability a place in the history of ethics, and he designates it as a special human virtue (Randall 1992). He makes human openness to a presence outside the self his main concern. For Marcel, 'the fundamental human experience and awareness of existence is communal' and 'existence in its higher forms is inseparable from intersubjectivity' (Randall 1992: 236). The crisis of 7/7 threw us off guard and towards each other, and we all experienced different ways of being with each other in a world now suddenly turned upside down. It is important to note that this changed way of being with others after 7/7 was not some ideal situation in which 'unconditional positive regard' for fellow humans blossomed, nor was it a matter of oversentimentality. Relating to others after trauma is usually characterized by friction, irritability, anger and conflict, as well as coming together harmoniously to create and take refuge in safety. The aftermath of 7/7 was no different. People struggled with life and with each other, but ultimately, they pulled together to heal, recoup and protect.

From a purely Heideggerian perspective, one might have expected a significant number of the rescue staff to have come to feel personally confronted with their mortality and to have sought to rethink their life choices. (This may well be what happened to members of the public who were affected by the bombings.) Instead the spirit of comradeship which prevailed among staff at the time would appear to have prevented this later, personal anxious confrontation with mortality.[6] This could be viewed, in Heideggerian terms, as 'falling' in with the 'they'. Binswanger's emphasis on the importance of the social dimension of human existence and Buber's view of a person as emerging in and through relation with others offer an alternative understanding to what seems to have happened after the July bombings. As I perceive it, a positive sense of community developed through shared experience and understanding among TfL staff and, through it, the emergence of persons more open to one another.

Notes

1   See Babette Rothschild's *Help the Helper* (2006) for further details on compassion fatigue and vicarious traumatization.
2   This text deals mainly with the trauma first aid service. For a comprehensive outline of differential diagnosis between different stages of traumatic shock, see *DSM-IV* (APA 1994); Rothschild (2000).
3   The triune brain offers a context within which we can discuss shared heritage between humans and other animals. It seems a useful metaphor for delineation of categories of brain functioning and less useful as a topographical map of the brain. Accelerated technological advances are now allowing scientists an increasingly better view of the working brain. MacLean's theory is continually criticized and updated by neuroscientists (Damasio 1999; LeDoux 1999).
4   By connecting to one's breathing, establishing a 'safe space', progressive muscle relaxation (described by Schiraldi 1999), muscle toning (Rothschild 2000), teaching how to achieve self-hypnotic trance, autogenic training (Schiraldi 1999) or practising dual awareness (Rothschild 2000, 2003). The non-traumatized are able to 'maintain awareness of one or more areas of experience simultaneously' (Rothschild 2000: 128). For example, I may recall the unpleasant way I parted with my daughter this morning while also noticing how much I am enjoying the heat of the sun on my face. Holding dual awareness is not so easy for those shocked by a traumatic experience. The memory of an event (flashback) can take over and, unable to maintain the awareness of the fact that the event is not happening right now, they may feel as if they are experiencing it all over again. Rothschild helpfully explains a protocol which teaches the client to simultaneously maintain the awareness and discrimination of past (traumatic event) and present (safety). Dual awareness is a prerequisite for safe trauma therapy as it stops clients being sucked into the vortex of traumatic re-experiencing.
5   Interestingly, those train operators who, on that day, performed relatively simple routine tasks which their training had prepared them for, reported hypervigilance-related symptoms in the weeks following 7/7, but did not appear to suffer from the guilt and shame feelings commonly experienced by trauma survivors. They were prepared; they had a remit. Hence the outcome didn't seem 'out of synch' with their aspirations. They were not 'failures'.

6   Editor's note: It is not uncommon for older cancer patients to express their embarrassment at coming for counselling, contrasting what they regard as their present, reprehensible anxiety with their time in the war, where they 'just got on with it'. On reflection, they invariably see the difference as lying in the wartime comradeship – 'we were in it together', in contrast to their lonely experience of cancer.

References

American Psychiatric Association (APA, 1994) *Diagnostic and Statistical Manual of Mental Disorders, DSM IV-TR*, 4th edn, Washington DC: American Psychiatric Association.

Buber, M. (1996 [1923]) *I and Thou*, trans. Smith, R.G. (1937), 2nd edn 1958, Edinburgh: T. & T. Clark.

—— (2002 [1938]) 'What Is Man?', in Buber, M. *Between Man and Man*, trans. Gregor-Smith, R., London: Routledge.

Calhoun, L.G. and Tedeschi, R.E. (eds) (1999) *Facilitating Posttraumatic Growth: A Clinician's Guide*, Mahwah NJ: Lawrence Erlbaum Associates, Inc.

Damasio, A. (1999) *The Feeling of What Happens*, New York: Harcourt, Brace.

Frie, R. (1997) *Subjectivity and Intersubjectivity in Modern Philosophy and Psychoanalysis*, New York: Rowman & Littlefield.

Habermas, J. (1985) *The Philosophical Discourse of Modernity*, Cambridge MA: MIT Press.

Heidegger, M. (1962 [1927]) *Being and Time*, Oxford: Blackwell.

Heidegger, M. (2001) *Zollikon Seminars*, Boss, M. (ed.), Evanston IL: Northwestern University Press.

Herman, J (1992) *Trauma and Recovery*, New York: Basic Books.

LeDoux, J. (1999) *The Emotional Brain: The Mysterious Underpinnings of Emotional Life*, London: Phoenix.

Levine, P. (1997) *Waking The Tiger: The Innate Capacity to Transform Overwhelming Experiences*, Berkeley: North Atlantic Books.

—— (2006) *Trauma through a Child's Eyes*, Berkeley: North Atlantic Books.

MacLean, P. (1990) *The Triune Brain in Evolution*, New York: Plenum Press.

Mitchell, M. (1991) The Police After Lockerbie: What Were the Effects?, in *Police*, 23: 30–31.

Randall, A. (1992) *The Mystery of Hope in the Philosophy of Gabriel Marcel 1888–1973. Hope and Homo Viator*, Lewiston: Edwin Mellen Press.

Rothschild, B. (2000) *The Body Remembers: The Psychophysiology of Trauma and Trauma Treatment*, New York: Norton.

—— (2003) *The Body Remembers Casebook: Unifying Methods and Models in the Treatment of Trauma and PTSD*, New York: Norton.

—— (2006) *Help for the Helper: The Psychophysiology of Compassion Fatigue and Vicarious Trauma*, New York: Norton.

Sadler, W.A., Jr (1969) *Existence and Love: A New Approach in Existential Phenomenology*, New York: Charles Scribner's Sons.

Schiraldi, G.R. (1999) *The Post-Traumatic Stress Disorder Sourcebook: A Guide to Healing, Recovery, and Growth*, New York: McGraw Hill.

Tedeschi, R.G., Park, C.L. and Calhoun, L.G. (1998) Posttraumatic Growth:

Conceptual Issues, in Tedeschi, R.G., Park, C.L. and Calhoun, L.G. (eds) *Post-traumatic Growth: Positive Changes in the Aftermath of Crisis*, Mahwah NJ: Lawrence Erlbaum Associates, Inc.

Turner, E.J. (2007) email message, 12 January.

Turner, E.J. and Diebschlag, F. (2001) Resourcing the Trauma Client, in Spiers, T. (ed.) *Trauma: A Practitioner's Guide to Counselling*, Hove, UK: Brunner-Routledge.

Ursano, R.J. and McCarrol, J.E. (1990) The Nature of the Traumatic Stressors: Handling Dead Bodies, in *Journal of Nervous and Mental Disease*, 178: 396–398.

van Deurzen, E. and Kenward, R. (2005) *Dictionary of Existential Psychotherapy and Counselling*, London: Sage.

van Deurzen-Smith, E. (1997) *Everyday Mysteries: Existential Dimensions of Psychotherapy*, London: Routledge.

MEANING

Meaning is at the heart of existential therapy (Viktor Frankl even called his form of existential therapy 'Logotherapy' – 'meaning-therapy'). Meaning goes hand in hand with understanding, with discovering and selecting possibilities, with freedom of choice and responsibility; it underlies fulfilment and emptiness.

According to Heidegger, we always encounter a situation with a certain understanding of it and in a certain mood. The way we are 'attuned' at any given moment affects our understanding: if we are wearing 'rose-tinted spectacles' the outlook will be rosier than if we are feeling depressed. This affects the meaning we attach to situations, to the world around us, to our existence.

The work of therapy involves the exploration of meaning – the exploration of what is meaning-ful for clients: their relationships; their core values and beliefs; their hopes and ambitions; their losses and regrets; their fears and anxieties.

It may involve the exploration of the client's experience of meaninglessness and the emptiness, anxiety and even despair that may accompany it – so powerful is our need for meaning.

It may involve the client's experience of feeling that the world 'has been turned upside down' (e.g. by a loss, a diagnosis of HIV, etc.) and nothing is 'like it was'. It involves looking at what 'normal' meant and still means, yet cannot be, and the new sort of 'normality' that may lie ahead.

It may involve the uncovering of hidden meanings: 'why?' not just as cause or explanation, but as 'making sense' of a situation.

It may involve the unravelling of stories the client once created to bring an acceptable meaning back into his life.

It involves the creation of new meanings: the exploration of new possibilities, the making of new choices and priorities.

6

MORTALITY AND MEANING IN REFUGEE SURVIVORS OF TORTURE AND ORGANIZED VIOLENCE

Dick Blackwell

Mortality is overwhelmingly present in work with survivors of torture and organized violence. In an important sense, it constitutes the context in which such work is undertaken and thereby shapes the work itself and the experiences of both the client and the therapist. There is, however, in the course of this work, in the meetings between therapists and clients, relatively little discussion of 'mortality' as the awareness that death at some point awaits each of us. Rather, it is the proximity of death in the past and present experiences of the clients and the pressures this creates for therapists that often becomes the focal point of the work.

The organizational context and the client group

The Medical Foundation for the Care of Victims of Torture and Organised Violence was founded in 1985 in London. Since then it has received more than 40,000 referrals and currently expects to see over 2500 new clients per year. These clients come from more than 80 different countries and range from the very old to the very young. They are refugees from a wide range of political systems and political and military conflicts. We are therefore concerned with a great diversity of cultures, political systems, religions, family structures and personal experiences. While it is possible to make a number of generalizations about the experiences of clients and therapists engaged in this work, it is always necessary to bear in mind the specificity, and indeed uniqueness, of each individual's experiences and of each individual's encounter in therapy. While virtually all our clients have undergone traumatic experiences of torture and violence, the specific events they have survived are very diverse. Some have been detained and tortured on only one occasion and for a relatively short time, perhaps only a matter of days. Others may have been in captivity for years, or may have been detained and ill treated on a number of occasions. The nature and extent of the violence to which they have been subjected will also vary, as will the injuries they have suffered physically, psychologically and in relation to their whole life trajectory, identity and their being-in-the-world.

Common to this wide variety of experiences is the ever present threat of death. Few people detained in these contexts can have any confidence at all that they will come out alive. Some have been explicitly threatened with death and some have suffered mock executions. When they escape the country to seek refuge elsewhere, their belief and their experience tend to be not only that they are fleeing from further persecution or torture, but that they are fleeing for their lives. This is a primary feature of the context in which many, if not most of them, find their way to the UK and subsequently to the Medical Foundation.

They then embark on the process of applying for asylum. This involves them in what they, and many of their therapists, experience as a Kafkaesque process which maintains a profound level of uncertainty as to whether they will be allowed to stay in this only recently arrived at place of safety, or whether they will be returned to face the horrors and indeed the death from which they have so narrowly escaped.

Many of them have family members who have been killed or who have disappeared and may or may not still be alive. Others have had to leave family members behind and remain uncertain as to how safe those family members are. Those who have managed to bring family members with them may fear that the whole family might be killed if they have to return. Friends, colleagues, neighbours and other members of their communities are also likely to have been killed or to remain in danger. The refugee in this country may be regularly receiving news from the home country, both about the continuing levels of violence, persecution and killing in general and about the fate of those known personally.

It is not only individuals who are lost in this context; it is whole communities, cultures and political movements. The individual refugee may be cut off from his community and culture through his geographical relocation. This is a personal loss which can be mitigated, to some extent, by the knowledge of the continued existence of that culture. But in some cases, the culture itself may be destroyed by war and persecution or transformed to the extent that it is no longer, in a meaningful sense, the same culture. Similarly, political movements, beliefs and ideals can be destroyed. It therefore becomes important to talk about the death of a way of life or the death of the meaning of an individual's life.

There are considerable variations in the situations in which our clients find themselves when they arrive in the UK: some are children who arrive alone; some are children with one parent; some with both parents and siblings. Some come alone as adults, or with spouses, or with children. In some cases three generations arrive together. Some are able to connect rapidly with a refugee community or with others from their own country or culture. Others remain isolated, either because of where they are placed geographically by the accommodation system available to asylum seekers, or because their experiences of persecution have left them suspicious of others from their own country. In such situations, some have the social confidence to make connections with neighbours or other members of the local community, while others again remain isolated.

I have begun with this outline of the variety of refugee experiences and the variety of clients and client experiences encountered in psychotherapy and counselling with victims of torture and organized violence, for two reasons: first, because I believe the context of the client's experience is always important in any form of counselling; second, because I want to emphasize the difficulties and dangers in making generalizations about any specific aspect of our clients' experiences. This holds true whether we are considering the effects of exile, the impact of traumatic violence, or the part played by issues or intimations of mortality. Generalizations have value only insofar as they are sufficiently general to allow for significant individual variations and provided that they are understood as generalizations, with all the problems and limitations these necessarily have. Every client must ultimately be encountered and understood in the uniqueness of her or his lived experience. Generalizations are valuable insofar as they assist us in the understanding of that unique experience, but dangerous insofar as they encourage us to assume or anticipate a level of homogeneity which denies the uniqueness with which we seek to engage.

It is also necessary to note that counsellors and therapists come from a variety of backgrounds, are of different ages, genders, sexualities, cultures and political orientations. Also, the therapeutic encounter takes place between clients and therapists and is as much a product of their work together as it is a result of the client's background, personality and prior experience. Similarly, the issue of mortality and the current threat to the client hang over them both and affect them both, albeit in different ways.

Levels of encounter

In order to consider the therapeutic context with refugee clients, I have proposed a four-level framework (Blackwell 2005). The four levels are: political, cultural, interpersonal and intra-psychic. They are levels of experience for both the client and the therapist, so, within this framework, it is possible to consider the experiences that client and therapist bring to the therapeutic encounter and the ways in which they experience themselves and each other in the course of that encounter. Furthermore, thinking in terms of this framework provides a way to consider the client's total experiential contexts and all the issues that might need to be addressed. To some extent, it also guards against becoming overly focused on one aspect of the client's experience and missing other important issues.

The clients' experiences at each of these levels can be further divided into experiences in their home country and experiences in the UK. So, for example, we can consider their experience of their home culture and their sense of identity within it and their encounter with and experience of UK culture and their struggle to deal with the differences. In a similar way we can think about their experiences of the politics of their home country – usually the cause of their predicament – and their encounter with the UK's politics, particularly for many of them as it relates to asylum seekers.

Considering mortality within this framework, we can see that the politics of their home country has brought them close to death. The UK political system offers them both the possibility of safety through asylum and the threat of death through rejection and deportation back to their home country. Their culture will have its own language and system of meanings about death, which will probably be different from those they encounter in the UK and those of the therapist. At the interpersonal level, they may already have lost friends and family members to violent deaths, which they may have witnessed themselves. Intra-psychically they are often in a state of shock; managing to stay alive and keep going, but scarcely able to think about what has happened, much less about its meaning.

At the risk of overcomplicating the framework, I have considered adding two more levels, religious and economic. I have previously included religion within the category of culture and there are good arguments for locating it there. However, its currently high political profile and its powerful embodiment of beliefs about life and death suggest that it may require a category of its own. Moreover, it could be argued that considering religion as part of culture is a more Western secularist view, whereas in other societies culture might be regarded as a derivative of religion. The category of 'economic' suggests itself because so many of our clients live in such poverty that basic issues of economic survival become a dominant part of their lived experience.

Death and the meaning of life

The issue of mortality does not so much arise in therapy with survivors of torture and political violence; it infuses it, permeates it at every level and casts a shadow over the whole therapeutic encounter. The clients' lives have invariably been threatened. In the context from which they have escaped, many others have died. Family members, friends, relatives and colleagues may also have been killed. While the clients may be bereaved, they may be unable to begin any sort of mourning process, so they carry the loss, perhaps unconsciously, unable to talk or even to think about it. These are the literal physical deaths.

But one's relation to mortality cannot be separated from the meaning one gives to life: torture, organized violence, flight, the search for safety and living in exile can involve the death of many meanings.

At the political level, many people find the central meaning of their lives in political activism. The defeat of a political movement or becoming disillusioned with one's political ideals can be experienced as a profound loss of meaning. What else is there now to do? What else is there to live for? Then there are clients who come to feel that their political activism has been the cause of death and suffering to their families, or who feel broken and defeated by their own suffering. Their politics are less a source of meaning than a focus of doubt and guilt and questions about what they can now do with their lives.

At the cultural level, there is the loss of a way of life which may have been taken for granted in the way it provided meaning and purpose. While religious and cultural beliefs and practices may be retained in exile, there will inevitably be tensions in the encounter with a new culture, especially when the younger generation begins to take up aspects of UK culture. But there may be even worse problems at the cultural level. In some cultures, it seems, a woman who has been raped becomes a non-person. Her husband should divorce her and she should throw herself in the river. The victim then faces a choice of accepting the stigma imposed on her by her culture, or having to challenge that culture and lose much of the safety and security, and perhaps sense of identity, with which it has provided her. Many enter what I call a state of 'cultural transition', caught perhaps permanently between their original culture and the new way of life in exile.

At the interpersonal level, the violent death of parents, spouses and children assaults the meaning of family life and the identity of individuals as husband, wife, mother, father, brother, sister, son, daughter. Family members can be so changed by their traumatic experiences that they are experienced as different people – their previous personality having been lost. The way in which the family may have been persecuted because of the activities of one member can introduce complex and often unconscious feelings of guilt and resentment, which in turn bring a loss of trust and security. Parents in any case feel terrible at having been unable to protect their children, and the children have lost their sense of their parents being able to protect them.

Intra-psychically, various conscious and unconscious beliefs and assumptions have been lost. The world is no longer a reasonably safe place, but a terrifying one. Anger and aggression are no longer manageable, but are unbelievably dangerous and destructive. Sleep is no longer a refuge, but an occasion when the monsters from the past come to life and the terrors and torments are relived. Often there is a sense of numbness, an inability to think about the overwhelming nature of the experiences. This numbness can protect against overwhelming feelings and fragmentation. Torture has been described as a way of killing a person while leaving him physically alive – a description which captures the sense of feeling dead inside which is akin to this numbness. Robert Lifton, in his description of the survivors of cities destroyed by atomic bombs, introduced the term 'psychic numbing' in a book entitled *Death in Life* (Lifton 1968).

Assaults on meaning at all these different levels are woven together, leaving the individual struggling to find meaning and purpose, or even an identity, beyond being a victim of all these assaults. The struggle is not so much to come to terms with the fact of mortality, but to find a purpose in staying alive (Frankl 1985).

Politics, culture and interpersonal relationships, however, can also be sources of survival and ultimately of a renewed sense of life. Survivors may cling to their political beliefs, or find a new political project that gives them sufficient meaning and purpose to keep going and to begin to rebuild themselves as individuals with a place in the world. Culture and religion provide not only beliefs but duties that enable individuals to keep struggling. Religion is particularly powerful in providing hope and comfort for clients who at times can find nothing else to live for. Interpersonally, families and family loyalties also sustain the individuals within them. 'I have nothing to live for but my children' is not an uncommon statement. Often it is reported as the only thing that stands in the way of suicide. Religions which forbid suicide frequently provide a similarly preventive function.

These struggles with loss and meaning are compounded by the struggle for asylum. Applying for asylum leaves many of our clients in a state of limbo for significant periods of time, sometimes months, sometimes years. In the course of this process, they can lose whatever faith they had in UK society and its institutions. They feel they are not believed, not trusted and not cared about. Whether they live or die is a matter of little concern to anyone. They are non-persons. They do not have a sense of being in the world, but one of non-being – an experience that compounds the sense of psychic death. They live in a constant state of anxiety. Sometimes it is repressed or dissociated from for periods of time, so that it is not talked about; but nevertheless it overshadows their lives and their therapeutic meetings. At other times, particularly when the times approach for the 'hearings' of their applications or appeals, the anxiety can rise to the level of panic. Throughout this time, the threat of deportation, which to them means virtually certain death, hangs over them. They live in its shadow. Again suicide is often considered, and held in mind as an alternative course of action to avoid being 'sent back'.

Therapists in this setting, whether working with individuals, couples, families or groups, must all work in the shadow of mortality, and are given cause to reflect on mortality and meaning. Whatever attitudes and beliefs the therapist brings to the therapy, the work itself makes certain impacts.

Approaches to therapeutic work

My introduction to the world of counselling and psychotherapy was as a volunteer worker in the 'Samaritans', an organization which provided what it called 'befriending' to those who were suicidal and despairing. There was no theory: just a practice of listening, accepting and responding empathically and non-judgementally. Although the practice had much in common with Carl Rogers' 'non-directive counselling', it was not derived from it but developed separately out of the attempt to respond practically to the needs of the suicidal. It rested on the discovery of the value of the spontaneous empathic response of untrained volunteers. The term 'befriending' emphasized that it was not a professional practice but an activity of 'being with' as a fellow human being. The question of mortality loomed significantly in this work as did questions of meaning and being and it was out of this that my interest arose in existentialist thinkers such as Laing, Sartre, Buber and Tillich.

I went on to train in group analysis and in family therapy. Group analysis is the analysis *of* the group *by* the group *including* the conductor ('conductor' is the title given to the therapist). It is relatively easy to recognize existential themes in this discourse and to speak of it in terms of the social nature of 'being-in-the-world' and the understanding and development of a person's 'being-in-the-world' through the individual and collective praxis of a therapeutic group.

In my early work with groups in a psychiatric setting, I realized that for many of my clients what really mattered most was not what happened in their therapeutic group, but what happened at home in their families. This took me into family therapy, which focused on the way that 'personality', thinking, acting and being are influenced by the dynamics of the family. I became aware of the extent to which 'being in the family' shapes or perhaps to some extent determines 'being-in-the-world'.

Family therapy also showed me some other important things. By conceptualizing the family as a 'system' and then striving to bring about change in that system, it was easy to become quite instrumental and deterministic in theory and in practice. At the same time, family therapy showed how language is used not only as a way of conveying information but also, and often more importantly, as a way of shaping and developing relationships. Most importantly, it established that language is only part of communication between people and that all sorts of non-verbal aspects of communication play a vital part, both in conveying information and in shaping relationships.

In my reading and application of psychoanalytic, and indeed of sociological and political ideas, I am aware of the need to recognize: first, the tendency towards determinism which problematizes the idea of human freedom; second, the importance of those aspects of human encounter which go beyond theory and perhaps even beyond words, which arise spontaneously and unpredictably, and which can only be approached through art, literature, music and perhaps humour. It is, however, possible to use psychoanalytic thinking and sociological thinking too, not in order to be deterministic in theory, or mechanistic in therapeutic practice, nor to establish a norm of health or social behaviour against which to calibrate pathology, but to understand the constraints on freedom and the deterministic factors contributing to a particular state of being in-the-world, in order to move beyond them.

It was working with survivors of torture and violence that impressed on me the need to think in terms of unconscious processes and repressed memories and feelings. I needed a language to talk about interiority and ways of dealing with events and experiences that were overwhelming and could not be consciously held in mind and processed. Many survivors displayed various levels of shock, and were unable to remember large parts of what had happened to them. It was only subsequently that they could remember certain events and the feelings connected with them.

It was also apparent that some clients could get therapists to feel things on their behalf, which they themselves were not in touch with.[1] These were often the so-called negative feelings of anger and rage, or fear and anxiety, shame and guilt, but also feelings of hope or pride in their achievement of having survived. Therapists would feel full of these powerful feelings, while the client had no sense of feeling these things at all. It only made sense to me in terms of the psychoanalytic concept of projective identification, whereby one person can project aspects of their experience into another person in such a way that the other person experiences the feeling on their behalf.

Moreover, it seemed clear that traumatic experiences provoked biological, or, if you will, instinctive responses, such as fight, flight and dissociation, over which the victim had no conscious control and produced subsequent symptoms such as nightmares, flashbacks, startle responses, non-specific anxieties, somatization, uncontrollable rage, depression and memory loss, some of which are listed as symptoms of post-traumatic stress disorder (PTSD). The problem with the PTSD approach lies not in its recognition of some of the results of traumatic experience, but in its failure to locate them in a more complex matrix of lived experience, which has political, cultural, interpersonal and intra-psychic meaning. My approach is not to ignore or deny psycho-physiological determinations in the construction of the personality and in the response to trauma, but to integrate them with sociological and material factors, all of which can be addressed in the complex gestalt of a living experiential therapeutic relationship.

R.D. Laing (1967) said that psychotherapy remained the stubborn attempt by two people to discover the wholeness of being human through the relationship between them. In the context of this work we could refocus it as the stubborn attempt to recover a sense of being human and of being able to survive; and, in that relationship, to struggle to think and speak about their experiences in order to find meaning in their survival and in their future.

Mortality and meaning for the therapist

In most of the settings from which the clients have escaped, human life has become cheap. People are killed casually and gratuitously. Sometimes they are killed because they are members of an ethnic group, sometimes because they are members of a political party, sometimes it seems they are just in the wrong place at the wrong time. They are caught up in political situations, civil wars, campaigns for democracy, or are living under a repressive regime, in all of which violence has become a routine way to solve problems. Sometimes it is not even a way of solving problems, but seems more primitively driven. And the violence is extreme. It is not just fighting opponents. It is torture and killing on a wide scale.

Those of us who have grown up in a society where certain freedoms are guaranteed find it hard to contemplate the lives of those who must forgo many of those freedoms to be able to live. It is those very freedoms that give substantial meaning to our own lives and are vital parts of our sense of being-in-the-world. We are also used to a society in which death still registers importantly as an individual event. Human life has a high value, each death is significant and the taking of a human life is an act of such gravity that we have abolished the death penalty as an act that a state can acceptably commit. Even during an overseas war in which many members of another society have been killed, the deaths of members of our own armed forces are still reported as individual tragedies. As a society, to varying extents, we share in a sort of collective denial of the deaths of people in other societies, some of them as a result of our own foreign policies. Or, while we may be aware of them, they do not impinge on us.

But working with survivors from these other societies, within the context of violence, torture and slaughter, therapists are necessarily confronted with these realities.

The apparent cheapness of life in these contexts raises further questions about its meaning. Along with our high valuation of an individual life, we place a high value on individuality, on individual personality and perhaps on the virtue of the human individual. To encounter, through our clients, political contexts where these values seem effectively to have been negated raises questions about our own ontology, our own assumptions about what it means to be human. Along with the cheapening of life, we encounter the capacity of some humans to dehumanize others. We encounter clients struggling to recover a sense of being human and at the same time we encounter the human capacity for destructiveness. The dehumanization of our clients began in the minds of other humans.

These questions reverberate through our own political, cultural, interpersonal and intra-psychic experiences and beliefs, and may give us cause frequently to reassess our own experiences and sense of being-in-the-world at all of these levels.

The presence of death in the therapeutic space

Death becomes a focus in the therapeutic session in a number of ways. First, in family therapy, members of the family who have been killed are experienced as powerful absences. It may be difficult to talk about them and particularly difficult to talk about their death. Yet the family seem to bring with them an 'absence' which is present with them in the room. What is needed in the therapy is the opportunity to talk about the dead person, or persons, and the manner of their death. This begins a process of grieving, which has been frozen in the traumatic and hectic process of flight and the struggle to find safety, shelter and a way of continuing to function on a day-to-day basis. Moreover, since mourning usually takes place in a social and cultural context involving friends, relatives, neighbours, etc., it readily becomes suspended or frozen in families cut off from those contexts. If the family can begin the process in therapy, they may be able to continue it together, provided they have established themselves in a sufficiently stable current living situation.

In group therapy, the room can feel filled with the people who have been lost by the group members. The extent of the loss and volume of the grief can feel overwhelming. But where therapists can survive with their own 'sense of being' intact and where they can enable the group members to share their grief and support each other, a mourning process can begin and develop in the group.

In individual therapy, the lost people can also feel present, though at other times the loss can be so powerfully repressed or dissociated from the family that the dead person or persons are seemingly forgotten about by both client and therapist. In such cases it can take time before the client feels able to begin to remember them and to allow his feelings about them to surface.

These are the cases where the death has already happened and is known to have happened. But loved ones may be 'missing', without their fate being known. Then one enters a strange world of possibilities and probabilities, of imaginings and fantasies, of hopes and fears. Death may be a possibility. It may be a probability. But who is to say for certain. So the anxiety and the pain of loss remain, along with fearful and horrifying fantasies; the possibility of mourning remains suspended in the absence of a definite death. The missing people can be present through their absences in the different therapeutic settings in the same way as those known to be dead, but all that can be addressed in whatever form of therapy this occurs are the agonies of the uncertainty.

Lastly, there is the threat of death to the client. The Medical Foundation has a three-pronged approach to its clients, addressing first their need for safety from further persecution, second their physical and material needs – for medical treatment, food, clothing and shelter – and third their psychosocial needs. The need for safety is addressed through the provision of documentation to substantiate their claim for asylum. This includes medical reports on their injuries and reports from those involved in working psychologically with them. Thus, in the course of counselling or psychotherapy, which is primarily to address psychosocial needs, the therapist may be asked to provide a report to be used in the application for asylum. At this point, therapists are aware that their report can have a decisive effect on whether the client lives or dies. The client may feel the same thing.

At the stage of first applying for asylum the pressure may be less intense, but as the process develops and the expectations of the outcome become more uncertain, the tension and stress in the therapy begin to mount – particularly where the danger of failure and deportation is looking increasingly likely. The therapist, having done her best, is left feeling impotent and helpless. The client is anxious, terrified, angry, numb and may be more or less in touch with all or any of these feelings. At this point there is little the therapist can do but 'be with' the client and try to think and talk about the situation. At the same time, it seems an inadequate response and the therapist may be unable to believe that she really has exhausted all possibilities, and so continues to feel that there must be something that can be done. The client is facing death, not because of an incurable illness or fatal injury about which the therapist knows she can do nothing and for which she bears no responsibility. Instead, the threat lies at the end of a process of which she feels she has in some way played an official part, and which is an official process of her society and her government for which she feels responsible. Moreover, it is at this point that the client may declare an intention to kill himself or herself if threatened with deportation. Is this the sort of suicidal feeling that might be responsive to counselling or psychotherapy? Is it indicative of a psychotic state? Is it clinical depression? Is it just a threat? Or is it a sensible and rational decision in the given circumstances?

It is at a point like this that what might be regarded as the normal process or praxis of therapy seems to stop. The sort of therapy that enables clients to deal with their past experiences and their present context and find a viable sense of being in the world seems impossible. The world is offering them no space for being in it, and the therapist is somehow part of that world. Yet it is precisely the point where the therapy must carry on and the therapist must find a way of being with the client and addressing the situation they are in.

At such times, it is important for the therapist to be in a team. It is almost impossible to bear these sorts of situations alone; the support and creative thinking of colleagues become vital. It is not just a question of mortality or the threat of the client's death. It is a far more complex web involving the politics, culture, interpersonal relationships and intrapsychic experiences of both the client and the therapist, and of the historical processes in the wider social and political contexts.

Mortality and human history

Mortality, as I have already suggested, does not occur in this work as a single issue capable of isolation. It is seldom addressed as such. Clients, and their therapists, are preoccupied with the struggle to stay alive and to find a way to live. They seldom contemplate the fact that they are mortal. Yet in a sense, while mortality is nowhere, it is also everywhere – a given fact on which everything else is predicated. The fragility of human existence, the uncertainty of life and the threat of death are central to the experience of becoming a refugee. So is the fact of death, which is the fate of many in the political contexts from which refugees have escaped.

Mortality in this context is not just an individual issue; it infuses the social context from which the individual emerges, the world in which the individual has his being. I mean this not only in the existential sense that life is finite for each of us, but that certain historical events dramatize more than others the precariousness of life. In certain political contexts, life becomes cheap and devalued on a massive scale.

Refugees and their therapists are brought together by historical processes – wars and oppression in one country, the possibility of asylum in another. Both are products of the political and cultural processes and they meet at a certain point in history. Human history is in some senses a history of wars, slaughters, genocides, torture and violence; a history of political deaths. Therapists working with survivors of torture and political violence encounter not just individual victims, but individual embodiments of these historical processes that have victimized them. They therefore encounter mortality not just as it is manifested in the life of one individual, but as it is embodied implicitly in the bloodier pages of human history.

An escape from death, or from the threat of death, can raise the issue of mortality in a way that affects the individual's sense of being-in-the-world. But the world in which they have their being remains substantially unchanged. It is their relationship to it that has changed. For refugees, it is the world that changes. And loss and death are woven into all the levels at which they experience and have their being within that world.

Note

1 Editor's note: For an alternative, existential understanding of this phenomenon, see Conclusion (pp. 220–1).

References

Blackwell, R.D. (2005) *Counselling and Psychotherapy with Refugees*, London: Jessica Kingsley Publishers.

Frankl, V.E. (1985 [1959]) *Man's Search for Meaning*, New York: Washington Square Press.

Laing, R.D. (1967) *The Politics of Experience and the Bird of Paradise*, Harmondsworth: Penguin.

Lifton, R. (1968) *Death in Life – Survivors of Hiroshima*, New York: Random House.

AUTHENTICITY

This concept has a central place in existential therapy. It originates in Heidegger's philosophy, where it refers to a specific stance which we can take toward our own existence. It demands that we acknowledge to ourselves the anxiety which the thought of our mortality stirs up in us. Heidegger argues that the thought of our own finitude is so anxiety provoking that our natural tendency is to run away from it: we busy ourselves with our everyday lives to forget all about it; and we 'tranquillize' and comfort ourselves with generalizations such as 'death comes to us all'.

As a society, we then develop all sorts of expressions (e.g. he's kicked the bucket) to minimize the event of death. We also tend to pretend to ourselves that death is something that really only happens to others. In Tolstoy's *Death of Ivan Ilych*, the dying Ivan reflects upon the syllogism: 'Caius is a man, men are mortal, therefore Caius is mortal.' It 'had always seemed to him correct as applied to Caius, but certainly not as applied to himself.'

Authenticity requires a resolve to face up to my lack of control over both my birth and my mortality, to stop pretending that death only happens to others. Far from being tied to a philosophy of doom and gloom, authenticity is tied to a philosophy of can-do and can-be (*seinkönnen*): for, Heidegger argues, an awareness of *my* own mortality opens up and 'discloses' the choices and possibilities before me. It allows me to see and develop my potentialities and 'own' my life. ('Authenticity' is from *autos*, '-self'.) This is why he says that 'death individualizes human existence'. To own your life is a heavy responsibility, yet it is also liberating: for it frees you from feeling that you have to fulfil in your life the expectations, ambitions and wishes of others. It frees you from the anxiety and shame that comes of worrying about what others may be thinking of you. Life is between your own self and your own conscience.

However, we are only human and cannot sustain an authentic stance; most of the time, we dwell in a state of inauthenticity (or 'falling'). We can only experience moments of authenticity ('moments of vision') – yet these moments can be decisive and life changing.

117

7

REFLECTIONS ON SUICIDE AND DESPAIR

John Heaton

Suicide raises many questions. There are philosophical and religious questions such as is it ever justified, and if so when? There are questions of management for those who run prisons and mental hospitals with concerns over the sort of precautions to be taken to prevent suicide attempts. Should we remove all possible pieces of clothing and anything else that could be used and put the person in a padded cell? Should this be done to anyone that threatens suicide or just to some? If the latter, then what are the criteria for the decision? How far can we trust a person not to attempt suicide? Does lack of trust increase the likelihood of attempts at suicide? What drugs can be given to prevent it? Should drugs be used at all?

I shall not discuss any of these important questions. I will concentrate on the position of a psychotherapist confronted with someone who consults him or her and is in despair, threatening to commit suicide, or is frightened that they will do so, or has made various attempts at it and feels that is the answer to their problems. In all these cases the person in despair has a problem about suicide. Obviously if they had determined to kill themselves they would have no problem and would not consult a psychiatrist or psychotherapist.

There is a basic distinction to make in discussing suicide: it has both a public and a private nature. One can be spelled out in words, whereas the other is more subtle and requires insight, understanding and experience. Suicide is a public act. It can be talked about and attracts talk and publicity; facts about it can be conveyed directly. Thus we can discuss the pros and cons of suicide, how terrible it is, wonder why it is increasing among particular groups of people, give instructions as to how to prevent it, make laws about it, and so on. If someone tells me their dreams, their thoughts and feelings, then this is a private matter between them and me and there may be all sorts of hidden communications going on between us. Suicide, however, is a very public matter even when it is done in a private space. It has public consequences – friends and relatives may be very distressed and perhaps feel guilty for years

119

afterwards; there may be serious economic consequences for the family; an increase in suicide among a particular group possibly indicates social problems that need remedying. There must be an inquest, as suicide is of public interest and has legal consequences which might include complaints against the therapist. If it can be shown that he had acted irresponsibly, been drunk at some of the sessions, tried to seduce the patient, or even been 'negligent' in his note-taking, etc. then the coroner can report the matter and the therapist could be in very serious trouble with his professional body.

So if someone is a serious suicide risk, I point out to them that it is not a private matter between them and me, a sort of private gambling game between us. I insist they give me permission to tell their general practitioner, if he does not know already, as he has responsibility towards the patient and is likely to be called out in an emergency. If the patient refuses me permission then I refuse to take them on, although I cannot remember anyone to whom I had to do this. I usually give them my home telephone number, pointing out, however, that I am not always available on the 'phone. With some people this is a great relief. Some have told me that they never realized it was so serious. They had been playing with the idea 'in their head' and it had frightened them, they were now brought down to earth.

The second aspect requires insight and understanding, as it is concerned with what drives a person to suicide; we have to understand the way the particular person sees his problem. Now broadly speaking, in suicide, we are concerned with despair, but how despair is understood is best conveyed through a personal relationship, as it has to be understood in the terms of that particular person. It is here that a huge gap arises between the existential–phenomenological tradition and therapies such as psychoanalysis, its offshoots, and cognitive behavioural therapy. The latter therapies are all based on the methods of the natural sciences. These depend on theories and doctrines which are public and have to be learned and accepted. Their theories and techniques can be conveyed directly to people, they can be stated in books and lectured on, they are public matters stating general truths and technical knowledge that any intelligent person can understand if they apply themselves.

The existential–phenomenological tradition differs in that it does not approach problems of human existence, such as despair, in a direct way. Despair is not simple and the capacity to understand it cannot be taken for granted. A person in despair may deny it or say he is in despair and not really mean it. For language can be used to conceal as well as reveal. Thus writers such as Dostoyevsky and Beckett convey great understanding of despair although they did not possess the technical knowledge of psychologists. There can be no certified authority on despair because the language we use to describe it must be interpreted and our interpretation depends on our own experience of it. What do we mean by despair? It has no fixed meaning to which we can point with authority.

Terms such as existence, passion, anxiety, despair, love are used to designate ways of living. They are equivocal as they are ways of assessing a life; they cannot be read off from what they appear to say, their meaning cannot be abstracted from their context. A dictionary is of little help in understanding them. Thus 'love' in the sentences 'I love chocolate', 'I love money', 'I love Betty' has a different sense in each case. Surely my partner, 'Betty', would rightly object if I loved her in the same sense as I love chocolate! There is no word that is necessarily and unambiguously a word of love, and many words and gestures can express it. Everything depends on speaker, context, intention; not so much *what* is said but *how* it is said.

So understanding despair is not a matter of learning something about a neutral object 'out there' but involves reflection on the part of the writer and reader, or indeed the therapist, who must understand that the meaning of despair is beyond the letter: it can only be conveyed indirectly. Indirect communication is directed towards its appropriation by the individual addressed. When we appropriate a communication we make it our own. It brings us home and only we can be the authority on that, your home is not mine. If we tell a person how to be happy, the meaning of life, the way to love, the way to be with a person in despair, then there is always the question as to how he takes the meaning of what we say. Are we merely stating our personal beliefs? Or are we concerned with the particular person we are addressing? With how the person appropriates what is said? For, 'How words are understood is not told by the words alone' (Wittgenstein 1967: par. 144).

Kierkegaard pointed out that the comic is an important form of indirect communication (Oden 2004). Thus:

> The comic is present in every stage of life, because where there is life there is contradiction, and wherever there is contradiction, the comic is present. . . . The comic interpretation produces the contradiction or allows it to become apparent by having 'in mente' [in mind] the way out; therefore the contradiction is painless.
>
> (Kierkegaard 1992: 513–516)

For example, a student who had studied Kierkegaard told me she had a patient who was paranoid and had not responded to conventional treatment. In the first two sessions the patient would not speak, but searched the room as she felt it was bugged and the information would be used against her. In the next few sessions the student spontaneously joined in the search. Soon there was a sense of engagement with the patient and they were both laughing at the absurdity of it. The comical had been acknowledged and the therapy took off.

There can be no external authority on these matters for they do not involve general truths. It was essential that the student engaged spontaneously with the patient. We do not prescribe humour! Personal meaning is inseparable from the embodiment of language. In spite of dictionaries and rules of grammar, we can never know what language means prior to its occurrence. We are given language only as it occurs and whatever meaning it has depends upon our perceiving it as such. There can be no authority that guarantees for us what a speech act means when it has a personal meaning. Concepts such as despair and humour call for a dialectical examination. That is, we attend to how the meaning of the concept changes as the subject, of which it is the concept, changes, and as the context in which it is used changes. 'Despair' means different things depending on its place in the person's life, on how they take it. The following comment by Kierkegaard illustrates the difference:

> In relation to a doctrine, understanding is the maximum of what may be attained; to become an adherent is merely an artful method of pretending to understand, practised by people who do not understand anything. In relation to an existential communication, existing in it is the maximum of attainment, and understanding it is merely an evasion of the task.
>
> (Kierkegaard 1992: 332)

The point is that people may easily imagine they understand when they do not. The criterion for understanding is how the person behaves in actual life. Thus we may have a joke explained to us and 'understand' it, but that is not the same as 'seeing' it and laughing.

The difference between mere pedagogy and existential understanding is illustrated by Kierkegaard in his example of the drill sergeant and the recruit who is talking in the ranks: 'The sergeant yells, "Shut up!" the recruit answers back: "Yes, of course, now that I know you want me to, I'll shut up!" ' (Kierkegaard 1967–75: par. 649). The recruit is merely a clever academic, he understands but does not 'get it'. He does not realize that how he must be on the parade ground is different from the lecture theatre. It is the same with matters of existence such as despair. They are not theoretical but problems arising from how we live, so lecturing about despair to a person 'in it' or applying a theory to him are out of place. There can be no final answer to matters of existence; seeing the world aright is not a possible achievement of any book, lecture, theoretical or dogmatic system; we must see for ourselves and at some point stand alone.

Despair

I will now turn to Kierkegaard's account of despair. This account of despair and its relation to suicide is heavily dependent on Kierkegaard's *The Sickness unto Death* (1980b) and the recent translation of Michael Theunissen's *Kierkegaard's Concept of Despair* (2005) in which he makes a rigorous reconstruction of Kierkegaard's understanding of despair, concentrating on its form of communication and the issue of the concept of despair (rather than the theological clothing in which Kierkegaard wraps it).

I shall not give case histories of despair as I agree with Hans Cohn that case histories are deeply misleading (Cohn 2002: 126). They are always written from one point of view, the therapist's, usually to illustrate his technical skill and often what a 'kind' and 'understanding' person he is. It assumes the goal of the therapist and patient is the same, it ignores their different perspectives. It mystifies the norms of the therapist which may conceal his interests and those of the group to which he belongs. History is usually written by the victor, but to understand despair we must see that there can be no victor. Freud's writing is full of metaphors of conquering, plans for cure, alliances with the weak ego, etc. The most famous being the motto to *The Interpretation of Dreams* (Freud 1954): 'Flectere si nequeo superos, Acheronta movebo' [If I cannot bend Heaven, then I will arouse Hell] (Virgil, *Aeneid* 7: 312). This is defiance – an expression of despair.

Let us turn to an analysis of despair, to show that it is a problem of existence and so can be hidden and difficult to recognize, both by the observer and the sufferer. According to Theunissen's reconstruction of Kierkegaard's analysis of despair, its principle is: We do not will to be directly what we are (Theunissen 2005: 5). That is, human beings may fail to be the beings they could be; they may fail in various ways to be truly human. This would be vacuous to take directly, so requires elucidation: (a) Who is this '*we*' about whom Kierkegaard speaks? (b) What does it mean to say we do not will to be what we *are*? (c) What does it mean to say we do not will to be *what we* are? (d) In what sense do we will all this *not to be*?

(a) The '*we*' referred to is the 'we' who live in the modern world, a historical 'we' who feel we have lost our original nature, are restless, divided, and often in conflict with ourselves and others.

(b) What we *are* is our specific concreteness, what we find ourselves to be, our bodies, dispositions and potentialities. It includes that in which we find ourselves, our life history, our specific relations with others, our family, society, and historical period.

(c) Not willing to be *what we* are means that we take a negative relation to *what we* are. We relate negatively to our particular determinateness. We are human and so have concepts of freedom and necessity, of finitude and infinitude. When these come together and are lived, they provide a framework for our lives. If they fall apart one or other may come to dominate; we then get various forms of despair that may lead to suicide. Thus we may want more than we can possibly have, to achieve some cherished goal that is beyond us, to have a partner who will never leave us, to have some impossible form of freedom; if these fail we may consciously despair. At one extreme, our freedom seems boundless, we may become manic, lost in possibility and the vortex of the future. At the other extreme, in depression, we drown in necessity and the vortex of the past. We are unable to envisage any possibilities other than the grimness that confronts us, we feel forced to go through the daily grind. It is similar with finitude and infinitude. We rebel against getting older and less desirable, we want constant bliss and we do not want to die now, but sometime later. Or we may live in terms of finitude: every choice and decision may appear pointless; we may lose all horizons except crudely finite ones, as if we and others were just things and processes which only have a use.

(d) Our *not willing to be* means that we do not want to accept our human-ness, we are in a state of revulsion against the limitations of our deter-minativeness – and not simply the bounds of necessity and freedom. We want to put an end to our freedom, our individuality, and our selves. We yearn for an inhuman existence, for human life has lost its meaning. This form of despair is more often found in older people who may see little point in being alive, especially if they feel isolated and are poorly inte-grated in their community. They may self-harm or commit suicide although no particular life events, such as a loss, may have occurred.

In all these cases there is a dogmatic imperative: we think we or the world ought to be different from what they are. We are addicted to what we imagine things ought to be and, if they do not turn out that way, we may lose hope and despair. We fail to attend to our singularity, to what is. We construct a hypothetical self that has little to do with our factical existence. The self in Kierkegaard is not an entity or a process, as it is conceived in psychoanalysis and even in some existential literature (van Deurzen and Kenward 2005). Spirit is the self and the human self is a relation that relates itself to itself and in relating to itself relates itself to another (Kierkegaard 1980b: 13–14). To understand the self as an entity or process would be, according to Kierkegaard, a form of despair, a not willing to be what we are, which is spirit.

However, as Theunissen (2005: 25–26, 36–37) has pointed out, Kierke-gaard is still under the influence of essentialism. Clearly it is the embodied person rather than his self which is to relate to itself, reflect on itself, or lose itself. Surely the self cannot be spirit as our embodiment would then be volatilized into an ideal. We are free, but at the same time bound by our physical bodies, upbringing and culture. It is this self-realization in which the person gradually unfolds and comes to be who he or she is that is so difficult to understand and accomplish.

Wittgenstein

Wittgenstein's life and writing can throw light on despair and suicide. He shows both an understanding of and an overcoming of despair and the wish for suicide. He was an admirer of Kierkegaard and was deeply concerned with despair and suicide for much of his life. He had four brothers, three of whom committed suicide. Otto Weininger, whom he greatly admired, shot himself on the floor of the house where Beethoven died. Many people in Vienna regarded this as an ethical deed and it inspired a number of suicides. According to Oswald Spengler this was 'one of the noblest spectacles ever presented by a late religiousness' (Monk 1990: 19–20). Wittgenstein for years afterwards felt ashamed that he had not dared kill himself. Finally, the great physicist Ludwig Boltzmann, with whom Wittgenstein was intending to study, committed suicide (Monk 1990).

Wittgenstein joined the Austrian army as a volunteer gunner soon after the First World War started. Throughout the war he kept a notebook where he wrote his thoughts about philosophy and his experiences. Some of these notebooks have been found and published. He felt that the experience of facing death would improve him: 'Fear in the face of death is the best sign of a false, i.e. a bad life' (Monk 1990: 141). When first glimpsing the enemy he wrote: 'Now I have an opportunity to be a decent human being, because I am face to face with death. May the spirit enlighten me' (McGuinness 1988: 221). He often complained of the difficulty of finding the courage to accept life as it is, to 'live for the spirit', when exhausted by cold, lack of sleep, an empty stomach, and enemy fire (McGuinness 1988: 220). 'Only death gave life its meaning' he wrote during his first days in an observation post, an extremely dangerous place to be (p. 240). His skill and courage were recognized by the military authorities and he was awarded many medals.

It was keeping up his spirit in the face of death that was important to him; he could easily have let himself be killed in a state of depression, as did thousands. If he lost heart, even if his soul flinched when he heard a shot, it was a sign of a false conception of life (p. 240). It is possible to see from his notebooks the many forms of despair that he fell into and struggled with; sometimes he was depressed and weak, more often he forced himself to face danger in order to become a decent human being as he conceived it.

All this affected his thoughts on philosophy. As Russell remarked, his attitude to philosophy was affected by the fact that it had to compete with the dogmatism of shells and bullets (Monk 1996: 227). Most of the *Tractatus* was written during active service in the 1914–18 war. His work was largely a clarification of the illusions of meaning which lead to various forms of dogmatism. Just as his struggle with despair and the fear of death were due to a false conception of life and so required clarification, so did his life with language. Dogmatic thought is despairing, as it is under the illusion that we can rise above our humanity, look down on our world from an illusory point, so willing that which we are not. For example, Freud makes a dogmatic claim when he assumes that all our thought and feelings are determined. This is a form of despair as it occludes human freedom.

The form of the *Tractatus* is similar to a number of works by Kierkegaard such as *The Sickness unto Death* (1980b) and *The Concept of Anxiety*

(1980a). They are compact, abstract and dialectical. They cannot be summarized, but each work has provoked, and is continuing to provoke, a large literature of commentary. The abstract nature of these works is a form of indirect communication as they cannot be definitely summarized, they do not form a system, but provoke commentary and interpretation; we have to work on them ourselves. A commentary is not the same as a text, it aims to reveal the meaning of the text, yet the text itself surely has meaning. So there is a tension between the text and commentary which is especially acute when the commentaries differ so greatly, as they do on the *Tractatus*. This tension is a form of indirect communication as it has to be interpreted by us, the readers. Similarly, when clients speak of despair, there is a tension between the language they use to express it and the language the therapist uses in describing it.

Therapy of despair

A crucial point in Kierkegaard's account of despair, one that is emphasized by Theunissen (2005: ix), is that there is no therapy for despair as such. We cannot show a person how to step out of despair, because he does not recognize it as such, he does not understand what it is, because it is the way he exists. We may take steps to prevent his suicide or give him drugs to change his mood, but that is not psychotherapy. What is needed is to operate descriptively rather than prescriptively. In other words we need genuine phenomenological insight into the matter, rather than interventions or interpretations based on a constructivist theory and this includes, of course, a theory of despair.

Now by description I do not mean an abstract academic description, a method that students can be trained to do. When we begin to speak or articulate our despair to some other person, then a dialogue is started that may lead to greater understanding of the phenomenon. The nature of despair can only be elucidated by indirect communication, because despair is a way of being in the world, it is the way a person exists and to remind the person of this requires reminders and prompting rather than intellectual constructs and discoveries. One may well pass an exam by regurgitating what one has been told, but this sort of approach to a person in despair can intensify the despair and drive him to suicide. Rather we must attend without presuppositions or sidelong glances to grounds or to instructions.

When we analyse despair, we begin to see what promises a remedy. We do not stipulate despair or relate prescriptively to it by making assertions but, in a finite and fragmentary way, gradually show the movements of existence that are blocked in it. When we can make these movements, then the despair is lifted. As we are dealing with a problem of existence rather than of knowledge, then mood or atmosphere are important. For mood is not a mere accompaniment of thought in problems of existence, it concerns the very atmosphere in which the thought is conceived and the person is living. Kierkegaard wrote:

> That science, just as much as poetry and art, presuppose a mood in the creator as well as in the observer, and that an error in the modulation is just as disturbing as an error in the development of thought, has been entirely forgotten in our time.
>
> (Kierkegaard 1980a: 14n)

Patients are more aware of the importance of atmosphere than therapists. I have often been told by people that they left a therapist because they did not feel that the 'atmosphere' was right. Their remark was not trivial as many therapists believe.

An important distinction that Kierkegaard makes is between 'despair over' and 'despair of' (Kierkegaard 1980b: 60–1n). The person who despairs *over* herself has a self relation that is beset by her despair. She despairs over that which binds her in despair. Thus, 'I am no good', 'I am a failure', 'I have lost everything', etc. She despairs over 'that she is as she is'. We despair over what we cannot have. Thus, if we despair over the unfaithfulness of a partner we despair that we have lost something.

Instead of feeling hopeless we can feel helpless. We despair *of* that which can save us from despair. We despair of our ability to obtain. We lose trust in possibility – 'nothing can help me', 'I cannot have children as I could not bear to lose one'. We despair of our own strength, of that which can redeem us of our own weakness and of the possibility of that which releases us from despair.

A further twist occurs in defiance, when we will to be what we are not. Thus, we may despair over the possibility of being helped by some other. We act as if we were unique and isolated human beings, as if we could master the future by breaking free from everything that is pre-given and need no help from anyone. A man who had made several suicide attempts, at his first interview with me, produced a carving knife and suggested that I cut off one of his fingers and then he would cut off one of mine; if I flinched less than him then I was worthy to treat him. This was an expression of defiance: he could not acknowledge me as a person who might help him. Another man, soon after starting therapy, would drive his car at full speed to a cliff edge in order to get over his fear of death; he would then be cured he said. This too is defiance. Instead of modestly acknowledging his fear of death and working from there, he tried to get *over* his fear. Many people in a state of despairing defiance do not consult anyone as this would be too humiliating for them. My impression is that defiance is commoner in men.

> To the extent that a person has the truer conception of despair, if he still remains in despair, and to the extent that he is more clearly

conscious of being in despair – to that extent the despair is more intensive. The person who, with a realization that suicide is despair and to that extent with a true conception of the nature of despair, commits suicide is more intensively in despair than one who commits suicide without a clear idea that suicide is despair; conversely, the less true his conception of despair, the less intensive his despair. On the other hand, a person who with a clearer consciousness of himself (self-consciousness) commits suicide is more intensively in despair than one whose soul, by comparison, is in confusion and darkness.

(Kierkegaard 1980b: 48–49)

Many people threaten suicide – 'That will show them!' The threat is used to manipulate people; they are not intensively in despair. They do not intend to kill themselves, they are not confronting their mortality. They are using suicide to avoid confronting their difficulties and to get what they imagine they want. Of course this does not mean that the threats should not be taken seriously for they may unintentionally kill themselves.

Some people try to kill themselves as it is the 'logical' thing to do; they too do not have a true conception of despair. Thus, a young man was sent to see me as he kept trying to hang himself. He told me he felt he was a ghost, but that if he killed himself, then it would prove that he was not, as ghosts cannot kill themselves. A good example of a 'logic' that is out of this world. He was in despair, as he idealized his life into a logical problem.

As Kierkegaard emphasizes, despair presupposes itself: despair *over* something presupposes despair *of* possibility. If someone despairs over the loss of a partner, this presupposes that they already unconsciously despair of possibility – the possibility, say, of living without her or of ever finding another. Anyone who despairs over something makes this 'something', which is a particular, into a totality. They have 'tunnel vision', a particular something, say a loss, is changed into the world in toto. 'My wife has walked out on me: I have lost everything.' They act as if something particular has taken on the appearance of the whole. This may lead to a total loss of meaning and is a form of dogmatism. So they despair *of* that which, rightly understood, can release them from despair.

Everything for the person in despair is represented as being *in* his consciousness, often in 'his head'; he is self-absorbed. For him being and thought are one. He imagines that the meaning of what he says or thinks is something correlated with it. 'I am a total failure', 'I have lost everything so I might as well kill myself.' These are dogmatic statements and there is no answer to them. Contrast: 'I have had depressing news' with 'I am depressed.' The former statement is a statement of fact that could be right or wrong. In the latter statement the person has assimilated a proposition to a name; he has named himself as 'depressed' and this is what he imagines he is. He cannot question as to whether it is true or not. He has framed his problem. Yet, to think 'I am a total failure' is meaningless. I may have lost my job and my partner but that is not the whole of my life. 'I am a total failure' has not the same meaning as a name – it does not define me in the same way as 'I am Peter'. Meaning is in the world. It does not correspond to words, but to their use in the expression of propositions with sense, to their application within the context of our active, everyday lives. To define myself as a 'total' failure involves confusion over the nature of conceptualization; in despair this leads to ignoring the possibilities for change.

In despair, suffering is often given a special meaning. Thus: 'I deserve to suffer, I am a worm'. Or suffering may be used to make the person feel special. For example, in Ham's opening speech in Beckett's *Endgame* he says: 'Can there be misery [he yawns] loftier than mine.' Suffering has to stop being used and become a simple fact of life. The person may, in desperation, try to get 'out' of his thoughts by taking drugs or killing himself, but this is a further twist of despair for there is no 'out' to get to. Suicide may be seen as a solution to one's unhappiness. 'Death seems the only way out of my hell.' It may serve as a punishment or a sacrifice: 'My child is dead, so I must be with her.' Or vengeance – 'That will teach them.' It converts suffering into action, as the impotence of despair has become unbearable. The act is towards a silence, a shelter from torment. Suicide tries to remove the absurdity of life rather than respond to it; the person is not prepared to, or perhaps able to, take responsibility for their life.

Clients in despair often say that no one can help them. It is vital to respect this and not say or imply that they can be helped. They may be full of bitterness and try to kill themselves as they can feel completely misunderstood by an enthusiast. Self-assertive zeal, well-intentioned remarks and idealization of therapy are out of place. 'I need a place from which I can hate; my last therapist was too nice, I identified with her and it all went dead' (the patient finished that therapy by making a suicide attempt). But that does not mean that the client is to be left to cope by themselves. They may come for many months repeating 'You are useless; no one can help me.' This is to be respected. The gist of my reply – though not my actual words, is 'That is how you see things, it is not how I understand them.' The crucial point is that they have a witness, another person, to listen and respond to their misery. It is only when a client sees that the therapist is indeed useless that they start recovering. They have begun to see her as a separate person relating to them, rather than a mere instrument to be used. A person in despair who recognizes herself as the source of the condition relates to herself in a way that is itself not in despair, she realizes that there is no 'out' to get to. By becoming aware of herself, that it is she that is in despair, she is able to take some responsibility, she is on the path of healing.

Therapists presuppose that the potential for healing is present in their clients. It is by reminding them of the nature of their own existence that new perspectives, and so possibilities, are revealed. We remind them of things they have forgotten, and of the obvious, we make up pertinent stories, point out paradoxes, in order to loosen their fixation on dogmatic forms of life. Every therapist will have their own style. The client will respond not merely to the words, but to the way they are said, the age, sex, physiognomy of the therapist. The listener must reflect on what is said, this is a task and involves decision, these will govern the way in which he appropriates the material. It is appropriation that is sought and so indirect communication is used. Finally, it is vital to remember that despair is a matter of existence; reading and knowing about it are of little importance for it is not purely a matter of knowledge:

> Let us imagine a first mate and assume he has passed with distinction all the examinations but as yet has not been out to sea. Imagine him in a storm: he knows exactly what he has to do, but he is unacquainted with the terror that grips the sailor when the stars disappear into the pitch darkness of the night; he is unacquainted with the sense of powerlessness the pilot feels when he sees that the helm in his hand is only a plaything for the sea; he does not know how the blood rushes to the head when in such a moment one must make calculations – in short, he has no conception of the change that takes place in the knower where he has to use his knowledge.
>
> (Kierkegaard 1993: 36)

References

Cohn, H.W. (2002) *Heidegger and the Roots of Existential Therapy*, London: Continuum.

Freud, S. (1954) *The Interpretation of Dreams*, London: Allen and Unwin.

Kierkegaard, S. (1967–75) *Søren Kierkegaard's Journals and Papers*, 7 Vols, trans. Hong, H.V. and Hong, E.H., with Malantschuk, G., Bloomington: Indiana University Press.

—— (1980a [1844]) *The Concept of Anxiety*, trans. Hong, H.V. and Hong, E.H., Princeton NJ: Princeton University Press.

—— (1980b [1849]) *The Sickness unto Death*, trans. Hong, H.V. and Hong, E.H., Princeton NJ: Princeton University Press.

—— (1992 [1846]) *Concluding Unscientific Postscript to 'Philosophical Fragments'*, trans. Hong, H.V. and Hong, E.H., Princeton NJ: Princeton University Press.

—— (1993) *Three Discourses on Imagined Occasions*, trans. Hong, H.V. and Hong, E.H., Princeton NJ: Princeton University Press.

McGuinness, B.F. (1988) *Wittgenstein: A Life*, London: Duckworth.

Monk, R. (1990) *Ludwig Wittgenstein*, London: Jonathan Cape.

—— (1996) *Bertrand Russell*, London: Jonathan Cape.

Oden, T.C. (2004) *The Humour of Kierkegaard: An Anthology*, Princeton NJ: Princeton University Press.

Theunissen, M. (2005) *Kierkegaard's Concept of Despair*, trans. Harshav, B. and Illbruck, H., Princeton NJ: Princeton University Press.

van Deurzen, E. and Kenward, R. (2005) *Dictionary of Existential Psychotherapy and Counselling*, London: Sage.

Wittgenstein, L. (1981 [1967]) *Zettel*, 2nd edn, trans. Anscombe, G.E.M., Oxford: Blackwell.

SUICIDE AND DESPAIR
Keynotes for therapy

John Heaton and Laura Barnett

- Clients in despair who consult a therapist about being suicidal have a problem with suicide (if they hadn't and were determined to kill themselves, they would not be consulting a therapist).
- Suicide has consequences for friends and relatives and possibly for the therapist. So if someone is a serious suicide risk, we need to point out to them that it is not a private matter between them and us, a sort of private gambling game between us. We also need to ask for their permission to tell their general practitioner.
- Despair, a sense of hopelessness and helplessness underlie suicide.
- Despair is a way of being in the world; it is the way a person exists. Therapists cannot learn the meaning of despair from books or training – this sort of approach to a person in despair can intensify his despair and drive him to suicide. Therapists can only attend to each individual client and seek to understand their individual experience of despair. Everything depends on speaker, context, intention; not so much *what* is said but *how* it is said.
- Despair is not simple: a person in despair may deny it or say he is in despair and not really mean it.
- Despair often arises out of an unwillingness to accept the reality of what human *being* involves: our mortality, our sexuality, the various constraints on our lives, our freedom of choice and the dilemmas that go with it, etc. We want to put an end to our freedom, our individuality and our selves. We think we or the world ought to be different from what they are.
- Kierkegaard makes an important distinction between 'despair *over*' and 'despair *of*': we despair *over* what we cannot have (e.g. a long life, a partner, more money, etc.), or what we cannot be (e.g. healthy, beautiful, etc.).
- We despair *of* that which can save us from despair: we forget that some

133

things are in our own hands to change. We lose trust in possibility. Hopelessness becomes compounded with helplessness.

- Persons in despair may have a 'tunnel vision', e.g. 'I am a total failure'; 'I have lost my wife, so I might as well kill myself.' The focus of their despair (their sense of failure, the partner they lost, etc.) becomes their whole world – nothing else and no one else counts.

- Suicide may be seen as a solution to one's unhappiness – 'death seems the only way out of my hell'. It may serve as a punishment or a sacrifice: 'My child is dead, so I must be with her'; or vengeance – 'That will teach them'. Suicide converts suffering into action, as the impotence of despair has become unbearable.

- There are no prescribed interventions, only an exploration of each individual client's way of existing. By exploring that particular client's despair, by seeking to understand it, we begin to see what promises a remedy: we can gradually show the movements of existence that are blocked in it.

- When clients are aware of their despair and can recognize that they are the source of the condition, they are already relating to themselves in a non-despairing way: they are taking some responsibility and are on the path of healing.

- Clients in despair often say that no one can help them. It is vital to respect this and not say or imply that they can be helped. But that does not mean that the client is to be left to cope by themselves. They may come for many months repeating: 'You are useless; no one can help me.' This is to be respected. The crucial point is that they have a witness, another person, to listen and respond to their misery.

8

THE EXPERIENCE OF WORKING WITH PATIENTS WITH A SHORT PROGNOSIS

Paul Smith-Pickard

In this chapter I have attempted to capture my experience of working with patients with a short prognosis in a large inner-city hospital. The work took place outside of a consulting room, either on an open ward or in a single room on a ward at patients' bedsides. The hospital context is an important factor, as working with the same client group in a hospice might be somewhat different. There would presumably already be some recognition and acceptance of the process of dying and death, whereas in the medical setting of a hospital, death is frequently regarded as failure.

It is not my intention that the chapter should be seen as a 'how to do it' guide, but seen merely as a reflection of experiences that have taken place over a period of time. I do not even offer these stories as examples of good practice. They are simply experiences from practice that led to what appeared to be significant moments of encounter and meeting on the journey towards death. They occurred as an upsurge of shared experience and connection that frequently gave a voice to what is often regarded as an unspeakable narrative in a cultural denial of death. The following stories are based on actual events and experiences, but they are fictional in as much as they are composite stories of many patients who are no longer alive, but who have left a lasting impression on me.

As the narrator of the stories and as an agent within them, I need to briefly contextualize myself as a psychotherapist within the field of psychotherapy. I trained and am registered as an existential psychotherapist. However, there are many diverse strands to existential thought. The approach is philosophical rather than medical and the broad scope of a philosophy of existence offers many ways in which to practise existential psychotherapy. My therapeutic practice is focused through images and ideas taken from existential thinkers and continental philosophy, particularly those of Maurice Merleau-Ponty (1908–1961), from whom I have absorbed ideas about the nature of intersubjective encounter. It is also informed to some degree by social constructionism, feminism and what has become known as a relational paradigm. Central to my practice is the recognition of the body as the site of our experience and that our experiences take place in a world of other people, where the world that I sense through my body at the same time senses the body I am. 'I am all that I see,' says Merleau-Ponty. 'I am an intersubjective field, not despite my body and historical situation, but, on the contrary, by being this body and this situation' (Merleau-Ponty 1996: 452).

I have chosen three stories that illustrate the impromptu nature of working in this context with this particular group of patients. I say this group of patients, but as the stories will show, the only common thing they share is being hospitalized and having a short prognosis. My first story concerns a young woman called Belinda who suffered from a chronic congenital respiratory disease.

'It feels like I'm going on a journey and nobody is coming with me'

I had met Belinda several times during her regular admissions to the hospital. She was approaching her eighteenth birthday, but looked and sounded much younger. Whenever she was admitted for treatment, the specialist team would inform me that she was again in our care. I would then visit her and attempt to offer her my help. Our conversations were very superficial and frequently interrupted by nursing staff. I felt ineffectual in my attempts to make a connection with Belinda. Regular hospitalizations had been part of her life since she was a young child. She appeared to feel at home on the ward where she was clearly a favourite with both the ward nurses and the specialist team treating her. There always seemed to be an aspect of Belinda that was unreachable. She was happiest when she was in a single room on her own with her telephone and her television and videos. She disliked the odd occasions when, due to bed shortages, she was placed on the open ward with much older patients. Despite this familiarity she resented being in hospital and having to undergo a fairly aggressive treatment regime. Many children with her condition did not survive as long, and her chances of reaching adulthood were slim.

On this occasion I walked through the ward, past beds full of patients with chronic conditions. The atmosphere on the ward, with its all too familiar sounds and smells of illness, was busy as usual. For some reason, the billowing curtains around many of the beds remind me of images from refugee camps. I never feel comfortable on this particular ward. At the nurses' station smiling faces show signs of strain and exhaustion. 'I'm here to see Belinda,' I say to no one in particular, as I check the whiteboard above the nurses' heads to see which bed she has been allocated. As usual she is in one of the single rooms at the end of the ward.

I knock gently and enter the room. 'Hi Belinda, I heard you were back in hospital and so I thought I would come and see how you are getting along.' I had no idea how I could be of help to Belinda and it felt as if I was just going through the motions of offering some unspecified assistance. Even the specialist nursing staff felt helpless in the face of Belinda's condition and the inevitability of her early demise. Her poor health had meant little schooling and limited socialization. Conversation was difficult and common ground hard to find. I was seeing her mainly because I had been asked to, and Belinda herself had no sense of why I might be there to speak to her, or how I might help her. I came as part of her care package. Like many of the patients that I came into contact with, she had little or no understanding of counselling and psychotherapy and indeed why should she? I felt like an imposter entering into her circle of carers.

We began talking about the videos she had been watching. She was bored and fed up with being in hospital and the conversation felt difficult as usual. One of her favorite videos was *The Prince of Tides*. She was asking me if I had seen it when the telephone rang and she answered. I motioned to her that I would leave to give her privacy, but she signalled that I should stay. It was her father on the line and, as she spoke to him, I witnessed a complete transformation. She became cheerful, optimistic about going home and full of vitality. I felt awkward about being present during this exchange and made again to leave, but again she motioned me to stay. When the call ended she immediately fell back into her heavy mood. 'That was my Dad,' she says in her wheezy voice, as if some sort of explanation was needed. I remark on seeing another Belinda when she was on the phone. She attempts to respond but is overcome by a violent fit of coughing. I wait and feel awkward and helpless as she slowly recovers her breathing.

> 'Yes well you have to be cheerful for them don't you? They think I'm in here to get better. So they expect me to be better,' she says as if explaining the obvious to me.
> 'And is that what you expect Belinda? To get better?'
> 'No. Not really.'
> 'Does it get any worse?'
> *She nods thoughtfully and then after a long pause:*
> 'They want to take me to Disneyland for my eighteenth.'
> *There is another long pause and I become acutely aware of her difficulty in breathing as I listen to her bronchial wheeze. I feel slightly awkward at witnessing this level of distress and vulnerability. It feels too personal, too exposing for her.*
> 'I'd like to go but it would be really difficult. I always wanted to go to Spain for a holiday. My aunt goes there a lot and she brought me some

dolls back . . . like Barbie with frilly costumes . . . got them in my bedroom at home . . . I just want to be 18 even if I have to have a party in here with this lot!'

She laughs as if we are sharing a private joke together and it restarts her wheezy cough.

'The way that you said that, Belinda, it sounded to me as if you are worried that you might not get to 18.'

'I will . . . I've got to. I can't not have my eighteenth birthday. I want my Dad to buy me a mini . . . can't drive, but that don't matter, I can still sit in it. It'll be wicked!'

Belinda has a big smile and rocks herself backwards and forwards on her bed looking straight ahead. After a long pause the smile fades and she says:

'I will be so pissed off if I die before I'm 18.'

'I think we all will be Belinda.'

She turns to look at me with a very serious expression that is accusatory, almost angry.

'Will you? So why are we talking about dying then? What started all this miserable crap off?'

'I think it was you saying that you had to be cheerful for your Dad when you know how serious your illness is. It just made me wonder what it is like for you Belinda to have to be cheerful for everyone else when you don't necessarily feel cheerful.'

She thinks for a while and then looking directly at me says:

'It feels like I'm going on a journey and no one is coming with me.'

After all the superficial and strained conversations we had gone right into the heart of Belinda's private world. We met several times again after this and I tried my very best to accompany Belinda on her lonely journey. Sometimes she wanted to talk at this level and at others it felt as if we had never shared this thought together. It was the sharing of the thought that seemed so important. It linked us together in a way that was both meaningful and painful for both of us. Sadly, Belinda never made it to her eighteenth birthday. She died just a few days short of it on a Sunday evening and I wasn't able to be there at the end. It was apparently a difficult death and the nursing staff were all traumatized. I helped them process their experience and felt surprised by their denial of Belinda's imminent demise. I felt very grateful for the time I had with Belinda at the end, where I felt that we had both met each other in a place that no one else seemed to be prepared to visit with her. It was as if Belinda also met herself on her journey at a place where she didn't have to abandon her reality, and could share it with another human being. We spoke about the unspeakable reality of her condition and her fears. It clearly didn't make the last moments of her short life any easier, but it made the final part of her life journey a little less lonely. I don't know if it would have helped if I had been there at the end. I am not a priest or a doctor. I was just being a psychotherapist trying to do what I could in the circumstances; to be present and meet another human being in a meaningful way. And in the process Belinda affected me at a deep level. I like to believe that we were both changed in some way by the experience but I have to accept that I will never know whether Belinda found it valuable.

We live in a culture where it seems that very few of us are prepared to look death in the face. When patients in acute healthcare have a short prognosis, it affects not just the patient themselves but all of those immediately concerned with the patient. This includes, as well as family and friends, the array of healthcare professionals into whose care the patient has entrusted themselves both physically and emotionally. There is frequently a gulf of denial and emotional self-preservation that opens up between the patient and those concerned with them when there is a short prognosis. Psychotherapists working with these patients sometimes have an opportunity to make a pact with them to be a travelling companion of sorts. On this journey, both of us may bear the acute anxiety of holding the space, facilitating a transition from patient to client, as we address and confront the unspeakable. This is raw psychotherapy where we share and bear with our client a painful intimacy that is often fleeting, comforting, and yet both terrifying and beautiful. It is raw because we have to leave the comfort of the consulting room and create a different style of therapeutic frame within the context of a hospital ward. This context is full of smells, sights and sounds that can be intrusive and disturbing. Any notion of an externally constructed therapeutic frame or assumed authority on the part of the therapist has no certainty here. It can be usurped and quickly demolished by the arrival of a junior doctor in a white coat with a draped stethoscope who, assuming you are a visitor or family member, ignores you totally by cutting across any dialogue that is taking place.

In a culture of 'evidence-based practice' how do we account for the work we might do, and how we might be, with a patient with a short prognosis? To me personally, it seems ridiculous and tasteless to attempt to measure the efficacy of psychotherapy with the terminally ill. However, I am not suggesting that one is not accountable. Far from it, as there are extremely sensitive ethical issues involved. The work is very difficult and demanding and there are times when one's presence is resented and rejected. We can also feel brutalized by the aggressive nature of illness and the reminders of the frailty of our own physicality, the potential for serious illness and our own eventual death. We may also feel outrage at the insensitivity of some of our medical colleagues who focus on pathogens rather than persons. The work is not easy and we pay an emotional price in doing it.

So what are we there for, and what is it that we are expected to provide? Is it to provide a palliative emotional intervention or to repair damage done by blunt medical information? Certainly there are times when patients are referred because we are expected to relieve the distress and even trauma caused directly by the experience of being hospitalized. However, there is more to it than soothing the patients, particularly those with a short prognosis who it may seem need soothing the most. In working with this group we are not looking for change in the client as such, although there may be moments of meeting that seem to be significant and which may change us both. What I am attempting to illustrate here is that something shifts and changes between therapist and patient that allows the patient to become a client. This shift is often subtle but needs to be recognized because it is at that point that therapeutic work can take place. The shift usually has a strong embodied sense of meeting and the significant therapeutic content may only last for several minutes. These are moments where something reveals itself in the interpersonal space between us. During these brief moments of meeting, the unspeakable reality of the person can sometimes enter into this space as both a spoken and an embodied narrative. These two aspects of narrative were evident in the following story.

Magic brings people together

I had a call from the sister on one of the neuroscience wards asking me if I would attend a man over whom they were very concerned. When I arrived on the ward, I was told that this patient had that morning been given the results of the biopsy on his brain tumour. His ageing parents, with whom he lived, had been present and had been very distressed by the bad news. The tumour was inoperable and he would be unlikely to live for more than a few months at most. The parents had left and the ward sister was concerned as the patient did not appear to have taken in or understood the information of his short prognosis.

Ronald was sitting up in bed wearing old-fashioned striped pyjamas. He looked to be in his fifties but there was something about his whole demeanour that seemed to belong to another era. Ronald embodied the post-war era of my own childhood. His was the only occupied bed in the side ward. He smiled and appeared very welcoming but somewhat vacant, as I introduced myself to him. I explained that I was a psychotherapist working in the hospital and that I had come to see him, first of all because he had agreed to see me, but also for me to see if I could be of any help to him. His response was a mixture of benign amusement and incomprehension. I began to share the ward sister's concerns. This man appeared to be totally disconnected from the reality of his situation and any thoughts about working therapeutically with him seemed overly optimistic. However, we were both here on the ward together and I decided that I would at least try and engage with him.

The afternoon spring sunshine was streaming through the window with a misplaced optimism. I asked Ronald if he minded me sitting on the edge of his bed to talk to him. I said that I understood that he had received bad news from the biopsy and also that I had been told that his parents had been with him. He confirmed what I said but without any sense of distress whatsoever. He answered all of my questions as if he wanted to please me and give me the 'right' answers. This was going nowhere. I was rapidly drying up and starting to feel disingenuous and awkward as I tried one last attempt to connect with him. I didn't really think about it. I just blurted it out:

'What do you like?' His response was instant.

'Magic,' he said. 'I like magic.'

I was totally thrown by this response. I couldn't comprehend what he had just said and it clearly showed. He, however, had suddenly come alive.

'What kind of magic?' I asked.

'Conjuring, I like doing conjuring tricks.'

In that moment the shift took place. We started the process of him becoming my client and I his therapist. I shared with him my own interest in conjuring tricks when I was young. We both became quite animated and I suddenly felt connected to him. The conversation was slow but we held each other's gaze throughout as if we had reconnected after years apart. His eyes sparkled and there was a feeling of warmth coming from him as he talked about doing his conjuring tricks for the residents in an elderly residential home. He spoke about how magic had been his passion in life, and how through it he had made friends and been noticed. We were able to talk about the fact that, because of his illness, he would not be entertaining elderly residents at Christmas again. We spoke about his parents' distress and how he felt about dying before them. He talked to me about what it felt like knowing that he was going to die soon, but not feeling as if he was dying. To him it didn't feel as if he was really that ill and the information didn't fit how he felt. He was not in denial about his death, nor was he terrified by the prospect. He simply accepted that this was what was going to happen to him, in the same way that he had accepted the narrow confines of the rest of his life. He would have preferred not to have the tumour, but he did and that was how it was.

He was an only child and his parents had always taken care of him. He had never left home and it felt appropriate to him that they should care for him in his death. At least, he said, he wouldn't be left alone when they died. It was unimaginable for him to live in a world where he was not with his parents and he felt a strange sense of relief at not having to deal with the death of his parents on his own. At times, we just sat in silence looking at each other with no words, but still communicating.

We ended talking about magic. 'I like to see the expressions on their faces when I do tricks. Being surprised by magic makes them happy. Magic brings people together.' There was simplicity to Ronald's world that he was able to articulate with great generosity as he shared it with me. His limited expectations for himself allowed him to more easily accept his short prognosis. He was right about magic, and it felt difficult leaving him because I knew that I would never see him again as he was returning to his local hospital the next day.

These two stories illustrate how the unspoken and unspeakable reality of death was able to find a safe respectful space to be heard and acknowledged as an aspect of these two people's reality. It is often very difficult for this reality to be shared with significant others. It is either too painful to face the reality, or else it is too difficult to find an adequate language. When there is a short prognosis, the process of grief may begin long before bereavement. For some, it is hugely beneficial for this grief to be shared intimately by facing the loss together, in what can be an extremely powerful and moving experience. The final story describes how it is sometimes possible for the therapist to facilitate difficult conversations between patients and significant others.

Coming out of the shadows

Karl had come to this country from South Africa to work temporarily as a teacher. Shortly after starting his new job he suffered from severe headaches which he put down to stress. They became acute after a very short time and he went to a GP who immediately referred him to the hospital. The biopsy produced the worst possible prognosis and now it was a question of Karl finding a flight back to South Africa before he became too ill to fly. He desperately wanted to go home to die surrounded by friends, rather than in an English hospital with strangers.

I found him propped up in bed in a darkened ward with his head swathed in a large dressing and bandages. I was not immediately aware of the man sitting beside him on a low seat in the shadow of the corner of the room. Karl was welcoming as it was he who had asked to see me. His thinking was deeply into problem-solving mode and the logistics of getting back to Cape Town. His attitude was very much: these are the cards I have been dealt; now how best can I play them? Karl was very open about how shocked he had been by the prognosis and how scary the whole thing was. He was 36 years old and felt that he was only halfway through his life. Now he felt a tremendous urgency to get back to South Africa. He had come into hospital to be diagnosed, treated and cured. Now that the third part of this was not possible, he wanted to get on with the next stage of dying, in his own home, where he would feel more in control of the situation. Karl gave me the impression that he was already taking a lot of control by being very focused, rational and unemotional. I wasn't sure why he had asked to see me.

At this point I became aware of the other man. His discomfort was tangible and I began to feel uneasy and somewhat unwelcome. His mood was in stark contrast to Karl's proactive stance. After a while I sensed that Karl was actively excluding this other man from our exchange. I experienced a dilemma. Did Karl want the other man there or did he want privacy? Should I try and bring this man out of the shadows? I had not established any contract with Karl and felt that I needed to clarify the situation. I asked the other man if he was a relative of Karl. He told me that he was a close friend and that he had arrived from South Africa the previous evening. His name was Peter, which he pronounced in a strong Afrikaans accent, and this was his first time in the UK. During this brief exchange I noticed two things. Peter became warmer and friendlier, while Karl adopted a very protective stance towards him. My sense was that Karl was attempting to protect a level of privacy between him and Peter, which my presence seemed to threaten. I didn't feel that I could be much help by following Karl's rational problem-solving stance and I had a hunch that there was something going on between these two men that they found difficult to connect with. After I had checked that they would agree for me to work with both of them present, I turned my attention to Peter and asked him how he was coping with Karl's sudden illness.

Peter, who was slightly younger than Karl, had been completely devastated by the news of the diagnosis and short prognosis. It transpired that in South Africa they had lived together as a couple and they were clearly anxious as to how this might be seen here in the hospital. I then began working with them as a couple and invited them to address each other rather than me. They were able to express their anger with the tumour that was devastating their lives and the seeming arbitrary injustice of the situation. They acknowledged how scared they were about how little time was left. They were also able to tell each other how much they meant to each other. They spoke about not wanting to spend any more time apart and how they would go through this tragedy together. Karl connected with his emotions and Peter connected with his strength. For my part I witnessed a complete transformation in these two men as they confronted their grief together.

Before I left them they thanked me for helping them speak to each other. They said that they had been avoiding their feelings by focusing on the arrangements for returning to South Africa. They were angry with God, with the airlines, the hospital, and life in general. It felt unfair because they had had so much to look forward to together. And now they were determined to do this one last thing together, not as a logistical set of problems to be solved, but as an act of love and a celebration of their feelings for one another. By being able to talk to each other and to communicate their fears and their anger, they had managed to bridge their gulf of denial and emotional self-preservation, in order to meet each other as loving companions on a journey.

In each of these stories there is something about feeling helpless and not knowing; and it seems that, in this vulnerability, the therapist is able to meet the vulnerability of the patient, who also feels helpless and unknowing. I have also spoken about the shift that needs to take place for therapeutic work to be done. It is the shift from patient to client, and it involves some sort of recognition and meeting of the other. I have often found that it involves some sort of risk on my part as the therapist to go with intuitions as well as disruptions and the unexpected. It involves being attentive with one's whole being and listening to one's embodied feelings and responses.

For me, the therapy and the therapeutic encounter are always co-constructed out of our shared humanity as a form of inter-experience. My perception of the client and of myself is always an embodied experience that sometimes resists being brought into spoken words in 'this magical relation, this pact between them and me according to which I lend them my body in order that they inscribe upon it and give me their resemblance' (Merleau-Ponty 1997: 146). I often think of the therapeutic encounter as a dance where we follow each other with subtle clues and where I pay attention with my whole being.

Working with patients with a short prognosis usually means that the encounter takes place on an open ward where many of the customary structures of therapy are dissolved. Time boundaries have to be flexible because this may be the one and only opportunity to meet, or there is a disruption by the medical team who assume priority over you. Patients may also be too ill for more than a brief meeting. Confidentiality can be a difficult boundary on an open ward and in a hospital environment generally, where there is a culture of shared information. The therapeutic frame becomes something that is held in the space between you and your client rather than externally constructed around you. The success or otherwise of this 'raw' therapy is extremely difficult to gauge, but it does seem that it is possible to recognize the patient–client shift and that, in the brief but significant moments of meeting, the unspeakable can find a voice that makes the journey less isolating.

References

Merleau-Ponty, M. (1996 [1945]) *The Phenomenology of Perception*, trans. Smith, C., London: Routledge & Kegan Paul.
—— (1997 [1964]) *The Visible and the Invisible*, trans. Lingis, A., Evanston: Northwestern University Press.

'RELEASEMENT', 'LETTING BE'
(*Gelassenheit*)

In this concept, Heidegger meets Buddhism, meets ecology. Heidegger distinguishes between two forms of thinking: 'calculative thinking' and 'meditative thinking'. We must bear in mind that thinking for Heidegger is never just a mental activity, it is related to how we live our lives and generally to our whole way of being-in-the-world.

'Calculative thinking' is the dominant attitude of our era: it does not simply refer to numeric thinking (adding up, weighing, measuring), but to how we approach the world. 'Calculative thinking' is a form of knowledge that tries to master the world: analysing, organizing, getting nature to reveal its secrets.

'Meditative thinking', on the other hand, attends to the way we dwell in the world. It is not proactive: it is not about willing; it is about waiting, not passively, but with openness. Its therapeutic value, to my mind, is as an antidote to the modern obsession with 'moving on'. 'Being stuck' and 'wallowing in it' are not the only alternatives to 'letting go and moving on'. Instead we can open ourselves to what may lie on the other side of our horizon, to other possibilities of our being, without necessarily forgetting what has been. Heidegger calls this 'releasing ourselves' to the 'region' beyond the horizon, letting it come towards us and allowing ourselves to meet it. 'Meditative thinking' says: all in its own time. It is also about letting beings be, as they are, and encountering them without always wanting to impose our stamp on them.

9

PALLIATIVE CARE, PASTORAL CARE AND COUNSELLING

Working together, learning from one another

Alison Diffley, The Revd Hilary Fife and Melanie Lockett

Alison Diffley (A.D.)

In my 19 years as a palliative care nurse I have noticed that, although the presence of palliative care has greatly expanded in hospitals, its role still remains a mystery to many patients, relatives and professionals. It therefore seems appropriate to begin by demystifying and defining it:

> Palliative care is an approach that improves the quality of life of patients and their families facing the problem associated with life-threatening illness, through the prevention and relief of suffering by means of early identification and impeccable assessment and treatment of pain and other problems, physical, psychosocial and spiritual. Palliative care ... affirms life and regards dying as a normal process; [it] intends neither to hasten or postpone death.
>
> (World Health Organization 2002)

While working as a palliative care nurse, I trained as a counsellor and now also work, part time, as a counsellor in primary care. These two roles are very different and while they are mutually enriching, they also present me at times with contradictions, dilemmas and their respective limitations.

In counselling there is a need to get to know the client as fully as possible, taking time to build a solid working alliance and develop the relationship. Yet, just as palliative care patients may not always have the luxury of time, neither do the professionals caring for them. In many cases, although patients may have been in hospital for weeks, referrals to palliative care are late and there may only be a handful of contacts with the patient before they die, or are transferred to their preferred place of care. There is frequently much ground to cover in a short time. My training as a counsellor was integrative and my years of working in close proximity with the terminally ill and dying have drawn me to the existential elements of that approach. Heidegger argued that we tend to offer one another 'a constant tranquilliza- tion about death' (1962: 298; 254). The general trend 'does not permit us the courage for anxiety in the face of death' (ibid.). This is particularly true in a hospital setting, where the promise of symptom control for when the time comes is offered to allay the fear of dying, and anxiety may be treated with medication. While palliative care takes a holistic approach to the person, I am still far more likely to recommend medication for anxiety in that capacity than I would as a counsellor.

Throughout this chapter we will step into the world of Kate, who is a fictional character whose issues have been drawn from the many real people we have cared for and the experiences they have given us.

> Kate was a fiercely independent 80-year-old lady who lived alone and had been diagnosed with cancer less than a year prior to her hospital admis- sion. Initially, she had responded to treatment, only to be diagnosed with disease progression.

One of a palliative care nurse's responsibilities is to discover, by means of careful assessment, the clinical problems and symptoms that patients are experiencing. Kate was struggling with pain, nausea, vomiting and above all profound weakness and it was necessary for me to work with her, her family and the multidisciplinary team in order to help control these symptoms.

Over the years that I have worked in palliative care, I have become aware of a shift in my approach to patient assessment and am now more comfortable focusing on their concerns. Previously my emphasis was on ensuring that I had covered the entire assessment and ticked all the boxes, stunting many potentially meaningful discussions before they had a chance to develop. These days I am happier to let patients lead the way, seeing myself in a facili- tatory role, and I believe this shift has been freeing for my patients and me.

Having two different professional trainings is not without difficulties. In my palliative care role I work as a member of a team and, although teamwork is fundamental to providing a good palliative care service, at times I feel frustrated as I can have different priorities from other team members because of my counselling training. My role is multifaceted and I must remain clear about my responsibilities, which involve advising on symptom control, dis- charge planning, liaising with other professionals and supporting patients, families and staff – all while carrying a bleep that I am obliged to respond to. These demands mean that prioritizing is important, though not always easy. I battle with the messages I received during my nursing training which are often in conflict with those received during my counselling training. During my nurse training the emphasis was on performing tasks, working hard and proving my worth by getting as much done as possible. As a consequence of this, at times I still struggle with the misguided view that time spent listening and talking to patients and families is a luxury.

In the past, I tended to work in a more task-orientated manner, which was neither facilitative nor helpful. I am aware that I sometimes revert to this way of working when under pressure, but believe that, as long as I am conscious of this, I have choices and can find ways around it. I may decide that today is not the day to enter into discussions, or that I am not the best person to facilitate them and at such a time would refer on to our cancer counsellor or chaplaincy team. I have learnt to bracket my own agenda so that I can be available to open my ears and facilitate meaningful discussions.

My counselling training has taught me the importance of boundaries; being mindful of boundaries helps me care for myself, as does working within a supportive team. However, it is frustrating that, as a palliative care nurse, I do not have the luxury of 50-minute appointments in which to create clear boundaries and give my undivided attention. Another essential ingredient in caring for myself and, ultimately, my patients is clinical supervision, facilitating my reflection on my practice. At times I feel stuck with patients and need to consider what may be happening; this may involve exploring and confronting my own issues. Many nurses do not have clinical supervision readily available to them, yet I believe that it has enabled me to continue to work with people who are dying and helped to guard against burn-out.

It was clear that Kate's disease was very advanced and her prognosis likely to be short. Kate was dying and one of the problems for her and those involved in her care was that this had neither been discussed with her nor acknowledged; in fact the professionals caring for her did not seem to have realized this was happening. Kate was bewildered, her body was failing her and she was all too aware of this. 'What is happening to me? I don't seem to be getting any better . . . sometimes I wonder if this is it.' Such thoughts and questions formed a large part of Kate's initial meetings with me in addition to addressing distressing physical symptoms. When these issues were gently explored with Kate, she spoke of feeling very unsure about her situation and was waiting for the medical team to tell her.

Over time I have become more comfortable with taking responsibility for initiating conversations around the possibility that death is approaching, but this is a big responsibility and can still at times feel overwhelming. Doubts can creep in: 'What if I'm wrong?' 'What if this is nothing more than a setback?' I have learnt to try to avoid dealing in absolutes. With Kate, I needed to discover what she thought was happening and I find this a gentle way of beginning to explore insight. Crucial to these kinds of discussions with patients is the role of empathy. I believe that if I can convey empathy and Rogers' other core conditions of unconditional positive regard and congruence I go some way to creating an environment in which patients can dare to share some of their experiences, whatever they may be. Although I am all too aware that I can't enter their world or know what they feel, I can open my ears to hear as keenly as possible and respond sensitively, communicating to them that I have heard a little of how it is for them and attempt to attune to their needs.

I am aware of the temptation in this kind of work of hiding behind standard responses. I know that at times, when feeling under pressure, this is still one way I can do my job, yet I know that I am not working to the best of my ability when I do so. However, I am only human and at times other pressures cloud my judgement.

> It became clear that Kate had always been able to rely on herself, but her body was letting her down now and relying on herself was no longer working; issues of loss of control and loss of identity were very much around and causing pain.

When I asked Kate to tell me what she felt was happening, she spoke of the fact that she had been gardening only a few short weeks before. This statement touched me. I sensed her comment held great meaning for her and that exploring it would help me understand more about her world. My counselling training has taught me not to simply accept statements. I let Kate talk more about her life. 'I've always managed so well and it hasn't always been easy, especially since Tom died, but I've tried not to be a burden. I hate being like this.' With Kate something about her determination to tell me that she was more than I was seeing and that her existence had meaning long before I knew of it connected with me. Kate seemed to need to let me know something of who she was as a person. This is a common need for people facing death whose roles have been eroded. This was not a time for me to offer her reassurance, attempt to make it better, or offer solutions, but to hear Kate's experience and her pain, both physical and emotional. For other patients, there will be different feelings that I need to be prepared to hear and bear witness to – perhaps rage, sadness, relief or disbelief.

When supporting patients and relatives, I am acutely aware of the part I play in their experience. When I look back at my own experience of being a patient or my children being patients, what I remember most vividly is when someone engaged with me in a way that represented their care and respect for me as an individual; the hardest thing was when I felt stripped of this. During my personal therapy, what I appreciated most in my therapist was her acceptance, support and genuine care which she communicated in small ways. I felt cared for and believe communicating that sense of care to be very important. This was what I tried to convey to Kate.

The medical team's attitude seemed to reflect Kate's own sense of being in limbo. They were keen to treat as actively as possible but were aware that their attempts were not succeeding; it was difficult for them to acknowledge that Kate was dying.

It is much easier for me as a palliative care nurse who, until this point, had had no involvement with Kate to stand back and see the bigger picture. It was therefore my responsibility to ascertain the medical team's thoughts and plans, suggest that Kate was now dying and help the team to consider where the emphasis of care needed to be.

What followed were careful discussions with Kate and her family about the progression of her disease. As a result, the emphasis was switched from active treatment to symptom management and supportive care.

People cope in different ways, some choose to talk only about physical problems. Denial is a common coping mechanism and one which can be particularly frustrating to work with. However, although I have a duty to explore and probe, I should never force content discussions. I am aware of needing to accept my limitations and I become ever more aware of the temptation of being drawn into omnipotence.

Kate was beginning to look at some key issues, to question the very meaning of her existence. She was not a member of any particular church, describing herself on admission as C of E but non-practising. However, she was struggling spiritually.

When teaching, I frequently talk of spiritual pain and the role we have in identifying it. I point out that spiritual pain may be indicated if people ask such questions as 'Why is this happening to me?' However, I add that it is seldom that obvious and patients' questions or comments around spirituality are frequently buried. Although I work at trying to be aware of when patients are struggling spiritually, I know that I am not always the most appropriate person and don't always have the necessary time or skills to facilitate discussions in great depth. Therefore I need to refer on to our chaplaincy team, as I did with Kate, with her consent.

The Revd Hilary Fife (H.F.)

The point at which the doctors say or the patient realizes that 'there is nothing more that can be done' (at least curatively) is the point at which one is forcibly confronted with the mystery we call death, with the mystery of the 'absolutely other' (Lévinas 1998: 63). If a person is still well enough to think and reflect, to be aware of the fact that they are dying, this can be the moment when the questions begin – questions of meaning, of value and of relationship. What meaning does my illness/suffering have? What (if anything) lies beyond death? Does God, the Other, exist and if so what is this God like? If something called 'Heaven' waits, do I qualify – has my life been good enough? It is one of the paradoxes of living and dying that we can find we have expended quantities of time and energy on many questions and challenges during life's journey only to realize that some of the most complex issues have been left until the end, when time to wrestle with them is very limited and hampered by weakness and pain.

I have found as well that it is a mistake to assume that people who have been devout believers throughout their lives are exempt from this struggle for meaning and hope in dying and death. All the major faiths have clearly formulated beliefs and teaching about death and life thereafter. The major faiths have between them a vast wealth of accumulated wisdom to help address the spiritual needs of the dying, as well as the ongoing concerns of the living. However, as Heidegger pointed out, there is a world of difference between acknowledging that 'one' must die and saying 'I' must die. (Heidegger 1962: 297; 253). There is a world of difference between expressing a belief in what happens at and after death while one is well, healthy and anticipating a number of years more, and looking at the possibility of finding out whether beliefs are true in a matter of weeks.

Modern palliative care can address many, if not all, of a dying person's symptoms, relieving them from pain. This then allows time and energy for the big questions: Why? Why me? What happens next? How do I want to use the brief time left? Are there things I want to put right? What things of significance or importance to me do I want to leave to those close to me? One prayer I sometimes use at funeral services contains the lines:

> We pray that nothing in this man/woman's life will be lost but will be
> of benefit to the world and that all that was important for him/her
> will be respected by those who follow.

The spiritual quest for meaning would seem to be a pressing concern for almost all dying patients regardless of whether they profess a particular religious faith. As Victor Frankl reminds us: 'Man is not destroyed by suffering but by suffering without meaning' (Frankl 1964).

It is into this process of questioning and exploration that a chaplain is often invited, both by people of faith and by those who would not call themselves religious. That was where Kate was when I met her. Through the support and care she had already received from the palliative care team she had been able to clarify what was going on and to be told openly and honestly that she was dying. Distressing symptoms were being addressed and because of the care of the whole person that had been offered, she was able to begin to focus on spiritual questions. An atmosphere where difficult issues could be faced had already been created – it was into an ongoing process that I was invited to enter, to share the next part of Kate's journey.

That initial meeting would be crucial. In other pastoral situations there is ample time to establish trust, not so in this case. My time as a hospice chaplain has taught me how brief a window of opportunity exists, how one can never take it for granted that there will be a tomorrow where thoughts can be further refined, explorations deepened. I also know that it is an invitation to tread on holy ground: holy because I am privileged to be asked to share in something so important and personal to the patient; holy because I believe God is already there, whether openly acknowledged or not.

There are potential pitfalls of which I need to be aware – even after my 14 or so years in this ministry. Kate, as every other patient I meet, will have invited me to walk with her, not to choose the route. I am there to listen and share, not preach and instruct. I believe that how I am, what she perceives me to be, is as important as what I say. Louf reminds us that the patient may hear God's word 'from the look on another's face or catch the sound of it in his heart' (Louf 1991: 91). I must set aside preconceptions, eschew easy or neat answers and, as far as I am able, enter Kate's world and be there with and for her. This is her journey not mine. Answers to her questions if they are to be found at all will be found together. God, if she is seeking him, will reach out to her in the manner and at the time that is right for her. Sheila Cassidy (1988) illustrates what I believe to be the essence of ministry to the dying in her book *Sharing the Darkness*. A series of four pictures shows doctor and patient and chaplain and patient. In the first two images the professionals have all the tools of their trade, the symbols of their expertise – uniform, books, pills, medical instruments, bible, cross and sacrament. In the third image these have been stripped away and patient and professional sit together simply dressed. In the final image both are naked – two vulnerable human beings sharing their humanity, their questions and their hopes. Words from scripture, prayer, sacramental ministry may turn out to be very significant during this shared journey, or they may not. What they must never be is something imposed to protect me from the pain Kate is experiencing or to ensure I keep well within my own comfort zone.

At our first meeting Kate told me that she'd never been very 'churchy', but that she'd always tried to live in an upright way. 'I'd like to think I always tried to treat others as I'd like to be treated,' she explained. We spoke of her early life, of her marriage, of her family and her pride in all of them. We spoke of the ordinary that was nevertheless extraordinary because it was her story and it was unique. As I listened, I was reminded of a colleague's account of a conversation in the hospice where he works. An elderly miner, an atheist, wanted in his dying to tell his story. My colleague listened as the story unfolded over several visits ending with a question: 'Has my life been any good? Will it do? (Gordon 2001: 112). An important part of that search for meaning is often a looking back, a sharing of the story of one's life, so that together its goodness can be affirmed, or at least moments of blessing and grace celebrated.

I was aware that Kate and her family were struggling with some of the unfamiliar words that were now part of their daily lives – the medical terminologies around medication, diagnosis, prognosis and so on. Though an efficient and accurate means of communication for the medical team, the use of such terms was less clear and helpful for them. Other colleagues were there to help 'interpret', but I was reminded of how the same problem can occur in the field of religion and spirituality. I found with Kate that it was possible to speak of God, of eternity, of redemption in other more familiar language – in the language of home, of family, of love. Words and concepts that had been so much a part of her life now became metaphors for that other home, for the love and welcome waiting. When Kate and one of her sons asked for a prayer, I chose one which used those familiar words and ideas that had become the bearers of other meaning and hope.

> On one occasion when Alison went to review Kate, a staff nurse mentioned that Kate was not her usual self and that she had become uncooperative. Alison found Kate agitated and distressed. Kate confided that she had had a most upsetting dream, but would not elaborate. Rather than explain her dual training which might confuse her role, Alison asked Kate whether she would like to see the cancer counsellor, who is used to listening to patients' dreams. Kate agreed to meet Melanie.

Melanie Lockett (M.L.)

I went to meet Kate knowing nothing about her except that her cancer had progressed, that the palliative care team had resolved some of her distressing physical symptoms and that she had had a distressing dream.

Many of the principles and boundaries I work with are not unlike those already described in this chapter by Hilary and Alison. Patients may choose to talk to one or all of us about their worries and preoccupations as death approaches. Although each of us works with a different emphasis, there is some overlap. My emphasis with dying patients is on their emotional well-being. I work within the limits of a patient's health and stamina and in a context that offers little opportunity for quiet and privacy – there is no place here for rigid frames.

My thinking and practice in this area is informed by writers such as Kübler-Ross (1970) and the many writings of Dame Cicely Saunders. As I walk towards Kate's bed, I focus on our common humanity. We are likely to have similar fears about the unknown, a similar need to feel loved, connected and not alone, some similar experiences such as loss, grief and helplessness.

By approaching Kate in this way, I believe that I am opening myself to her, hoping that she too will see what we have in common. (I describe more of my approach in Chapter 2, 'Reflections on Cancer Counselling'.) I am interested and care about what Kate thinks and feels, her uniqueness. I draw on my compassion for us both as human beings – she facing her death, me knowing that one day I too will confront my own. I hope that by being truly myself I will be able to establish a trust between us, so that Kate feels she can talk about her concerns. I prepare to meet not Kate the patient but the essence of Kate: I would like to try to understand what it means to be Kate. She starts telling me about the dream she had two nights ago – I do not attempt to interpret it, but listen to what it means to her. She had dreamt of the young soldier with whom she had had a relationship, before she met her husband, during the war. He later emigrated to Canada. She cannot talk to her family, yet she feels the need to talk about him, about what was and what might have been. This brings up other past hopes and regrets, but also an affirmation of her life's joys and achievements.

We have now met three times. As I listen to her, I become aware that her bouts of quietness and anger are outward signs that Kate is coming to terms with the end of her life. She is uncertain about what is happening to her, feels confused and dependent. Sometimes she quietly reflects, feeling tremendous sorrow about all that she has to leave behind. Sometimes she is angry and fearful. She is expressing the tension of having so many losses coming at once, while wanting to go on with her independent life. Kate is aware that I am listening intently, saying very little, giving her room to listen to herself. Occasionally I reflect back to her what I have heard, her sadness, sorrow, fear and anger. She worries about leaving her family and thinks she has left them too much to do after her death. I cannot ease this process for Kate, but neither do I need to feel helpless. I can express my compassion and be a witness to her struggle, helping her to make sense of her life at this time. I can connect with her in a very ordinary way so that she may feel less isolated and calmer in the knowledge that we all die and it is normal.

Working in the here and now with Kate is vital. There may only be the here and now, because, as the process of dying takes over, Kate may not be able to or want to make the effort to talk to me. Already Kate is often dropping off during the session and we are aware that every meeting could be our last.

A.D.

People have a lifetime of issues and I have to remind myself that I cannot bring about happy endings for all my patients. They cannot all die on good terms with everyone and at peace with themselves and the world. People often die as they have lived and this may not be in the way I or others would sometimes have them do it. It is important that they do it their way, and supervision can help me to clarify this. I need to remain aware of my assumptions and be open to people responding in unexpected ways.

Facing death, whether it is our own or that of a loved one, is exclusively a lonely and isolating experience. Frequently, I notice that people who are dying appear to turn inwards, I am not sure if this is simply part of the dying process, if there is a need to disconnect and disengage from relationships. Or is it the fact that no one can accompany us when we die and that we need to turn our attention inwards and prepare ourselves to face death?

M.L.

On my next visit, Kate was asleep. I stayed with her for a few minutes sensing that I would not see her again. I quietly told her that I had felt privileged that she had been able to share her thoughts and feelings with me. I chose not to touch Kate. She hasn't invited me to hold her hand before and so it seemed inappropriate to do so even at this poignant moment. I said, 'Go well' and wished her peace and left; I didn't see Kate again. Her health deteriorated, she turned inward and her children stayed with her until she died. Kate's story is not unfamiliar, but it is unique. Our sessions offered her a brief opportunity to feel the connection of another human being who was not 'doing' to her but 'being' with her. I am yet again left with a sense of awe about how people take leave of their lives. Kate had unfinished business of which she took notice in a dream and chose to speak about to me, a stranger. The work I have done with Kate and others helps me to live my life in the knowledge that I am mortal and that death is normal.

> Kate's family were angry. They didn't understand why their mother was suffering and were confused about the future and what to do for the best. Their ideas about death were coloured, not surprisingly, by previous experiences. Their father had died in pain many years previously and this had not been a good experience for them. They were very frightened that history would repeat itself.

A.D.

In my care of people who are dying, I believe in the importance of engaging in their world, listening and supporting them, holding both the reality that they are dying and the concept of hope, perhaps coming to fruition in, for example, relationships. I don't see it all ending with the death of the patient, but try to see the bigger picture. Frequently, as was the case with Kate, I need to pay attention to the family. I believe that we make a difference not just to the immediate problem: we can affect people's attitudes towards death and loss and their later experiences by giving them the best possible experiences now. We cannot alleviate their pain and struggle, but I believe that a good enough experience will in some way assist relatives with their own existential concerns around death. So I felt it important to explore Kate's children's previous experiences. This meant hearing their pain and paying attention to their concerns about Kate's symptoms.

H.F.

Through visiting Kate I too had met a number of her family. Some would take the opportunity of my being with her to take a break and head to the hospital canteen for coffee. From time to time, to allow Kate space to talk, her visitor would wait outside. In my experience, this can provide family and friends with the opportunity to seek spiritual support in a way that is comfortable for them – a brief conversation as I leave, before they return to the bedside. Questions such as 'Do you think she'll be reunited with Dad?' provide the opportunity for engaging with their need and distress and for establishing sufficient rapport for individual family members to seek support or to explore their own spiritual questions later on. The hospital chapel is kept open daily and for some of Kate's family, although not conventionally religious, it provided a 'sanctuary' – a place of peace to think and to reflect. In fact, on the night she died, having sat with her, they asked for the chapel to be open so that they could gather there as a family before going home.

Kate remained settled and peaceful, her symptoms for the most part well controlled. As she slipped into unconsciousness, her medications were administered via a subcutaneous syringe driver. This is a time when we can again be reminded of the mystery of death, for it is no longer possible to receive answers from patients about how they are feeling.

A.D.

In my work with dying people I frequently feel very humble and moved by them and their experiences. I often wonder if trying to gain some insight into the mystery of death itself has been part of the reason for my choice of work. It is interesting that I can feel exquisitely touched by people in the moment I am with them and that I can then struggle to remember them a week later. At times I find this troubling, but also wonder if this is part of how I manage to keep doing my job as a palliative care nurse. I have a sense that I am most effective when I allow myself to be touched by another and moved by them and their experiences. Yet I know that it is important for me to be in touch with how and why patients impact on me, so that I can separate my own issues, enabling me to continue to deliver a service and guard against burn-out.

The ward staff had got to know Kate and her family well and some were very upset. I facilitated a staff debrief to help them reflect on the care offered and on their own feelings about Kate and her death.

H.F.

The theology underpinning what I do is based on an understanding of a God, the Other, who does not keep a distance, viewing our joy and pain from afar, but who has chosen and chooses to get involved, to share, to suffer with us – to be compassionate. It follows, therefore, that while I also operate within clear boundaries of confidentiality, of respect for the patient's integrity and of ethics, 'professional distance' is not a phrase I would use. I think I would prefer 'professional closeness'. I believe that I have to share Kate's pain, to empathize, if my presence on her journey is to be of any value. The invulnerability of distance is not an option. Kate's pain is not my pain, but at times when she felt hopelessness, I felt helplessness. When she had shared her suffering, I left with sadness. That is, I think, how it has to be, but at times being there for Kate and for others can be very hard. It is therefore of great importance that I take care of myself, both emotionally and spiritually. That is a necessity, not a luxury, if I am to be of help. Within the field of chaplaincy, supervision or work consultancy is not given high priority and not all chaplains come from a tradition where the support and guidance of a spiritual director would be readily sought. However, from experience, I have found that regular supervision from an experienced chaplaincy colleague from another hospital trust, along with spiritual direction, has been invaluable. Being part of the multidisciplinary team is also crucial. There are areas of overlap in palliative nursing, a chaplain's ministry and the work of a counsellor and there are areas of shared understanding, expertise and experience. The regular multidisciplinary team meetings, along with more informal conversations, are an important source of support, insight and wisdom, as we seek together to work with patients at this crucial stage on life's journey – while still keeping to our respective professional guidelines regarding confidentiality. In my journeying with the dying, their families and friends, these words by Miguel de Unamuno (1864–1936), which I encountered by chance, have resonated deeply:

> Those who believe that they believe in God, but without passion in their hearts, without anguish in mind, without uncertainty, without doubt, without an element of despair even in their consolation, believe only in the God idea, not God Himself.

I have come to realize that for any chaplain privileged to be a companion to the dying, belief in the 'God idea' will sustain neither chaplain nor patient.

Strength and direction come from belief in God himself, and that is a place reached after considerably more challenge and questioning and usually over a long period, a lifetime. Sometimes a person's dying really can be like Mr-Valiant-for-Truth crossing the river to enter the celestial city in John Bunyan's *The Pilgrim's Progress* (2005), leaving the chaplain and everyone else around humbled, uplifted and hope-full. More often dying, as being born, is more complicated and more painful. There is no place at the bedside for dishonesty, and I have found there can be no place before God for dissemblance either. So when I bring those I am caring for to God in prayer, as I usually promise to do, the content of that conversation can contain a lot of questioning, of struggle, of emotion – including anger. I am coming to realize that not only is that all right, but it is essential, if my relationship with God which underpins all I do and my ministry within the hospital are to have integrity.

References

Bunyan, J. (2005) *The Pilgrim's Progress*, Ülrichsville OH: Barbour.

Cassidy, S. (1988) *Sharing the Darkness*, London: Darton, Longman and Todd.

Frankl, V. (1964 [1946]) *Man's Search for Meaning: An Introduction to Logotherapy*, trans. Lash, I., London: Hodder and Stoughton.

Gordon, T. (2001) *A Need for Living: Signposts on the Journey of Life and Beyond*, Iona: Wild Goose.

Heidegger, M. (1962 [1927]) *Being and Time*, trans. Macquarrie, J. and Robinson, E., Oxford: Blackwell.

Kübler-Ross, E. (1970) *On Death and Dying*, London: Tavistock.

Lévinas, E. (1998 [1947]) *Le Temps et L'autre*, Paris: Quadrige/PUF.

Louf, A. (1991 [1974]) *Teach Us To Pray*, trans. Hoskyns, H., London: Darton, Longman & Todd.

World Health Organization (2002) *Improving Access to Palliative Care*. www.access2pall.care.org-uk/definition

SPIRITUALITY

Nietzsche's famous saying 'God is dead', Sartre's virulent atheism and Camus' emphasis on the absurdity of existence have together conveyed the impression that existentialism has no room for spirituality. This is a misapprehension: Kierkegaard's and Gabriel Marcel's thought were deeply rooted in Christianity; Buber's in Judaism.

What characterizes existentialism is a questioning of received values, customs, assumptions, dogmas and beliefs, and a rethinking of them for oneself. Thus, even those existential philosophers who were religious did not conform to established tradition.

Lévinas enlarged upon Nietzsche's famous quote: 'The God of onto-theo-logy may well be dead, but is he the only God – are there not other meanings of the word God?' That is, is there not another way in which spirituality and a religious dimension can enter our lives? Existentialism covers a whole spectrum of answers to that question. What all existential philosophers agree about is the importance of personal engagement with the question and firm commitment to one's own chosen views.

In my work with people who have been faced with their mortality, the question of God often arises in various guises: 'Why me?' 'What have I done to deserve this? or else 'I know there was someone up there looking after me.' 'I know I've been given a second chance.' As an existential therapist, I see my work as giving clients the opportunity to explore their religious or spiritual beliefs, doubts and feelings in the safety of their ignorance of my own.

10

WORKING WITH BEREAVEMENT

In the midst of life we are in death

Sarah Young

Introduction

How do we cope when someone close to us has died? Suddenly the child we have loved and nurtured so adoringly has at the age of 20, so full of life and promise for the future, been killed in a car crash. Our partner of 40 years who has been friend, lover, companion and the mainstay of our life is no longer there to share the minutiae of our day. The mother we depended on so completely, who always dropped everything to be available, is not there now to meet our needs, to share our joys and miseries. Despite knowing that we will all die – the one certainty we share – death can come as an overwhelming shock, shattering our way of being and leaving us stricken with grief; a grief that can be so unbearably painful that it more or less immobilizes us. Many of us cope with our grief with the support of friends and family. But for some, outside support is deemed necessary by the bereaved person themselves or those close to them.

We now live in a culture where the 'bereavement industry' or more accurately the 'grief industry' – since this is what bereavement counsellors are dealing with – has grown enormous. There are numerous services offering bereavement counselling, many providing their own training. Courses in bereavement counselling can be remarkably brief, as in an afternoon workshop, or as extensive as a full diploma course. A few weeks after a patient's death, most hospices routinely offer counselling to those who have been bereaved. Despite the now commonly held belief that grief is the normal response to being bereaved – in this context, through the death of a relation or friend – counselling is seen as a necessity for large numbers of the bereaved. Bereavement is considered one of the most stressful experiences in our lives – the death of a spouse being rated the highest (Holmes and Rahe 1967). The charity Cruse Bereavement Care, the largest organization in the UK specializing in bereavement, receives close to 200,000 contacts a year and has numerous branches, volunteers and publications. Bereavement has spawned a vast literature which would fill a substantial library. There are several journals focusing on bereavement, for example, *Mortality, Death Studies, Journal of Loss and Trauma.* Thanatology, the study of all aspects of mortality, generates a huge body of research.

How did it all begin? Freud's classic paper 'Mourning and Melancholia' (1957 [1915]) described grief as a normal defence against the trauma of loss. Grieving involved the withdrawal of emotional ties (libido) to the deceased, so-called 'decathexis'. Lindemann (1944) is said to have coined the phrase 'grief work' and to have been the first to discuss 'anticipatory grief'. His study of those bereaved after a fire at the Coconut Grove, a nightclub in Boston where 492 people were killed, revealed a remarkably similar 'grief syndrome'. Following his research, social scientists began to study the grief process in earnest. George Engel (1961), employing a medical model of grief, characterized it as a 'disease', believing this would facilitate study into the area and would improve medical management of people who had been bereaved.

It is perhaps fair to say that the beginnings of the present-day 'grief industry' and making a 'special case' of bereavement counselling followed the pioneering work of Elizabeth Kübler-Ross in the USA with the publication of her seminal book *On Death and Dying* (1970). Kübler-Ross drew attention to the process of dying and described a five-stage grief model. In a climate of repression and denial, her work was considered revolutionary at the time and she did much to improve the care of the dying. Her classic five stages (denial, anger, bargaining, depression, acceptance) became the model for bereavement counselling. In the UK, the psychiatrist Colin Murray Parkes is largely responsible for the growth of bereavement services. With the publication of *Bereavement: Studies of Grief in Adult Life,* now in its third edition (1998), he brought to the forefront the need for services to support the bereaved. Drawing on attachment theory (Bowlby 1969), Parkes described four dimensions of grieving: shock and numbness; yearning and searching; disorientation and disorganization; resolution and reorganization. He also drew attention to feelings of guilt and anger that can feature so prominently in the grief process.

In a move away from the stages of grief, Worden (1991) described the tasks of grief. By focusing on the tasks of grief, we are given a more active view of grief work, rather than the somewhat passive stage model. The four tasks are: to accept the reality of the loss; to work through the pain of grief; to adjust to an environment in which the deceased is missing; to emotionally relocate the deceased and move on with life. It seems we have almost come full circle in that, along with Freud, we now consider grief to be a normal if highly complex process involving both 'psychological' and 'physical' components. There is indeed a large body of research showing the physical effects of bereavement, such as impaired functioning of the immune system and excess mortality from heart disease in people who have lost a spouse (McChrystal 2004). The stage models, if taken too literally, tend to undermine the complexity of the bereavement process and its individual nature.

Our response to the death of someone close to us is dependent on many factors, not least our relationship with the deceased. Parkes (1998) highlighted three groups of factors which influence the grief process: antecedent factors, such as childhood losses, relationship with the deceased and mode of death; concurrent factors such as socio-economic status; and subsequent factors as in social support and new life opportunities. But of course we must be careful not to make assumptions. Someone with good social support and a secure background may be overwhelmed by the predicted and peaceful death of a pet.

Paradoxically, despite the voluminous literature on bereavement and despite being constantly bombarded with images of death on television and in newspapers, death is still something of a taboo in our society. In Britain, death has become medicalized, institutionalized and hidden away, with most deaths occurring in hospital. Advances in medicine have 'given rise to the belief that death can be put off, postponed, held in check or even conquered permanently' and death is frequently seen as 'medical failure' (Laungani and Young 1997: 219). When communities were more closely knit and deaths occurred in the home, with the dying person surrounded by family and friends and the body laid out in the front parlour, we were closer to death. Now, even if death occurs in the home we are able to quickly distance ourselves from it. I can recall the speed with which my father's body was removed from home and taken away in the back of the funeral director's hearse, placed alongside the empty bag for the next body to be collected. None of the family wanted to witness his departure. Open expressions of emotion in our society tend to be discouraged and funerals are often quite restrained, frequently private ceremonies. Children are usually protected from viewing a dead body (of course some adults too avoid this) and are kept from the reality of death, even though they have been 'socialized into a culture of violence, destruction and death' (Laungani and Young 1997: 222). We no longer have formal periods of mourning or show that we are grieving by wearing black or an armband. As long ago as 1965, Gorer, in his classic study of grief and mourning in Britain, argued for a return to these rituals and made a plea for more openness about death. (The above is, of course, a description of the dominant culture as other cultures in our society may behave differently.) How do we become more open and accepting of death? How can we make death more personal?

Making death our own

Why do you fear your last day? It contributes no more to your death than each of the others.

(Montaigne 1946: 109)

In his compelling novel *The Picture of Dorian Gray*, Oscar Wilde (1949) describes the exquisitely beautiful young man Dorian Gray and his attempt to avoid ageing and deny death. On viewing a portrait of himself, Dorian makes a fateful bargain. He sells his 'soul' for eternal youth. The stunning 'Adonis' of the portrait will wither and age while he retains his beauty. Dorian abandons himself to every sin his profligate mind can devise and while he remains youthful the portrait ages. Dorian manages to circumvent the existential conflict between his awareness of the inevitability of death and his wish to continue to be (Yalom 1980). He perfects the art of living 'inauthentically' and strives to forget Being (Heidegger 1962). Dorian immerses himself in the world of things. He lives in the 'deathless' world of art and collects endless gorgeous treasures, jewels, embroideries and perfumes, and marvels at the way things are. In this state of forgetfulness of Being, that Heidegger describes as inauthentic, we are unaware of the authorship of our lives, we flee, we 'fall' and are tranquillized and carried along by the 'they' (*das Man*). We are concerned about the way things are rather than that they are.

Heidegger refers to human existence as Dasein, meaning 'being there and open to all there is' (Cohn 1997). To be mindful of Being, we are open to existence and all that this implies. We marvel that things are, we are mindful of the responsibility we have for our lives, we recognize our self-creation and we accept the future non-existence of ourselves. Dorian was not prepared to accept this and he refused to recognize the future and his inevitable death. The present was his main concern and he absorbed himself in what was actually in front of him. He regarded the past as relatively unimportant and the future as merely what would soon be present. This was demonstrated in Dorian's desire to form a new movement which would teach man to 'concentrate himself on the moments of life'. In contrast to this, in moments of authenticity, we are aware of both past and future, of what we were and of the future before us (its finiteness, uncertainty, the choices it holds).

Heidegger teaches us that death is not separate from life, something that occurs at the end, an event that comes upon us at a future moment. He was not concerned with death itself, since we cannot experience death. Rather, Heidegger was concerned with our attitude towards our death, not death as an event but death as the end of all our experience. His analysis leads to the recognition that death, or rather 'being-towards-the-end', is always with us, affecting how we lead our lives. Death is there from the start and death is in life: once a moment is gone it cannot be had again, we are always dying. Death being the last possibility makes impossible any further possibilities. If we can truly grasp this we are more likely to take up on our possibilities. Rather than lead the safe comfortable life we have created for ourselves we will take the risk and do the things of which we have only dreamt. In this way the prospect of certain death can be life enhancing rather than life denying.

At the same time, 'death is the possibility of the absolute impossibility of Dasein' (1962: 294; 250) and as such it is anxiety provoking. Our anxiety before death means that, for the most part, we live as if we were going to live forever. We plan for tomorrow and attempt to make our lives as secure as we can, forgetting contingency and limitation – we live inauthentically. When my son was in his infancy and thought to be ill with a potentially fatal disease, my experience of living changed dramatically. Life became an intense and vibrant experience. Every moment I experienced a level of anxiety as heightened as it is possible to imagine. I felt as if my skin had been turned inside out, so raw and sensitive did I feel. But of course life cannot be lived at this level and as soon as my son recovered I once again became 'forgetful of Being' and was back with the 'they', planning the celebration of his first birthday, immersing myself in the everyday diversions of life. I learnt through the experience that consideration of death enriches rather than impoverishes life.

In recognizing our-being-towards-death we can find strength and purpose in our lives. In denying and avoiding our mortality, we close ourselves off from Being, and we pay a price for this in terms of our freedom. This freedom includes, in particular, 'the freedom to actively relate or avoid such a relation to our own being, to our very own humanity' (Condrau 1998: 31). If we had 'unlimited time available, nothing would be urgent, nothing would be important, nothing would be real' (p. 106). For a moment consider a life without death – life loses some of its intensity. Anxiety and the fear of death are ubiquitous. Anxiety in the face of our freedom and fear of the possibility of 'no-longer-being-able-to-be-there' encourages us to 'recognize that death calls upon us to take over our existence' and to 'live it in freedom and self-responsibility' (pp. 106–107). Is it possible that if we were to become more open and accepting of death, more courageous in facing its inevitability, then we would not only enrich our own lives, but we would also be better able to cope with the death of someone whom we love?

Bereavement counselling

Bereavement, from the Old English word *bereafian*: to rob thoroughly.

Maureen had rarely, if ever, thought about her own death or the death of others. This was revealed in her long and painful struggle to come to terms with her husband's death. 'I never thought he was going to die.' She and Jim had been married for 38 years and had been quite an isolated couple with few friends or family. Both were retired and neither of them had many interests. Maureen often repeated that 'they lived for each other'. She found it impossible to accept that Jim was not coming home, though she could acknowledge it: 'I do know he is dead.' She continued to live as if Jim were still alive. One year on from his death she would lay the table for two; his pyjamas were still neatly folded on his side of the bed.

There is no need to describe Maureen's response as 'pathological' or to regard her as stuck at a particular stage. Like all of us she was capable of enormous self-deception and could hold two contradictory beliefs – preparing a meal for two, at the same time knowing Jim was dead. We explored her grieving within the context of her whole existence. It has been argued that our problems stem from a conflict between the ontological givens of our existence (that we are embodied, that we shall die, our ultimate aloneness, etc.) and our response to them (Yalom 1980; Cohn 1997). Maureen saw that she had clung to Jim all her life, partly in the vain hope of protecting herself from its inevitable insecurities. She became aware of the extent to which she had restricted her life by making Jim her sole focus. Eventually, though it was tinged with pain, she was able to take some pleasure in her freedom and she became less frightened of taking on responsibility for herself. She remembered activities that had interested her as a younger woman and bravely entered into a more engaged existence, for example, joining a sewing group and making a patchwork quilt.

> Despite her supportive children, family and close friends, Anna felt almost intolerable loneliness when her husband died. She began to question her very existence: 'Why am I here?' 'What is the point?' Later, her grief became compounded with feelings of guilt, as she acknowledged to herself some resentment towards him; at the same time, she also wished she had been kinder to him. She berated herself for not being stronger and 'getting over it'. She felt a year after his death she should be better, forgetting that she had lived most of her adult life with her husband. She was surprised at how angry she felt at the futility of existence. Again and again through her tears she shouted, 'It is so stupid, so stupid. All that worry and anxiety and it ends like this, what is the fuss about?'

The absurdity of existence, so powerfully described by Camus and Sartre, was right before her. Slowly she began to explore her resentments towards her husband and realized that she had frequently felt bullied and ignored by him: 'We did what he thought best.' She started to recognize her part in this and how for the sake of peace she had allowed him to dominate. This realization helped her to rethink her own priorities for her life, bringing some meaning to the questions she had asked herself in her grief and despair. Her sense of the absurdity of existence stayed with her. She felt she had 'lost her innocence', life had no intrinsic meaning, yet finding she was able to construct her own meaning was a freedom she now appreciated.

Guilt is frequently described by those who have been bereaved – guilt for surviving, guilt in relation to the deceased (as with Anna), guilt for failing oneself and so on. But rather than seeing it as a stage or task of grief, existential thinking allows us to accept it as an inevitable aspect of existence – we are forever falling short of what we might be. Adjusting to a partner's death can be further complicated if the relationship was in some respects deeply unsatisfactory.

> When I first met Martin he was overcome with grief, constantly tearful and hardly able to function. Two years previously he had given up work to care for his terminally ill partner of 12 years. Six months after Roy's death, Martin was finding it difficult to leave the house or be with other people: 'They are all superficial and don't understand.' He described his relationship with his partner in the most idyllic terms: 'Nobody could believe how incredibly strong and special our relationship was.'

But not long after we met he began to reassess his relationship with Roy and went from idealizing it to seeing it quite differently. His partner had been 'selfish and they had always done what he wanted', he had 'been a fool to do so much for him'. His tears were no longer tears of grief, but of anger. His perception of all his relationships shifted and he became cynical about everyone's motives, including, of course, mine – though initially this was hotly denied. The world he had created was falling apart and he felt utterly disillusioned. Over many months Martin came to take a more 'balanced' view of his relationship and he began to re-engage with life. He recognized how important it had been for him, both before and during Roy's illness, to idealize their relationship. How else could he justify 'all the giving', both financial and in terms of affection? Again our capacity for self-deception was illustrated, knowing something is the case and at the same time convincing ourselves it is not.

Heidegger argued that the death of others can give us no understanding of our own death. But the death of another can bring us face to face with our vulnerability and mortality. Inevitably, the existential theme of facing our mortality emerges again and again in bereavement work (as it often does in therapy).

> Sally nursed her sick father until he died and she was with him when he died. She witnessed the fragility of our hold on life, our powerlessness. She managed to carry on with her life as a mother and teacher, but, one year on from his death, she began to think she was 'going mad'. Her constant worries about her own health, the health of her children and husband began to become obsessive. She was finding sleeping difficult and could not stop herself from imagining scenarios where a member of her family died.

In talking through her fears, Sally began to be less caught up in them. Despite missing her father, she was also able to celebrate his life and all that he had meant to her. Her confrontation with mortality left her more able to appreciate every moment of her existence.

While for some, like Sally, death brings a radical shift to their way of being, others seem to carry on regardless in the same vein:

> Janet came for counselling when she was in her late forties. She had been involved in a minor accident which had left her with a back injury and she had had to spend several weeks at home convalescing. To her utter amazement she had found herself overwhelmed with sadness and constantly tearful: 'I am completely worn out with crying and I don't really know why I'm crying.' Janet was a competent business woman who led a busy social and family life, caring for her husband and two children. Over the months, we explored and 'unpacked' her life, the disappointments, the hurts, the rejections, the sexually ambiguous relationship with her father and, as it became clear, most importantly her mother's early death. Janet was used to being in control and rarely had time to worry about 'things you cannot change'. Her mother had died at a young age when Janet herself was in her early twenties and just married. Janet had 'just got on with life.' 'You have to, don't you?'

Janet had dealt with all these experiences by 'keeping busy', but once confined at home for back-rest she could no longer hide in her busyness/ business. Janet quickly recognized her tendency to divert herself from anxiety and pain. I began to think she had read Heidegger, so well did she describe falling in with the 'they' – be it working long hours or having a casual affair. She realized how this tendency limited her relationships: 'I never really let anyone in – until now.' When she wept for her mother, she rocked with pain. It was as if her death had just occurred. The power of her 'delayed' grief was almost overwhelming for us both. When Janet returned to her job and busy life it was, she felt, with a new understanding of herself that would allow her to experience difficulties rather than 'stay on the run'.

Time, proverbially, heals; for most grieving people the pain lessens with time. There has been a great deal of discussion in the literature with regard to how long grieving should last until it is considered 'complicated' or 'pathological'. But how long do you grieve for your adored son killed at the age of 17, your enchanting four-year-old daughter or your husband of 60 years? There appears to be a great deal of pressure in our society to get over loss as quickly as possible with the minimum of fuss. I have been struck how often bereaved clients say 'I shouldn't still be feeling like this.' 'Why am I still crying so much?' It seems they feel they should be over their grief in a matter of months, despite having loved the deceased person over a period of years or a lifetime. Bereavement counselling can facilitate the acceptance of feelings of grief and 'normalize' the experience. Clients are extraordinarily grateful to know that they are not going mad and are allowed to feel what they feel. It does no harm to recognize that death happens in a moment, but its aftermath can last a lifetime.

The particular difficulty of mourning a parent who has been abusive can be highly confusing and problematic – it can also be a very long process. The contradictory feelings of both love and hate that are so powerful in their intensity may lead to doubts about one's sanity.

'I went completely mad after my mother died,' James told me at our first meeting. He absolutely adored his mother and he movingly described how she was part of him. 'She was like my skin,' he said as he touched the skin on his arm. But alongside the closeness, his mother's addiction to alcohol had led her to be horribly abusive towards him. Her threatening and manipulative behaviour towards a young boy, whose father had left when he was in his infancy, was excruciating to hear.

It seemed as if James was beginning to tolerate his contradictory feelings better and to acknowledge the paradoxical nature of life and living but, without any indication of wishing to end our relationship, he abruptly stopped coming to sessions. Paradox seemed to be at the heart of his difficulties, but to fully acknowledge his negative feelings was perhaps too much to tolerate.

The focus of this chapter is bereavement counselling informed by existential–phenomenological thinking. In one sense this is 'non-sense' since, from an existential perspective, it is recognized that everything is connected and we cannot isolate bereavement out as a separate experience from all others. We might also argue that there is no necessity for a specialist training for bereavement work, since all therapy involves dealing with loss of some kind or another. As the above vignettes have attempted to show, all experiences are explored in relation to each other and to the whole context of our life – and that includes not only our present experience, but also the influence of the past and our expectations of the future. It is that whole context that affects the way we cope with the death of someone close to us and that we need to take into account when working with bereaved clients.

Existential thinking recognizes that any understanding is always partial and limited and that finding answers or gaining complete resolution is rarely, if ever, possible. The models and stage theories discussed earlier throw some light on the grieving process, but like all theories they limit understanding and reduce experience to what can be explained. By trying to fit experience into a prescribed model, we are in danger of losing sight of the experience itself. In my attempt to maintain a 'phenomenological attitude' I strive to remain as open as possible to the person I am seeing, to gain some insight into their unique experience. Of course I cannot enter any situation without a multitude of assumptions, but I try to set aside some of my pet theories about how things should be and temper my prejudices. However, some existential assumptions, for instance, that we all face the same 'givens' of existence and that we co-constitute any relationship, not only inform how I am in any encounter, but are also fundamental to my work and my life. These I do not set aside.

Ingram *et al.* (2000) argue that traditional theories of bereavement simplify a 'very complex and rich experience'. Their postmodernist perspective is closer to an existential understanding: 'Grief work is an idiosyncratic phenomenon which involves individuals identifying their own tasks of mourning, negotiated through the process of everyday living' (Ingram *et al.* 2000: 72–73). It is the 'work of a life-time' requiring the 'continual re-negotiating and constructing of meaning' (p. 79). This sits well with the fundamental existential assumption that I create my own world and that this world is in constant flux, I am not a fixed thing. If this were not so, what use would therapy be? To witness our capacity for change is one of the most rewarding aspects of this work.

I have learnt a great deal about human courage from working with bereaved clients and from my relationships with other volunteers at the hospice. In all the stories I have been privileged to hear, I recognize something of myself and my own difficulties, and there are aspects with which I identify. I gain in learning about myself and this in turn affects my relationships and how I treat others. Above all, I learn to value my relationships and I attempt to appreciate every moment. In our society, despite all the constant reminders of death, we can still be lulled into the expectation of living out our potential lifespan. We know this may not be the case, but we live as if it were or as if we might live forever.

I believe that, as therapists, we need to be aware of what leads us to work with a particular client group. In choosing to work as a bereavement counsellor, as with everything, my motives were mixed. Seeking meaningful and gratifying work certainly was one of them. I am in the fortunate position of being able to do some voluntary work and there is an element of attempting to assuage my own guilt and shame at being in that comfortable position. There may also be a desire to be seen to be doing something worthwhile – 'sanctity rooted in vanity'. Other motives, I suspect, include my own experiences of bereavement and, in particular, those that occurred at a young age. I received some early lessons that it was not appropriate to show an emotional reaction to death. I remember feelings of confusion at being told I should not show my feelings. In fact, I realized I was being told that it was not even appropriate to have those feelings. Death was to be hidden, kept from view and no emotional outpouring was appropriate. Since then, I have often thought we need a greater acknowledgement of death; a fuller appreciation of what our own death and what the death of others means for us and an acceptance of the open expression of grief.

Conclusion

Live this day as if it were thy last.

(Anon.)

If this chapter and book do anything, it will be to remind us, as Heidegger did, of our mortality, to which for the most part we only pay lip service: 'It happens to us all.' 'My time will come.' Other euphemistic statements like 'he's kicked the bucket' or 'popped his clogs' help to distance us from death. In some respects the Victorians were more able to acknowledge death, with their period of mourning, the clothes, the rituals and the respect they showed towards the grieving.

> The certainty of death is perhaps the most unacceptable dimension of existence. What is intolerable is not only the constant threat of our mortality but also the acceptance of our finiteness. We do not wish to give up our illusions of omnipotence or our hope of immortality. We may extend these attitudes to any kind of separation or loss. To live as if we were immortal, to ignore separation, to refuse to mourn our losses, are all poignant instances of living inauthentically.
>
> (Cohn 1997: 126)

But living 'authentically' is an ideal beyond our reach. Heidegger (1962) described our everyday existence as inauthentic. Despite the constant reminders of our fragility and the fleeting nature of existence, we manage to deny or at least to avoid acknowledging the inevitability of our own death and of those we care about. We live under so many threats to our existence and to the planet itself through war, accident or terrorism. Yet, for the most part, we manage to live distracted lives, forgetful-of-being, caught up in the everyday. It has been suggested that in Western society we learn of death in the abstract: 'knowledge of death is in the head; neither the heart nor the eye experiences it directly' (Parkes *et al.* 1997). If it is possible for us to develop a more personal awareness of death, if we can show more acceptance of death in our lives and allow for the open expression of grief, the process of grieving itself will perhaps be less problematic – and the need for bereavement counsellors will diminish.

Bereavement counsellors are now rushed to the scene of a disaster and their services are available countrywide so that, in one sense, the bereaved are being encouraged to express themselves. Yet, paradoxically, a bereaved person can feel isolated and shunned: Susan frequently bemoaned the fact that no one would talk about her dead husband. 'It was as if he had never existed.' How often do we hear ourselves or others saying 'I don't know what to say' to someone recently bereaved? As bereavement counsellors, we are possibly filling the gap that ritual mourning left, but we may also be taking grieving out of the community and into our counselling rooms. Inadvertently, we may be part of the problem: we are preventing death from being brought back into our lives.

References

Bowlby, J. (1969) *Attachment and Loss, Vol. 1: Attachment*, London: Hogarth Press.

Cohn, H. W. (1997) *Existential Thought and Therapeutic Practice*, London: Sage.

Condrau, G. (1998) *Martin Heidegger's Impact on Psychotherapy*, Vienna: Mosaic.

Cruse Bereavement Care. www.crusebereavementcare.co.uk

Engel, G. (1961) Is Grief a Disease? A Challenge for Medical Research, in *Psychosomatic Medicine*, 23: 18–22.

Freud, S. (1957 [1915]) Mourning and Melancholia, trans. Strachey, J., *Standard Edition*, Vol. XIV, London: Hogarth Press.

Gorer, G. (1965) *Death, Grief and Mourning in Contemporary Britain*, London: Cresset.

Heidegger, M. (1962 [1927]) *Being and Time*, trans. Macquarrie, J. and Robinson, E., Oxford: Blackwell.

Holmes, T. and Rahe, R. (1967) The Social Readjustment Scale (SSRS), in *Journal of Psychosomatic Research*, 11: 213–218.

Ingram, J., Hunt, K. and Robson, M. (2000) Grief: A Complex, Unique and Rich Experience, in *Changes*, 18.2: 69–82.

Kübler-Ross, E. (1970) *On Death and Dying*, London: Tavistock.

Laungani, P. and Young, B. (1997) Conclusions I: Implications for practice and policy. in Parkes, C.M., Laungani, P. and Young, B. (eds) *Death and Bereavement Across Cultures*, London: Routledge.

Lindemann, E. (1944) The Symptomatology and Management of Acute Grief, in *American Journal of Psychiatry*, 101: 141.

McChrystal, J. (2004) *How Insecurely Attached Adults Respond to Bereavement in a Primary Care Setting: Health and Health Care Seeking Behaviour*, unpublished PhD thesis, University of Westminster.

Montaigne, M. (1946 [1580]) *Essais*, 1, XX, Paris: Bibliothèque de la Pléiade.

Parkes, C.M. (1998) *Bereavement: Studies of Grief in Adult Life*, 3rd edn, Harmondsworth: Penguin.

Parkes, C.M., Laungani, P. and Young, B. (eds) (1997) *Death and Bereavement Across Cultures*, London: Routledge.

Wilde, O. (1949) *The Picture of Dorian Gray*, Harmondsworth: Penguin.

Worden, J.W. (1991) *Grief Counselling and Grief Therapy*, 2nd edn, London: Routledge.

Yalom, I. (1980) *Existential Psychotherapy*, New York: Basic Books.

BEING IN RELATION, ALONENESS AND DEATH

There are two fundamental strands within existential thought that appear to be mutually contradictory: on the one hand, human existence is in-relation, it is a 'being-with', and on the other, there is the concept of existential isolation or aloneness. Yet, paradoxically, both can coexist without contradiction: it is indeed an important aspect of existential therapies.

Heidegger stresses that we are always in relation, even when we try to avoid people we are in relation – avoidance becomes our manner of relating. In that sense 'being-with' and 'being-in-relation' are fundamental aspects of human existence.

There is also a sense in which we are fundamentally on our own. The most obvious is our death; no one can die *my* death. The way I approach it is my 'ownmost possibility'. It is a possibility which I can seize (and that does not mean letting myself die or committing suicide). I can confront my mortality and decide what I want to do with my life. This is why Heidegger says that 'death individualizes human existence'. Or else, it is a possibility that I can try to avoid exploring. I can busy myself with things or seek assurances in the comforting talk of others (see 'Authenticity', p. 117).

Cancer patients, however supported they may be, often express their sense of isolation as they go through the various stages of their 'cancer journey'. It is frequently at the end of the treatment that the journey becomes most lonely, when family and friends heave a sigh of relief and say 'You're all right now, let's put it all behind us and move on.'

Dick Blackwell's description of refugees (Chapter 6), who live with the guilt of uprooting their families through their political involvement and causing them distress, is another such example of both isolation and relation.

11

WORKING WITH BEREAVED PARENTS

Ann Chalmers

And can it be that in a world so full and busy, the loss of one
weak creature makes a void in any heart so wide and deep that
nothing but the width and depth of vast eternity can fill it up!
(Charles Dickens, *Dombey and Son* 1847)

Living through the experience of the death of their child is something no
parent ever expects to do. There was a time when child death was expected
and people lived in the knowledge that it was unlikely that all their children
would survive infancy. Today in the West we exist in a world of significant
medical, scientific and technological advances, in which we have expectations
of longevity and of being able to watch our children grow and develop into
adulthood. Our hope is that our children will not have to deal with our death
until they are independent and no longer reliant on us as parents for their
safety and well-being. The death of a child therefore challenges our assump-
tive world in the most profound way. It also challenges therapists, who can be
faced with myriad issues, not only in terms of what bereaved parents may
present, but also in terms of their own beliefs, thoughts and feelings about
children, childhood and parenthood.

This chapter takes a phenomenological approach: it does not seek to fit
the experience of bereaved parents within any grief or bereavement theory,
but to describe what it can mean to have lost a child. My description represents the distillation of over 15 years of listening to and working with
bereaved parents. The chapter also considers the experience of the therapist
coming alongside parents who encounter this unique type of loss.

The bereaved parent

The nature and complexity of the parent–child relationship is such that the
death of a child is unparalleled in relation to other losses we may experience
throughout life. For any parent, the death of their child is an event completely against the natural order and the pattern they expect their lives to

follow. No one expects to have to bury their child, and nothing can prepare parents for this untimely death at whatever age and for whatever reason it occurs. Our children are always our children, regardless of their age. In this context, the definition of child extends far beyond the commonly accepted sense of the word. From early pregnancy loss to the 90-year-old mother whose 65-year-old son dies, one particular feature is common to the parents' experience – the feeling that this should never have happened.

Everyone's grief is unique and there is no 'right' way for parents to grieve. Their grief is a normal reaction to the death of their child. Parents are often taken aback by the duration of their grief which, because of the unique nature of this loss, most experience as never truly reaching an end. A parent's grief is not just for the loss of what they had with that child, but for a whole future that will never be lived. Throughout life the parents are likely to revisit their loss and experience that loss taking on a different significance, when what would have been key milestones for their child and their family are reached. This does not indicate that their grief is in any way unresolved, but simply that a new aspect of that loss has presented itself:

When we got to the stage of our life where all our friends' children were getting married, although our daughter had been dead for almost 20 years, the pain of knowing I would never walk her down the aisle was unbearable.

(Mark)

Each parent's unique grief response will be determined by a number of variables, not least the unique relationship and degree of attachment they had to the child, and what meaning they attributed to their relationship with that child. Past experiences will impact upon their ability to survive this loss. No death happens in isolation and past losses, particularly those which have not been worked through, will combine with the circumstances of the death, the personality, belief systems and support network of the parent, to have a significant bearing on how each individual responds. This can have implications for the parents' relationship, with couples frequently assuming that, since this is a loss that they share together for a child they have in common, the grief will be the same. Yet grieving the death of a child is a solitary experience. Each parent will grieve in their own way, in their own time, and the noticeable differences in the intensity, expression and duration of their grief can leave partners feeling very isolated and misunderstood.

While sudden death is accepted as particularly shocking in nature, it can never be assumed that parents whose child's death was anticipated will have a less intense or prolonged grief response. Children often surprise their doctors by surviving far beyond expectations and in these situations parents may have been lulled into a false sense of security, in denial that the death would ever really happen. The circumstances surrounding the death are, however, often significant in determining the nature and focus of the grief response.

Pregnancy loss is characterized by the loss of a dream, the fantasy baby, a shortage of memories that are shared with others and a lack of acknowledgement as a significant loss. Its impact is frequently devalued by others, with significance often attributed to the number of weeks gestation the pregnancy has reached. Where parents have taken the decision to terminate a pregnancy because of anomalies in the baby, their grief can be complicated by the fact that they have been involved in making a 'choice' to end their child's life. This can also be true where parents have agreed with doctors that treatment should be withdrawn from their sick child. Baby deaths that occur in utero and unexpected stillbirth bring with them the horror of physically carrying the dead baby and of subsequently giving birth to death. In these situations and those where an infant dies suddenly and unexpectedly, the parents, in the absence of any clear explanation, are likely to go over and over the events leading up to the death.

Sudden deaths of children through illness or accident plunge parents into the world of autopsies and inquests. Violent and accidental deaths often attract significant police involvement and intrusive media attention, with the added distress this brings to families. Death of their child by suicide has immense consequences for parents, with feelings of stigma and self-blame often seen as the predominant emotions. Where a child has had a life-limiting condition, the parent–child relationship is likely to have assumed a deeper level of intensity with parents even more closely involved in the daily life of their child. There may be strong feelings of anger towards an independent adolescent who refused to comply with their treatment regime. If parents have been unable or unwilling to communicate with their child about the child's impending death, there are often regrets as to what was unspoken.

The parents' experience will also be determined by a number of variables. The age of their child at the time of death is not significant in terms of any hierarchical sense, where the loss of a baby might be thought to be less than the loss of an older child, but it is likely to be significant in terms of how others respond to the parents in relation to that loss. There is undoubtedly greater social acknowledgement of the death where a child has lived for a time and others knew the child. In situations of pregnancy loss or death of a baby at or around the time of birth, parents often experience little acknowledgement, a commonly held yet largely erroneous assumption being that a little amount of life in some way equates to a little amount of loss for the parent.

The younger the child, the more involved a parent is likely to be in the daily life of that child. At this stage in life, a parent's identity is so closely linked to their child, being known often not by their own name but as 'Amanda's mum', 'Tom's dad'. Deaths during adolescence can be particularly difficult because of the relationships, ranging from ambivalent to hostile, that abound at this time of vying to establish independence and maintaining the necessary boundaries. Parents who have had a close involvement in their adult child's life will also acutely feel the loss of the parenting role. There is often, however, a diminished level of acknowledgement where elderly parents experience the death of an adult child who had a family of their own. The adult child's partner and own children are frequently the main focus of attention and sympathy from others and the significance of the loss for their elderly parents may not be as readily acknowledged.

The age of the child is also likely to determine the aspects of the loss that might be particularly significant to the parent. Parents often view babies and younger children as an extension of themselves in a physical sense, and may describe the loss in very physical terms, being experienced as 'an amputation', 'losing a part of myself', feeling incomplete and 'unwhole'. The unconditional love that a young child gives is seldom replicated elsewhere in life. Parents who are used to their home being filled with their child's voice and presence can experience hallucinations of seeing or hearing their child. For some these are a comfort; others express the fear that they are 'going mad'. On the death of their adult child, many parents express the loss of someone they consider to be their 'best friend', their confidant.

Research has indicated that the age of the parent also has some significance in determining their ability to manage this type of loss. The ability to adapt is more evident in younger parents, while older parents have been found to be less likely to recover from the experience of their child's death (Stroebe *et al.* 1993: 285–299). This may be due to younger parents perhaps having other children to look after or being able eventually to go on to have another child. Bereaved parents are only too well aware that the gap in their family can never be filled or the dead child replaced. But in these situations parents are more likely to have to engage in the restorative behaviour viewed by Stroebe and Schut (1999: 197–224) as being equally important as loss-oriented behaviour in contributing to a healthy outcome in situations of bereavement:

> The other children gave me a reason to go on – they still needed to be washed, dressed, fed, taken to school. They were my reason to get out of bed on those days when all I wanted to do was pull the covers over my head and be alone with my thoughts of my son who had died.
>
> (Sarah)

Perhaps older parents who are no longer directly involved in looking after their children, or no longer working, find it more difficult to achieve the necessary balance between grieving and getting involved in other activities which divert attention to other things in life. Having other children, however, can be a source of concern for many parents when a child in the family has died. Explaining to siblings what has happened is a major issue. Most parents will never have had any cause to think about how they might do this.

> What about our surviving children? How do we explain to them something we do not understand ourselves?
>
> (Louise)

While the dead child's siblings may be a reason for the parents to carry on, it may also be that parents modify the extent to which they express their grief in order to protect the other children in the family. Children are equally adept at protecting their parents and, as a result, many emotions within the family may go unexpressed. The challenge of still having to parent and deal with siblings' grief, while managing a huge loss themselves, can be enormously difficult for parents in the early days following their child's death. Responding to what can be exceptionally direct and frequently repeated questions from their other children can be particularly demanding.

The cultural background of the parents, as well as their faith and religious or spiritual belief system, will strongly influence how they deal with issues of death and dying. Given the diversity within particular faiths and cultures, it is unwise to assume how this will impact on their grief. It is also unwise to assume that faith will be a comfort at this time. For many parents their faith is indeed the very thing that gets them through the dark, awful days, weeks and months following their child's death. Others will rail at a God who could have allowed their child to die and may even experience a loss of faith which compounds the huge loss they are already facing. Brian and his wife Pat had very different responses following their daughter's death:

> I'm not a religious person, but I felt very, very angry with God. Pat started going to church, which she hadn't done before and I would drive her there in the car and wait for her. The priest said to me one time, 'Why don't you come in?' and I said, 'I don't speak to your God, because your God took my daughter.'
>
> (Brian)

For many parents, their self-esteem is crushed when their child dies. Their confidence in being able to be in control of their destiny, in their ability as a parent, is dealt a huge blow. Their heightened awareness of seemingly happy families around them only serves to increase their sense of stigma that they somehow have failed to protect their child from all harm. The parenting role is one of responsibility for their child and, regardless of the fact that death can occur no matter how vigilant and caring parents may be, parents often blame themselves and see themselves as having failed in that parental role, the endless 'if only' serving to reinforce the feelings of self-blame and guilt. Could it be that the apparent randomness of the occurrence of these events is so frightening to contemplate that assuming responsibility, however painful, affords parents more of a sense of control? The complexity of situations where a parent's actions did in some way contribute to the death of their child – for example, driving at speed, leading to an accident in which the child died – is immense. This can also be true in situations where ambivalent or negative feelings about a pregnancy preceded a baby's death, with mothers in particular feeling huge guilt:

> It was such a shock to find out I was pregnant. When our baby died, I was haunted by the fact that I had cried when I saw the result of the pregnancy test.
>
> (Angela)

Often parents are haunted by recurring thoughts of what they should or should not have done and it will complicate their grieving process, if these feelings are not given voice and worked through. Feelings of guilt and blame can also be exacerbated by others' lack of acknowledgement of the child's death, usually because people simply do not know what to say or do and consequently may tend to avoid the bereaved parent.

Parenting instincts are not extinguished by death. The role of a parent is to nurture and protect children and those instincts are likely to continue for some time after a child's death. It is not at all unusual to hear parents voice their concerns about their child being alone or being cold in their grave, or to express the very natural wish to be with their child. This seldom means they are in denial of the reality or are likely to take their own lives, although this should be explored. Most likely is that, for a period, life holds very little meaning for the parent, unable to trust a world in which something like this could happen:

> I became so fearful of life, the future, everything. Suddenly the world became a very frightening place. I felt like I had been put aboard a run-away train, against my will. It was careering down a track to a place I didn't know, a place I didn't want to go and I couldn't get off.
>
> (Jan)

'Why?' is a question that is never satisfactorily answered for parents bereaved of a child, and they are likely to engage in an endless search for meaning in a desperate attempt to make some sense of what has happened and regain some control. Yet no reason is sufficient to explain to a parent why their child had to die and no answer will ever be adequate to justify why they have to live the remainder of their lives without their child. The realization that their lives and their family are irrevocably changed can lead parents to question whether they will ever be able to learn to live again in the face of such a loss. For these parents, 'normal' life is a life that is forever changed:

> As we held her that night, we were acutely aware that nothing could ever be the same again. Up until then had been normal life and from that moment on represented our changed lives which would never feel normal again.

> (Madelaine)

Adjusting to life without their child is a monumental task for parents. Mothers and fathers have their own unique relationship to their child. The difference is seen most markedly in pregnancy loss where the mother has the unique experience of carrying the child within her and the unique bond that this physical closeness brings. Although fathers are often very involved in a pregnancy, attending scan appointments and antenatal classes, their relationship with their child is different at this stage. With a child that has lived for a time, there is likely to be less difference in the nature of the relationship each parent has with that child. However, the special meaning that child holds for each parent is unlikely to ever be exactly the same.

Differences in how the parents' grief manifests are likely to determine the way others respond to them. Mothers are frequently perceived to be the 'chief mourner' when a child dies, the father's grief often being overlooked and treated as secondary. Where mothers are regarded as having lost someone they loved, fathers often describe their experience as being treated as having lost someone they were responsible for:

> I went back to work soon after the funeral. Everyone asked how my other half was doing, but no one asked me how I was. I wanted to have a T-shirt printed with great big letters saying 'She was my daughter too'.

> (Andy)

This may result from the fact that women are more likely to be preoccupied with their dead child, to be talking and expressing their feelings and exhibiting behaviour that is more loss-oriented in nature. Women are also more likely to have the kind of relationships with friends where feelings can be shared. In contrast, men tend to behave restoratively in grief, directing their attention to things that keep them busy and distract them from feeling the pain of their loss:

> I went back to work quite quickly and started putting in more and more hours. While I was there I suppose I could pretend life was normal,

whereas when I was back home, the reminders and the grief were just everywhere.

(Phil)

Fathers can become very concerned at the intensity and duration of their partner's grief, fearing for her emotional well-being. She is usually desperate for him to share some of his feelings about their child, but he is unlikely to do this for fear of overwhelming her. As well as feeling protective towards his partner, a father may also resist talking about the child in order to protect himself and avoid confronting his painful emotions:

There was no closeness. I knew the closer I got to Pat the more she'd want to talk about it. Pat would get so frustrated with me not wanting to speak about it, but I couldn't. I couldn't face it.

(Brian)

This can be misinterpreted by their partner as uncaring, not missing or loving the child as much as they do, perhaps even as not grieving. Seldom will this ever be the case. However, this can lead to problems in their relationship which at best will be temporarily strained and at worst may be irreparably damaged, exposing the parents to further loss:

We almost split up. It wasn't that we didn't love each other; we just couldn't live with each other.

(Sue)

The all-consuming nature of grief makes it very difficult for either partner to be objective about what may be happening in their relationship, particularly in the initial stages, and at this time the couple may need the therapist to hold that observing function. The death of their child may, of course, simply exacerbate pre-existing relationship difficulties. Couples who find a way of sharing their feelings can, despite facing such immense loss, find themselves drawn together in this shared tragedy and ultimately survive with their relationship intact.

Single parents who lose a child may have no one with whom they can share their grief. If they have other children to look after, they may effectively find themselves forced into a restorative way of being that means their feelings go largely unexpressed. In this situation, counselling or attending a support group may provide the only environment in which single parents feel they can allow themselves the 'luxury' of expressing their feelings about their child's death.

The way we 'project ourselves' upon our future – our existential projects, our dreams for the future – influences our present way of life (Heidegger 1962;

Sartre 1969). When a child dies, parents' dreams are shattered. Children are our connection to the future and parents lose that future they had mapped out, together with the image they had of themselves in that future, which can now never be as they had envisaged. Where a first or only child dies, their social status and identity as parents is challenged and often their experience is of a crisis or loss of that identity. They know they are parents, but they are unlikely to be perceived as such in a world that sees them alone with no child. Celebrations such as Mother's Day and Father's Day can be particularly painful. For bereaved parents, the question so commonly asked – 'How many children do you have?' – becomes such a difficult one to answer. Do they acknowledge their dead child to almost certainly be met with an awkward silence and a swift change of subject, or if they have other children do they answer only in terms of their living children and perhaps then be left with feelings that they have somehow denied their child? What is certain is that part of the parent's identity will always be that they are the parent of their child who has died.

The therapist

There exists a general consensus that the death of a child is a particularly difficult loss to bear. Everyone tends to feel vulnerable in the face of untimely death, but when that untimely death is the death of a child, the very thing that most of us find unbearable to even contemplate is brought sharply into focus. Therapists who work with bereaved parents are likely to be put in touch with their own innermost thoughts, feelings and anxieties about their own children – those they already have, those they may hope to have in the future, the children they may not have been able to have in life for whatever reason. They are also put in touch with their own mortality and the anxiety this may provoke. We know that 'death comes to us all' but in saying this we turn death into an 'indefinite something' which does not feel personally threatening. Our clients' loss may confront us with our death as a possibility that feels real and very much our own (Heidegger 1962: 297; H. 253).

Each individual client will come from a family that has its own culture, its own way of managing issues of death and dying. As therapists, we need to work within the context and framework of that culture. This can be particularly challenging where the way in which the family reacts is alien to our own deeply held beliefs and values. Issues in relation to children and parenting tend to bring out strong reactions in all of us as to what is 'right' and appropriate. Similarly, we usually hold strong beliefs as to what is appropriate at the end of life. The combination of children and death is a potent mixture and its potential impact on the therapist should not be underestimated.

It is not at all uncommon for therapists, regardless of whether they are parents themselves or whether they have never had any children, to feel overwhelmed by the enormity of their client's loss and the rawness of the grief they witness. The emotions can be so powerful and the experiences being recounted and lived through so devastating, that parents do not know how they will survive. It can also be difficult at times for therapists to see how they can possibly survive the experience of being in such close proximity to feelings of this magnitude.

When the death of a child is the focus of the work, feelings of inadequacy abound. An existential–phenomenological stance excludes any reliance on learnt theory and skills, and the sense of security these may offer the therapist. Working with parents who have experienced this type of loss is therefore likely to challenge therapists who cannot necessarily rely on existing knowledge to steer them through this encounter. Therapists frequently feel powerless to help in the face of such a loss, mirroring their clients' sense of powerlessness in having been unable to save their child from death. Feelings of inadequacy and failure in the therapist can emanate from the recognition that this is a situation that cannot be made better, for nothing can bring the child back. This is a direct reflection of the feelings of inadequacy and failure that parents so often experience in having been unable to protect their child from illness, from harm, from death. Nothing can take away the excruciating pain which parents go through. Being in the presence of such intensity of emotion – and staying with it – is extremely demanding on the therapist.

Just as parents can experience the loss of their child in a very physical sense, it is not uncommon for therapists to experience a very physical reaction to the overwhelmingly powerful stories and emotions expressed by bereaved parents: palpitations, tightness in the chest, a constricted throat, a sickening sensation in the pit of the stomach have all been described. Therapists may be told terrible stories and hear horrifying things, with the result that they can be left with dreadful images that are difficult to erase from their mind. Confronted with the reality that a child's life can end, therapists are likely to experience periods of being considerably more fearful in relation to their own children's safety and well-being, having been exposed to parents' stories. In their therapeutic work they may come to withdraw from a genuine encounter with the client and his pain, and with their own existential vulnerability:

> Every time I saw a particular client whose teenage son had died, I became overwhelmingly tired and literally could barely keep my eyes open. It was only when my supervisor asked me, 'What is she telling you that you can't bear to hear?' that I realized the parallels in our families were just too close for comfort.
>
> (Anna)

What we as therapists can offer our clients is a normalizing of their experience in the face of what they often perceive in themselves as 'madness' and containment of the multitude of frightening and overwhelming feelings they present. But we face a number of challenges in attempting to do this. How do we offer normalization in a way that does not diminish the uniqueness of our client's experience? And how do we stay congruent and at the same time offer containment of feelings that we ourselves experience as totally over-whelming? For the therapist confronted with such situations, these can feel like mutually exclusive states, but perhaps that need not be the case:

> It mattered to me that my counsellor looked visibly moved the first time I told her how my son had died. It was the most awful thing that had ever happened in my life and seeing that she was affected somehow validated my feelings and the enormity of my loss.
>
> (Cheryl)

In situations of child death, clients may feel anger towards their therapist by virtue of the therapist's association with the organization or agency that is seen as the repository of blame or guilt for the child's death (e.g. hospital-based counselling). Hindmarch (2000: 159) also recognizes that in working to rebuild the bereaved parent's self-esteem, the therapist may for a time become the ideal parent that the client either wished they had or would like to be for their children.

The enduring nature of this type of loss has challenged conventional thinking about the process of grieving. This loss, arguably more than any other, highlights the validity of the more recent understanding of grief which recognizes the notion of 'continuing bonds'. Klass *et al.* (1996: 197) acknow-ledge that there is a continuing bond and ongoing relationship between the bereaved parents and their dead child; that death does not seem to sever this bond. Parents need to find a way to integrate their dead child into their lives, to find an appropriate emotional place for that child, which enables them to carry on functioning and living without their child, at the same time main-taining a sense of their child's presence in everyday life in a way that differs from when the child was alive.

How often are we driven as therapists to move our clients on and how does this sit with the bereaved parent's need to maintain a continuing relationship with their dead child? It is not unusual for therapists new to this work to question whether there can indeed ever be any resolution to these situ-ations of loss. The challenge for the therapist is to be able to distinguish between a continuing bond that is a healthy one and one that may represent a denial of the reality of the child's death, the latter being a significant con-tributory factor in unresolved grief. Memories of the child and rituals are important aspects of maintaining these continuing bonds. What therapists must guard against are their own assumptions or perceptions of what is appropriate. Actions such as repeated visits to a grave or leaving a child's room unchanged must be considered in the context of how the parent is functioning otherwise in life and may not in any way be indicative of an unhealthy attachment to the dead child.

Knowing ourselves, our own stories, our own triggers, can support us in this demanding work. To display congruence and empathy, we must be prepared to allow ourselves a degree of vulnerability and seek to find the mid-point between being totally invulnerable – where we will be unaffected by what we hear or witness – and being totally vulnerable – where we will have a high level of permeability and be overwhelmed by what the bereaved parent brings. Being self-aware and knowing where our vulnerabilities lie is essential in supporting parents bereaved of a child, as is good supervision.

For my own part, it was the very experience of giving birth to a stillborn son – without doubt the most significant loss of my life to date – that brought me to this work. Effectively giving birth to death effected within me an immense transformation in relation to my long-held fears of matters of death and dying, having had no previous experience of significant bereavement. My son's death enabled me to embrace this unavoidable aspect of life, rather than flee in terror from all acknowledgement of it. In the years following his death I was drawn to the field of bereavement work, having greatly valued the support I had received. My own training as a therapist was integrative. However, my experience of losing my son and confronting the questions of existence – questions of life and death and the meaning of existence – has brought the existential aspect of my therapeutic work further to the fore. It has highlighted the value of exploring, in the face of our mortality, the possibilities that lie before us and the choices we have (Heidegger 1962), and emphasized the importance of finding meaning for our losses and our lives (Frankl 1964).

It was naive, however, to imagine that experiencing the loss of one of my children would obliterate all fears for the safety and well-being of my surviving children that this work has the potential to engender. Working in this field exposes the therapist on a daily basis to the fragility of life. No amount of exposure will ever render me totally immune to the natural anxiety before death most of us carry (whether we are prepared to face up to it or not), nor to the deep-seated fear that I might lose another of my children. My own experience has, I believe, enhanced my ability for empathy and understanding, but it has also highlighted how personal an experience this is. Every parent's grief is unique. Where parallels do exist, maintaining a healthy awareness of the potential for overidentification with clients is essential. Supervision that is both challenging and supportive has been invaluable in this regard.

Involvement in this work has given meaning to my son's brief life. For a time, being engaged in work that I loved as a result of the tragedy that was his death did not rest easily and took some working through, but it has been significant in helping me integrate his loss into my life. Despite the often intolerable pain and anguish of this type of loss, parents bereaved of a child can and do survive.

References

Dickens, C. (1847) *Dombey and Son*, London: Odhams Press.

Frankl, V. (1964 [1962]) *Man's Search for Meaning*, trans. Lash, I., London: Hodder and Stoughton. (First edn 1946.)

Heidegger, M. (1962 [1927]) *Being and Time*, trans. Macquarrie, J.R. and Robinson, E., Oxford: Blackwell.

Hindmarch, C. (2000) *On the Death of a Child*, Abingdon: Radcliffe Medical Press.

Klass, D., Silverman, P. and Nickman, S. (eds) (1996) *Continuing Bonds: New Understandings of Grief*, Abingdon: Taylor and Francis.

Sartre, J.P. (1969 [1943]) *Being and Nothingness*, trans. Barnes, H., Abingdon: Routledge.

Stroebe, M. and Schut, H. (1999) The Dual Process Model of Coping with Bereavement, in *Death Studies*, 23.3: 197–224.

Stroebe, M., Stroebe, W. and Hansson, R. (1993) *Handbook of Bereavement: Theory, Research and Intervention*, Cambridge: Cambridge University Press.

THE UNCONSCIOUS REVISITED

The British School of Existential Therapy proposes a therapy that does not involve the unconscious in any way. What does that mean? It would be absurd to claim that there is no such thing as unconscious feelings and thoughts: we cannot possibly be forever conscious of all that is going on for us. What it denies is the existence of a place or system that differs from consciousness in the nature and dynamic of its content. It does not accept a system of drives, phantasies and repressed emotions, with its own rules and mechanisms, that plays a major role in our existence.

It does accept that we have thoughts, feelings, projects, memories, ways of relating towards ourselves and others of which we are not aware, because we have not chosen to shine light upon them.

Besides, Sartre asks how thoughts and feelings would become repressed. How can there be a 'censor' who is sufficiently 'conscious' to be aware of what needs to be 'unconscious' and repressed?

How then does existential therapy explain transference, projective identification, etc.? Does it deny their existence? Because existential therapy is holistic and does not separate body, mind, soul, environment, it cannot conceive of a psyche with intra-psychic and inter-psychic processes. Existential therapy does not deny the existence of certain phenomena such as the strong feelings that clients may have for their therapists. It sees them as real feelings for the therapist, which can be explored and understood in terms of the particular client's embodied being-in-the-world, present, future and past. (On an existential understanding of projective identification, see the Conclusion.)

AND WHEN THE THERAPIST OR SUPERVISOR DIES . . .

Bernice Sorensen

As therapists and supervisors, are we mindful of the existential fact that we are, each one of us, going to die and yet cannot predict the time? And are we sufficiently aware of the possible impact of our death on our clients and supervisees? This chapter explores these two questions through an enquiry into the experience of clients and therapists who have lost, through death, either their therapist or their supervisor. It also asks what we as therapists and supervisors can learn from their experience and whose responsibility it is to bring the therapist/supervisor's mortality into the therapeutic space. This research has its roots in my own sense of existential frailty. It seeks to highlight some of the choices we as therapists face as we confront our mortality, and the way these may impact on our clients and supervisees.

My interest in this topic initially grew from my own experience of being diagnosed with breast cancer in 2001, while working as a counselling trainer, supervisor and therapist. During this time I had the support of both my supervisor and therapist and made certain decisions, based on what I believed was appropriate for the people involved in my practice as well as myself. Thus I chose to tell both my counselling trainees and supervisees about my cancer, but I chose to withhold this information from my clients. These decisions were based on the fact that my prognosis was good and therefore I believed my clients did not need to know my diagnosis, or experience the anxiety I thought that might engender. In hindsight, I am sure many were aware something was going on when I became increasingly tired through six weeks of radiotherapy, but few commented other than to say I looked washed out. Conversely my counselling trainees were told about my visits and treatment and knew each time I had to go into hospital for an operation. They remained supportive, but again in hindsight I did not give them as much opportunity to explore the effect this may have had on them as I think I would now. Finally, I also informed my supervisees. Some chose to end, despite the fact that I continued to work with minimal disruption, but the word cancer, for some, had too many negative connotations. At the time I felt confused and hurt by their response, but now I understand it much more. Others stayed, I suspect more out of loyalty than for any opportunity I offered to use the situation therapeutically. In other words, I do not feel I dealt particularly well with any of these groups with what, for me, was a life-changing episode. Subsequently, I have found similar resonance in the difficulties other people have had in knowing what to do for the best in similar circumstances. In doing this research, I have heard and read a good deal of material that has certainly influenced my practice. I hope that in future I will be more mindful and more prepared concerning the impact of terminal illness and death on the therapeutic alliance.

The Schopenhauer Cure

I describe myself as an integrative psychotherapist, as my trainings have incorporated psychodynamic, humanistic and existential modalities. Having always enjoyed Yalom's fictional therapeutic writings, I read *The Schopenhauer Cure* (2006) in the hope of receiving some interesting insights into the impact of a facilitator's death on his therapeutic group. Despite the fact that this is a very entertaining and informative book on a number of different levels, I was disappointed when the book ended with the death of the therapist. Yalom concentrates primarily on the ongoing impact of the facilitator's diagnosis on his group, rather than the effect on the participants, once the facilitator had died. My research examines the impact of the death of a therapist or supervisor on clients and supervisees.

The research

In order to understand people's experience of losing a therapist or a supervisor through death, I sent out information about the research to colleagues who had suffered such a loss or knew others who had. I received a total of 22 replies, many from therapists who had themselves lost a therapist, but the majority (17) were from people who had lost a supervisor, which gave an interesting juxtaposition of experience. I am indebted to Diane Voller (2003) whose research offers an interesting parallel to my own. Her research was solely on clients whose therapists had become ill, and many of her participants were themselves therapists. Eight clusters of themes emerged from her findings about a client's experience of a therapist's illness, briefly summarized here:

1   The therapist's avoidance or denial of illness (although the client often sensed a problem).
2   The powerful impact on clients of such an experience.
3   Negative feelings towards the therapist, including anger, guilt and selfishness.

194

4 A reversal of roles which, for the client, could be experienced on a continuum from disorientating to damaging.
5 Clients' questioning of trust in the therapeutic contract.
6 Clients' parallel life experiences of ill health, loss or abandonment.
7 The question of clients' own mortality, brought into sharp relief by their therapists' experience.
8 A sense of isolation for the client whose therapist was less or no longer available.

Many of these themes emerged in my own research, as I shall demonstrate below, and applied to both the loss of a supervisor and a therapist. I have loosely themed my findings under three headings: the impact of death or knowledge of a terminal illness on the therapeutic/supervisory relationship; opportunities to prepare; and how the experience has influenced practice.

The impact of death or knowledge of a terminal illness on the therapeutic/supervisory relationship

Diana Voller carried out her research as a consequence of her own experience of her therapist's illness. The research completed, she thought the therapist had fully recovered, but subsequently discovered that she had since died. She told me:

> My experience of losing my therapist was one of the most profound experiences of my life. At the time, I was extremely sad and angry, resentful and felt abandoned and relieved.

This mixture of emotion was exemplified in my co-researchers' responses, not surprisingly perhaps, as death nearly always produces paradoxical feelings. These include shock and disbelief, anger and resentment, guilt, depression and withdrawal, acceptance and resolution. However, both the context of the death and the unique relationship (whether it be therapist, supervisor or group facilitator) can be particularly powerful because of the nature of the investment placed on them by the survivor. Dilemmas manifest themselves even before death and are illustrated here by Andrea, whose supervisor became ill and subsequently died:

> I had been in supervision with him for a year when I was informed by telephone that he had broken his hip and would be unable to meet with me that week. I had a horrible foreboding that he might die and I was reminded of my grief for my uncle, who had died a few years previously following a broken hip. On the other hand, I knew others who had recovered from similar injuries at similar ages. I knew the importance of

195

the patient getting back on his or her feet as soon as possible and my fears grew as he suffered in hospital. I kept in telephone contact with those who visited him often, but did not visit myself. I wanted to see him, but I didn't want to intrude. I thought about him a lot and I wrote to him and sent a card. It seemed so little, but I also did not want to impose on him. Although I felt very close to him in our supervisory relationship, nevertheless this was a professional relationship and I felt that I just didn't know him well enough to visit him in hospital.

(Andrea)

We see Andrea experiencing many of the experiences that Voller (2003) describes: a sense of foreboding of the death; the parallel experience of her uncle; wanting to visit, but fearing intrusion; and finally a sense of isolation with the experience. Unfortunately, like so many of my co-researchers, Andrea was not immediately informed about the death and only learned about it when she returned to college: 'I was numb with shock. I still feel dizzy when I think of the shock.' The shock of a belated discovery exists even where there has been the opportunity to say goodbye, as Celia describes:

I know that the ending was acknowledged fully on both our sides and that I wrote him a letter of thanks. I knew that his illness could lead to his death but somehow imagined he might have many years in declining health, rather than an early death. It was some years after that, when I found myself in the company of one of my co-workers from the agency, that I discovered that my supervisor had died. I remember feeling very hurt that I had not been informed – it seemed very uncaring not to let me have such an important piece of news. Somehow though, I think I might have known anyway – I had deduced it and somehow accepted this – but it was the retrospective discovery of it that somehow threw me.

(Celia)

Celia went on to explain how hurt she still felt, and angry that the agency had not informed her. Even though she had seen a 'Sold' sign on his house and guessed he might have died rather than moved, she still felt very upset and taken aback that she had not been included in knowing about his death. Justine also experienced a similar sense of trauma when her therapist died, despite having finished working together:

The death was sudden, and unexpected. I was glad we'd finished and had a chance to say goodbye. He had been my first therapist . . . and I'd been to his wedding . . . So I felt I'd lost an important influence in my life.

I dream about him from time to time, and if he'd been alive, I would have been back to see him.

(Justine)

The significance of the role of both therapist and supervisor is illustrated by all my co-researchers. Anna, now retired, remembered that as a trainee generic case-worker she was 'abandoned' by her therapist, only learning of his move when she knocked at the door for her appointment. Despite the fact that he had warned her that he would only be available for three months, it did nothing to allay her devastation:

Although I 'worked through it' subsequently and I now can only imagine the distress I know I then felt and acted, I am sure that it left me deter-mined never to strongly attach to a therapist again. It would have helped if he had told me himself – even by phone – but I do not think the early warning of the probability of departure helped at all.

(Anna)

Although this therapist was not ill and did not die, the impact of the sudden loss of relationship had, as we can see, an enormous impact with regard to trust. Kate talks about this relational aspect further, concerning her super-visor. She felt anger and guilt when her supervisor finished because of her partner's ill health:

The first time I lost my supervisor was a shocking experience as my supervision was terminated by letter with immediate effect. I felt angry at being abandoned, then felt guilty for being angry and rationalized the experience because of the situation. My rationalizing went something like this, 'How can you be angry when someone is very ill and needing the care of your supervisor? You are a mature adult and this is not the end of the world. You can find another supervisor.' I then suppressed the angry needy part of me and reverted to defensive strategies of coping and cutting off the pain of abandonment. It rekindled my rage towards 'bad' mother, by whom I felt abandoned. It reinforced my belief that I had to be self-sufficient and rely on myself and it reinforced my mistrust of powerful figures. I felt unable to look for a supervisor and was unwilling to be vulnerable with such a person. For about three years after this, I relied solely on peer supervision and I set up three lots of peer supervision, so that, if one or even two didn't work out, there would be someone there for me.

(Kate)

Like Anna, Kate's loss prevented her from trusting in the therapeutic/ supervisory alliance. Her own personal history came into play, seeing her supervisor as her abandoning mother and leaving her to feel she must cope on her own. Similarly, Chloe's supervisor became ill just before her move from London. Despite the fact that Chloe would have ended anyway, having the matter taken out of her control mirrored past events and made the whole experience very painful:

> In the week I was due for supervision, a friend of hers telephoned me to say she was ill and would therefore not be able to see me. I knew my supervisor had problems with her back and I assumed something connected with that had got worse. We met about a month after her initial cancellation . . . and she said she would be closing her practice for a while. I still did not take in that this was our last session, until I mentioned something about getting in touch again. Only then did I realize that this was the end. I felt stunned, stupefied, not really able to grasp what felt to me like an unexpected ending. I had so not wanted to understand that this, like the end of my marriage, was for ever . . . There was something dreadfully ironic about being confronted once again with not being in control of what happens in relationships . . . As I sat on the bus going home, I felt disembodied, all feeling and no substance.
>
> (Chloe)

It is almost as if the therapeutic relationship parallels issues of loss in our own lives. This was also noted by Voller (2003): 'The therapeutic relationship can embody what we may have entered into the therapy relationship to avoid.'

Another interesting aspect arising from my interviews is the incidence of multiple losses of therapist/supervisors to the same person. Three of my co-researchers suffered multiple losses. Lisa lost two supervisors through death. The first loss, although traumatic, was a 'gift'. She describes her supervisor's attitude as 'beyond-the-call-of-duty, unto death'. Even though it was harrowing at times, they were both able to share the responsibility of keeping the 'dying' in the relationship. So too with her next supervisor who was 87 when Lisa began supervision with him. She had been mindful of his age and, after six months, realized that she had been protecting him; 18 months later their supervisory relationship was terminated due to his admission to hospital. When I interviewed Lisa, her newest supervisor was undergoing treatment for cancer and once again she had needed to find another supervisor temporarily.

Arianna has also experienced multiple losses. Her first supervisor, a man, died in 1990, three years after starting her own practice. She stopped working for a time and felt 'very numb' but, she says, she still carries him 'in my head'. The second death happened in 1996 – a tutor and supervisor the same age as herself. The third supervisor had an accident and is still in hospital on the long journey of recovery. Arianna feels that this one may have had less impact on her simply because she now has several different avenues to use for supervision. One thing is clear, therapist or supervisor loss has an enormous impact on the client/supervisee. The death of a therapist or supervisor confronts clients/supervisees with their own mortality and may awaken their anxiety (Heidegger 1962). In addition, without the support of the therapeutic/supervisory relationship they are faced with having to rely on themselves for exploring their choices and taking decisions (even if it is only to find another therapist/supervisor or form of support). The loss of a therapist/supervisor confronts clients/supervisees with their own existential isolation, freedom and responsibility.

Opportunities to prepare

Lisa was able to say goodbye to her supervisor in the hospice. This transformed her loss into a 'gift'. Yet, even where the ending was complete (Celia, Justine, Lisa), the loss of the actual person was still profound. Where clients/supervisees did not have a prepared ending and were not informed of the death, as in Andrea's case, it was much worse. Some felt that although opportunities to prepare had been available they had been obscured by confused boundaries or by either party's denial of the situation. June had first seen her therapist as a supervisor, and continued working with him until he died:

I had a very enmeshed relationship with my therapist who saw me as 'the daughter I always wanted, but never had'. I started work with him, as a supervisee, when he was 76 (I didn't know his age when I started and he seemed much younger) and continued until he died, suddenly from a heart attack, when he was 86. During the ten-year period that I knew him our relationship transformed from supervisee, to client attending three to five times a week, to friend, to carer of him and his wife, who died four months before him. When he died, I was devastated, losing my 'Good Father' and my secure base. During the course of our work together, he had often talked about the likelihood that he would die before me. I was always very fearful and tearful when he broached the subject. He had wanted to prepare me, but I had been in denial. That ten-year period of my life, and his death, changed the direction and the decisions that I made about my career, marriage and spiritual path. It was both healing and wounding.

(June)

June's therapist attempted to prepare her for his death, but the enmeshed relationship prevented this in any real way. Megan's supervisor chose to keep her cancer to herself and Megan knew nothing about it until she died. She now feels resentful at this lack of preparation:

> After a few years, my supervisor began to cancel sessions and some-times conduct supervisory sessions lying down. When I enquired after her health, she always told me she had a chronic back condition. I found it difficult to ask other people who knew her what might be the matter, as I felt bound by my loyalty to her and the confidentiality agreement we had made. Out of the blue, it seemed to me, I heard from my manager, that she had died; she spoke about the arrangements for the funeral. She had died of cancer, with which she had been battling for many years. The immediate impact was one of extreme shock. This was followed by anger and feeling deceived and let down. When I went to the funeral, I was amazed by how many people attended and the other aspects of her that I had never known. She had existed for me in an enclosed bubble.
>
> (Megan)

Therapists usually play a significant role in a client's training to be a therapist. Similarly, a supervisor plays an important role with trainees or newly qualified therapists, holding a significant position on a personal and professional level. Ella's therapist was also her group therapy leader and she had no preparation at all for his death. She was able to mourn with her group but the group disbanded after a year of a new facilitator:

> I had been with my therapist for over a year when I learnt that he was dying. During my time in therapy, he had encouraged me to train to become a therapist. I started and loved it, but towards the end of my first year of training, he became ill and died about a month later. I was both devastated and angry, as I felt abandoned and thought I would never be able to continue without his support. I had been seeing him once a week, one to one and was also in group therapy with him, so the loss of two sessions a week was tremendous. I knew he was ill, but was assured that it was all under control. A phone call cancelling my next session came very unexpectedly and a further message a few weeks later confirmed that he was dying. No preparation at all, plus denial on my part that this could be happening.
>
> (Ella)

Having an opportunity to say goodbye, even if only after death, seems particularly important. The opportunity for this is usually a result of other people's involvement in the therapist/supervisor's life and practice. Julia's supervisor went into hospital but she was kept informed and was able to go to his funeral and memorial service. As she had already chosen a new supervisor who knew him, she was able to talk about him and appreciate their work together:

> I fully expected he would recover until the very end. I did not go to see him. I was lucky, in that I knew someone else who I had earmarked as a supervisor, should I ever need to change. On a personal and professional level his death was shocking. I grieved deeply for him and thought about him all the time for about a year. I still want to talk to him – he had a range of intellect, understanding and approachability that I deeply admired. He changed the way I worked as a counsellor and had a lasting impact on me. His death did not alter the profound difference he made to me. I went to his funeral and memorial service, which allowed me to say goodbye. My new supervisor, who was also his supervisee and friend, and I spent a lot of time talking about him and still speak about him often – reflecting how he might have addressed an issue.
>
> (Julia)

Perhaps the most poignant story was from Maja. After 18 months, her therapist told her that she had had breast cancer in the past and now had metastases and required more treatment. Role reversal is clearly seen in Maja's story, as are the difficulties she had to attend to when she realized she could no longer burden her therapist with her issues. However, at the end, Maja was able to care for her in a way which facilitated closure for both of them:

> I was completely devastated – we had four sessions to work through this before she went for treatment. It's still hard to write about it in coherent sentences. Here are some words – sad, angry, pissed off, why her?, it's not fair, filled with dread, no control of the ending. We talked about another therapist and I knew I needed to continue to see someone. I was gently handed over to someone who she respected as a therapist and who was also a friend of hers. There was a feeling of safety in this. We agreed that I would return to seeing her when she had finished her treatment – something which I really hung on to for the next six months. My 'new, temporary' therapist was great and I was able to talk freely with her about her. I did go back after six months, but she told me that she was still ill and did not know what the prognosis was – I continued to see her for some time but it wasn't the same. I was a qualified nurse by now and there were issues of not wanting to 'burden' someone I knew was very

unwell. I tried to talk about this with her, but I never resolved it. In the end she had to stop practising. I went back to the temporary therapist who became permanent and is still there!!!

One day I was doing an extra shift in the radiology department. An ambulance crew arrived with a woman who was very unwell and required a palliative treatment – it was my former therapist. Her partner was with her. She was in my care for about four hours. She was conscious and knew me. I had the privilege of using my skills to care for her in that short time period. It felt very odd, me being in the helping role with her. All the time I was looking after her, I knew that this was the last time that I would see her and I was struggling with the right words to say to thank her for helping me face some real demons. I was able to hold her hand, look into her eyes and say a thank you I truly meant. She went back to the hospice and died early the next day.

(Maja)

How can the experience of losing a therapist/supervisor through illness or death influence therapeutic practice?

Most of my co-researchers for this chapter are therapists and supervisors. One might expect that the death of a therapist/supervisor would be more easily managed by such a group, but both my own and Voller's research show this not to be the case. As therapists, our own therapist and/or supervisor usually has a valuable place in our lives, and this may need to be more fully acknowledged by existential therapists. Much has been written about the particular quality of the therapeutic relationship in existential therapies and the potentially transformative power of such a relationship (van Deurzen 1998; Mearns and Cooper 2005; Spinelli 2006, etc.), yet perhaps insufficient attention has been paid to our existential needs for attachment (e.g. Yalom 1980). The reality is that the illness or death of a supervisor or therapist has a huge impact, facing us as it does with our own vulnerability and mortality, our professional and existential isolation, our freedom of choice and our responsibility. We inevitably invest a great deal in the person of the therapist/ supervisor and find it extremely difficult to accept their vulnerability and the change of status which illness engenders. Similarly, awareness of the therapist's ill health and mortality changes the therapeutic contract, even to the point of a role reversal. This can be very traumatic for clients or supervisees and inhibit their use of the therapeutic/supervisory alliance. On the one hand, they may try and protect the therapist/supervisor, yet feel abandoned and vulnerable, or they may try to normalize the situation, or even deny what is going on. However, denial by either party is often manifested in dreams, premonitions and forebodings. The person surviving the death of the therapist/supervisor is left with a variety of feelings on the grieving continuum. Clearly, some co-researchers had not come to a place of integration and I believe this underlies the diversity in the following statements regarding practice.

I asked my co-researchers if their own experience had impacted on what they felt they might do if they were to be diagnosed with a terminal illness. Interestingly, not everyone had reflected on this until I posed the question, although some had put procedures into place for certain situations, such as an accident. First is Anna a senior retired practitioner:

> I am mortified to report that, when I was in practice, I do not think I did discuss the possibility of temporary/permanent inability to continue the contract – either with clients or supervisees. That, despite the fact that at the end I was into my very early seventies. I did have a list of clients and supervisees with essentials – phone, address, short note as to how they should be informed and the likelihood of them needing face-to-face or phone support. I gave this to a consenting colleague to take responsibility should anything happen to me and I kept it up carefully, each time I was going away on a break.
>
> (Anna)

This was the most common response, while other people took this further by having a therapeutic will which stated how they wanted their clients to be contacted, how to dispose of clients' notes, etc. When it came to actually talking about death, people working from an existential perspective said they brought up this issue regularly, but differently:

> As an 'existential' therapist there is an emphasis on acceptance of contingency, uncertainty, insecurity, anxiety, limitations, death, etc. which is implicit or at times explicit. If I had a terminal illness (don't we all?!) and was having to finish working with clients/supervisees, I would discuss it with them fully/frequently (what it means for them, me breaking our agreement, having agreed it is for them to decide on ending, my death, their death, etc., etc.) and depending on their needs make provision for them and invite them to my funeral?
>
> (Sienna)

> I work as an existentialist and I talk about death all the time. My husband died recently and I had to cancel all my client work. I am presently in New Zealand for three and a half months and my clients and supervisees have had to find alternatives. I could be of no help to them other than to let them know what had happened. It is life – it is what happens – we

have to get on with it. I hope that I may work with at least some of them again – but who knows.

(Julia)

Many also said it was not possible to prepare clients or supervisees for death. However, there was a general consensus from people who had been through the experience of losing a therapist/supervisor, that having someone who could take on one's therapeutic work was beneficial to the clients/supervisees involved. On a more personal level, some people spoke about how they would like to inform their clients/supervisees themselves and how that could be managed, raising issues of congruence and authenticity:

If I found myself in this situation, I hope I would be able to be authentic, open and straightforward in my communication to my clients – and that together we could look at the impact it would have, what would need to happen next, etc.

I would hope to have the time (medically speaking) to let them know personally. I have given my supervisor a list of my clients' names and numbers, in the case of my death. However, if I was ill, but knew I was dying, I would hope to be able to speak to these clients myself. I am saying this at a time when I am healthy and well!

In all honesty, I think this is very hard to predict. I know what I would like to think I would do . . .! I would like to tell my clients and supervisees my situation; hold in mind and constantly monitor the effect it may have on our working alliance and the balance of power, as well as the relational changes this may make. I would also need to be mindful of the effect of the treatments and whether I wanted, or could continue, to work. I am also aware of how little I use disclosure in my practice and how hard it would be for me to bring any illness and diagnosis that I may have into the counselling relationship. Thinking about this alone has alerted me to issues of power and its close proximity to my interpretation of congruence. This is indeed very interesting!

Partly, I think, I would hope to work through to an ending and that I would be able to bear the rage of my client/supervisee and that we could experience the loss together. But of course I might not be physically or emotionally capable of doing this. As friends and colleagues experience illness, retirement and death, I realize more and more that it may not be possible to end well; I realize that clients and supervisees may feel angry and abandoned, as I felt, and guilty and all those confused feelings, and it may not be possible to work through it, even partially. I hope, because of this experience of mine, that I would be aware of all the confusion of feelings that my clients might have, and be able to offer them an opportunity to express something of this, whilst acknowledging the universality of death, chronic illness, ageing and other unpredictabilities in life.

Final considerations

A piece of research carried out by Kathy Raffles (2004) on the issue of therapists' fitness to practice (FtP) highlighted that practitioners are not always able to self-regulate 'in times of stress or crisis'. Her research was prompted by her own experience of illness and the necessity to close down her practice. In doing so, she realized how little guidance and support is available from professional bodies. Her research with other practitioners who had found themselves in a similar situation demonstrated the dilemmas around acting professionally and ethically, while attempting to face personal vulnerability. Her recommendations led her to conclude, among other things, that: 'In addition to future regulatory conditions, as practitioners are bound by requirements relating to their respective professional body, it would be best practice for each body to have their own version of what constitutes FtP' (Raffles 2004).

Ultimately perhaps, our professional organizations would provide information to help us make decisions concerning whether, what, when and how to tell clients and supervisees about illness and impending death (though this may not sit comfortably with an existential position!). General guidance would also be immensely helpful on the practicalities of such things as a therapeutic will. My co-researchers' experiences have helped them reflect on their own 'fitness to practice' in the event of future crisis, in particular illness and impending death. Although painful, it was a profound experience for them all in different ways. I have also reflected on my own experience and realized how difficult or even impossible it is to get it 'right'. There are so many dilemmas. However, what seems to emerge from this research is that preparation, contingency plans and an acknowledgement of our own vulnerability make a significant difference to clients and supervisees:

My therapist died only 18 months ago, it probably crosses my mind most days even now. For me it wasn't a discrete experience, more of a process. Now I feel glad and grateful and it's had a lasting impact: to have had the therapeutic experience I did, to have had that time with her, I can see things more from her point of view and am more understanding of why our ending was as it was. I also can understand my part in it and am less blaming of her for withdrawing from me and realizing that I also had difficulty confronting it. At the time, I was just devastated, upset, angry, and not in a position to reflect in the way I can now. As a result of this experience, I have more respect for the profound nature of what occurs in therapy relationships and am more tentative in my work. I think by 'tentative' I mean that I am more attentive to making sure it is grounded in existential awareness, i.e. that I do not inadvertently set up an illusion with clients of safety/continuity that, being human, I cannot possibly guarantee or sustain.

(Diane)

References

Heidegger, M. (1962 [1927]) *Being and Time*, trans. Macquarrie, J.R. and Robinson, E., Oxford: Blackwell.

Mearns, D. and Cooper, M. (2005) *Working at Relational Depth in Counselling and Psychotherapy*, London: Sage.

Raffles, K. (2004) *Fitness to Practice*, unpublished doctoral thesis, London, Metanoia.

Spinelli, E. (2006 [1997]) *Tales of Un-knowing: Therapeutic Encounters from an Existential Perspective*, Ross-on-Wye: PCCS Books.

van Deurzen, E. (1998) *Paradox and Passion in Psychotherapy: An Existential Approach to Therapy and Counselling*, Chichester: Wiley.

Voller, D. (2003) *The Client's Experience of Illness in the Therapist*, unpublished MA dissertation, London, Regent's College.

Yalom, I. (1980) *Existential Psychotherapy*, New York: Basic Books.

—— (2006) *The Schopenhauer Cure*, New York: Harper Perennial.

PHENOMENOLOGICAL

Phenomenological is an adjective that is often hyphenated with 'existential'. Yet, in my experience, even existential therapists are frequently unclear about its meaning. For Husserl, the father of Phenomenology, it is both a philosophy and a method. As a philosophy, phenomenology claimed to be *the* philosophy of knowledge: it aimed to explore the essential structures of all conscious experiences and the contents of these experiences. This meaning does not concern us here.

As a method, phenomenology is the method of choice of existential philosophers and therapists: it seeks to find out 'what it's really like' rather than depending on learnt theory and assumptions (e.g. 'grief theory'). It is characterized by a return to phenomena as they appear to us, a return 'to the things themselves' (without assuming that something more important or more real stands behind them); and it describes these phenomena in such a way as to clarify their essential meaning. By describing the experience of, e.g. losing a child, getting a diagnosis of HIV, becoming a refugee from violence etc., the contributors to this book are being 'phenomenological'. They are seeking to offer the essential meaning of these experiences.

There are two distinct phenomenological methods. Husserl's method ('transcendental phenomenology') involves a process of 'reduction'. Reduction here does not mean 'making smaller' but 'bringing back' to the observing self, temporarily divorced from the world with its scientific viewpoint, its assumptions and influences. Spinelli (1989) advocates a Husserlian phenomenological method for existential therapy.

Heidegger altered Husserl's phenomenological method considerably. Its aim was no longer to describe our mental operations and their objects, but human existence and its world. So, far from 'bracketing' the world like Husserl, Heidegger's method of 'hermeneutic phenomenology' enjoins us to be aware of ourselves as being-in-the-world in our work; to use it carefully as clues and starting points for further enquiries. Hans Cohn (1997, 2002) favours such a Heideggerian method, as do, explicitly or implicitly, most of the contributors to this book.

13

DIALOGUES

Buber, Rogers, Lévinas and the therapeutic relationship

Laura Barnett

Through their dialogues, this chapter looks at three thinkers at the margins of existential philosophy and therapy who revolutionized the way we look at relationships and at the other: Martin Buber, Emmanuel Lévinas and Carl Rogers. Although Buber's *I and Thou* (1996) is familiar to many, I shall offer a brief summary of Buber's thought before turning to his dialogues with Rogers and Lévinas.

Martin Buber (1878–1965)

There are two main strands to Buber's thought – it is a meditation on both human nature (a 'philosophical anthropology', a search for an ontology of man) and on man's relation to God. Fundamental to his view of man are the two poles of 'distance' and 'relation': we need to set others and the world at a distance to be able to observe, engage with and relate to them. There are two ways in which we relate to others and to the world around us: we can relate to the other as to an object (observing, experiencing, using), thus maintaining that 'primal' distance; or else we can seek, with our whole being, to relate to the other, while affirming him in his otherness. The latter kind of relationship, Buber argues, is what defines us as 'persons' rather than mere 'individuals'.

Buber encapsulated these two attitudes in the two 'primary words' *I–It* and *I–Thou*. It should be stressed that 'Thou' is the 'familiar' form of the personal pronoun (German 'Du', French 'tu'); and that Buber is not saying that we relate as I–It towards objects/animals/nature and I–Thou towards men. It is a matter of our personal attitude: 'To man the world is twofold in accordance with his twofold attitude' (Buber 1996: 48). For Buber, these two different attitudes to the world and the other are not psychological dispositions, but ontological[1] dimensions and ontic possibilities of man and 'the between';

they represent the 'two poles of humanity'. Buber argues that we are constantly in a 'double movement' of 'estrangement' from and 'turning' to 'the primal Source': 'every isolated *Thou* is bound to enter the chrysalis state of the *It* in order to take wings anew (Buber 1996: 128).

For Buber, God cannot be reached by looking away from the world or staring at it, but only through our everyday, embodied living, in relation, in the world. This is where the two strands of Buber's thought merge, for: 'Every particular *Thou* is a glimpse through to the eternal *Thou*; by means of every particular *Thou* the primary word addresses the eternal *Thou*' (Buber 1996: 99). The two strands of philosophical anthropology and relation to God also come together in Buber's concepts of 'destiny' and 'meaning'. 'The world . . . is divine destiny. There is divine meaning in the life of the world, of man, of human persons, of you and me' (Buber 1996: 108). Far from implying that man need only stand by and fatalistically let life take its course, it is a philosophy of engagement with life and of decisive, 'effective action'. The free man 'believes in destiny, and believes that it stands in need of him . . . it awaits him, he must go to it' (Buber 1996: 81).

The 1957 Buber–Rogers dialogue

In 1957, Buber gave a series of lectures in the USA to psychotherapists and others, which culminated in a now famous dialogue with Carl Rogers, given before an audience of 400 people. (References to Rogers and Buber in this dialogue will be given as D followed by the page number from Anderson and Cissna 1997.)

Carl Rogers needs no introduction among therapists. With his emphasis on the 'core conditions' of effective moments in therapy, he introduced to the therapeutic world a 'person-centred' approach to therapy. In 1959, he was one of the speakers at the Symposium on Existential Psychology (May 1961: 85–93).

Buber studied psychiatry for three semesters under celebrated professors including Wundt and Bleuler, as he 'wanted to know about man . . . in the *so-called* pathological state' and examine the possibility of establishing 'the real relation between what we call a sane man and a pathological man' (D: 20–21). He followed with interest the development of psychoanalysis and of a new breed of therapists who seemed less theory-driven and more concerned with the therapeutic relationship itself (Binswanger, Trüb, Boszormenyi-Nagy, Farber and Rogers). What particularly attracted other therapists to Buber was his elaboration of what constitutes an I–Thou dialogical relation.

Buber and Rogers both firmly believe in the healing power of 'dialogue' and 'meeting', as both the means and the goal of therapy (Buber 1999d: 242; Rogers' core condition 1, 1990a: 221; goal 1990b: 419; 1990c: 179). While they both agree that we live in an I–It world and cannot possibly avoid it, even in therapy, they try to avoid an I–It type of therapeutic relationship – a theory-bound approach, observing, analysing, labelling the other, applying learnt methods. They value the therapist's presence and 'attitude' above the use of techniques and skills (Buber 1999d: 237; Rogers' core conditions 3, 4 and 5, 1990a: 221).

I would like to focus on what Buber and Rogers see as three of the characteristics of 'I–Thou moments' and 'effective moments in therapy' respectively: namely, 'making present', 'inclusion' and 'mutuality' (Buber), and 'empathy', 'transparency' (later named 'congruence') and 'equality' (Rogers).

In reply to Rogers' 'impertinent' question 'How have you . . . gained such an understanding of the human individual, without being a psychotherapist?' (D: 17), Buber disclosed the deep influence on him of the First World War and the murder of one of his close friends. He had found himself imagining it concretely, 'not in an optical way alone, but . . . with my body' (D: 23). He called it 'imagining the real'. It was a 'decisive' experience for Buber: 'I felt, "Oh, something has been done to me" ' (D: 24). There is, however, a similar way of being towards the other that can be cultivated. Buber used the expression 'making present'; Rogers later called it 'empathy' (although not at the time of the dialogue). For both thinkers, it involves stepping into the other person's shoes, as it were, while keeping a sense of one's own identity. Both also stress the significance for the client of realizing that the therapist is attempting to view things from within his experience (Buber 1999a: 15; Rogers' core condition 6, 1990a: 221).

Buber and Rogers both speak of a mutuality of effective change in such situations. We cannot enter a relation with the hope of the other changing without expecting to be changed ourselves. For Buber, the I–Thou relation, as we saw, is an experience of mutuality. However, when it comes to 'professional relations' such as psychotherapy and teaching, Buber sees limits to that mutuality – as indeed does Rogers (Anderson and Cissna 1997: 30).[2]

The psychotherapeutic relationship is intrinsically an unequal situation, Buber argues, for the other has come to you for help; there is an inequality of roles, function and power. Besides, whereas you can try and see things 'from his side' as well as your own ('inclusion'), he can only see them from his own (i.e. he cannot practise 'inclusion'), he cannot see you and 'cannot have or give' 'this kind of detached presence' (D: 35).

> *Buber*: You are not equals and cannot be. . . . I see, you *mean* being on the same plane, but you cannot be (D: 38).
>
> *Rogers*: Well, what you've said certainly stirs up lots of reactions in me (D: 39).

Rogers argues that the client's way of looking at his experience, however distorted, has equal 'authority' and 'validity' with the therapist's own (D: 41); a view that Friedman, the moderator here, later expressed concisely as 'no voice is without value, no witness without reality' (Friedman 1992: 121). He adds that whereas, from the outside, 'in the world of I–It', the therapeutic relationship may appear to be an unequal one, from within, it 'is something immediate, equal, a meeting of two persons on an equal basis' (D: 45).

> *Buber*:   Hmm. Now, Dr Rogers, this is the first point where we must say to one another, 'We disagree.'
> *Rogers*:   Okay (D: 46).

And yet their views are not mutually contradictory here. It is interesting to note how, in what we could expect to be a paradigmatic Buberian 'dialogue', Friedman, a Buberian par excellence, does not practise 'inclusion' and repeatedly misrepresents Rogers' views, and how Buber and Rogers can miss each other at times (e.g. re: equality; transparency; Rogers' unusual use of 'reciprocal'; Buber referring to Rogers' 'method'). There are, however, points on which Buber and Rogers do hold opposing beliefs: e.g. regarding the possibility of a personal dialogue – one that Rogers fully endorses and Buber cannot accept, since to his mind (but not to Rogers') it lacks the essential element of 'surprise' (D: 69–73).

A truer dialogue develops around Rogers' core belief in man's 'self-actualizing tendency' – one in which Buber and Rogers listen to each other, hear the similarity of their views and meet despite their 'somewhat different' perspectives:

> *Rogers*:   When you get to what is deepest in the individual, that's the very aspect that can most be trusted to be constructive or to tend toward socialization (D: 80).
> *Buber*:   I would put it in a somewhat different manner (D: 81). I'm interested . . . in the so-called bad, problematic [person] . . . if I come near to the reality of this person, I experience it as a *polar* reality (D: 82). For what we may call the good, is always only direction. Not a substance (D: 85).

From a psychotherapeutic perspective, Buber's 'confirmation' is close to Rogers' 'acceptance' (later 'unconditional positive regard'). However, Buber understands 'acceptance' as referring to the person as he now is and 'confirmation' as accepting him in his potentialities, whereas Rogers uses the same word 'acceptance' for both. This difference is small, despite the vehemence with which Buber expressed it (D: 94–95). On the other hand, 'confirmation' is coloured by Buber's religious convictions, bringing an additional element into the therapeutic relationship. For 'confirming' means 'I can recognize in him . . . more or less, the person he has been . . . *created* to become' (D: 91).

The dialogue ends with another instance of 'mismeeting'. Buber misquotes Rogers, replacing Rogers' 'person' with 'individual'. He then sets off at a tangent on Jungian individuation and concludes 'I'm *against* individuals and *for* persons' (D: 104). Rogers' response 'correct' sounds like the modern-day frustrated, misunderstood teenager's 'Whatever!' Although there was much ground for celebrating commonality, sadly, a repeated lack of 'inclusion' gave rise to misunderstandings and did not allow dialogue, such as they valued it, to develop fully.

Emmanuel Lévinas (1905–1995)

A Lithuanian Jew, Lévinas attended both Husserl's and Heidegger's lectures before emigrating to France. Lévinas repeatedly acknowledges his 'still now irresistible' admiration for Heidegger, while condemning the latter's unforgivable allegiance to National Socialism, 'which nothing can ever dissipate' (EN: 220).[3] Lévinas' philosophy can be viewed as a response to Husserl and Heidegger and a meditation on biblical texts, in the aftermath of the shoah (see note 23, p. 35), in which most of his family were murdered. Heidegger never engaged with Lévinas or his work. What concerns us here is Lévinas' response to two major themes of Heidegger's *Being and Time* – that human beings are unique among beings in that they can question themselves about their own being; and that it is 'death' that 'individuates' a person (see pp. 13–15 or 'Authenticity', p. 117).

Lévinas' crucial claim is that what leads a human being to question his 'essence'[4] is the appearance of fundamental otherness in the world, of *alterity* – the otherness of 'the feminine', of 'filiality', death, infinity or, more concretely, of the other human being before me. Lévinas focuses on the otherness of the other, as it is manifested in the face, *le visage*, of the other before me.

When I look at the face[5] before me, I can either observe its features, or I can respond to the way it calls unto me: in the face before me, I may then see the 'Stranger', 'vulnerable', 'naked' and 'poor', yet 'commanding me' and 'teaching me' how to respond. In my freedom, yet without any willing or choosing on my part, I have now become 'responsible' for him, unto death. I cannot hand over this responsibility for him to anyone and in that sense it defines me irrevocably.

Thus what individuates a person is not his 'death' (as in Heidegger), but his responsibility for the other. It is that responsibility that takes man beyond mere self-centred enjoyment and 'essence'. This way of being *'for the other'* is 'beyond egoism and altruism' (AE: 186): it does not arise out of a need for enhanced self-esteem, 'a guilt complex', 'natural kindness' or 'a tendency to self-sacrifice' (DOTL: 209) – these would involve some intention on my part. Lévinas thus defines my relation to the other as primarily ethical, 'asymmetric' (the other is above me, in his defencelessness he commands me) and non-reciprocal (any responsibility he may feel for me is *'his* business' [EI: 94]). Lévinas expresses that relation as *'je-vous'*, 'I–You' (where the 'You' is the polite form of the pronoun, not the familiar form as in Buber).

Buber–Lévinas: a dialogue

Over a period of almost 40 years, Lévinas repeatedly sought to situate his work in relation to Buber. Unlike Buber and Rogers, Lévinas and Buber share what appears to be a similar background. Both were central European Jews and refugees; both were philosophers who focused on the ethical encounter and sought 'to locate the essence of the human *outside* the realm of consciousness and knowledge' (Calarco 2004: 250–251); both introduced God into their respective conception of human relations. They also seem to tell a similar story, in similar language.

Lévinas, we saw, speaks of man at first fully engaged in his enjoyment of the world until the appearance of the Other: 'The epiphany of the face as face opens up humanity' (TI: 234). Otherness, 'alterity' creates a 'fission' in my very heart and brings 'dis-quiet' (MT: 126). I now feel called, 'chosen' to be responsible for the other and to respond 'Here I am, send me!' (Isaiah 6: 8, cited DOTL: 220). No one can take my place. The Other therefore defines me irrevocably and gives meaning to my life and death.

For Buber, 'without It man cannot live. But he who lives with It alone is not a man' (1996: 52). Thus, 'we *begin* as individuals and we become *persons*' (1999e: 166) 'by entering into relation with other persons' (1996: 85). In such Thou moments 'shattering security' (1996: 51), man knows not how the relation came about, yet he feels that his life has now become 'heavier . . . with meaning' (1996: 140); he is both 'chosen' and 'choosing', for 'all revelation is summons and sending' (1996: 147). He senses the 'mighty responsibility of love' (1996: 139). His Thou defines him (1996: 44).

For both philosophers, speech articulates the relation and demands a response: response–responsibility (Buber 1999b: 108; Lévinas AE: 80, 149). Speech is also an opening to God, yet when we speak of God, 'the said' (Lévinas), the language of It (Buber), betrays what we are saying, though, in the other that speaks, the 'trace' of God remains (Lévinas AE: 150).

And yet, though Lévinas and Buber seem to express a very similar view of being-human as being-in-relation, there are deep underlying differences. This may partly explain their rocky dialogue. Lévinas oscillates in his misrepresentation of Buber's views between almost turning them to ridicule and, on the contrary, papering over the cracks of their differences in a 'totalizing' manner that should have been anathema to him. Buber's responses are, not surprisingly, rather dismissive (see Bernasconi 2004).

The two philosophers' exchange of views was cut short by Buber's death. While we can speak of Lévinas' 'personal dialogue' with Buber's thought, in the sense in which I have used this expression throughout the book, one can hardly call it a 'dialogue' in the Buberian sense, let alone in an ethical, Lévinasian one (*pace* Bernasconi 2004: 97). There is, to my mind, a far greater difference between Lévinas and Buber than there is between Buber and Rogers. Indeed, I would argue that the gap between their views is unbridgeable. Lévinas' 'asymmetric' I–You relation, in which the Other stands above me and commands me, crystallizes a fundamentally different position from Buber's I–Thou. It stresses a view of otherness as radically other, transcendent; it expresses the contrast between Lévinas' vertical ethics, starting from the other and Buber's horizontal ethics, starting from oneself.

Besides, whereas Buber wanted an ontology of the interhuman (1999a: 15; 1999f: 216), Lévinas sought to offer a phenomenology of the 'face-to-face' that was not grounded in the 'panoramic view of being', but was 'otherwise than being and beyond essence'. For Lévinas, 'the origin of signification is ethical and not ontological' (Cohen 2004: 245).

This is not the place to develop the fundamental differences between Buber's 'We' and Lévinas' concept of justice; between 'the eternal Thou' and 'Illeity' – their respective relation to God within man's relation to man; nor between their different approach to Judaism. Lévinas liked to quote Dostoievski's 'Each one of us is guilty for everything and everyone before everyone and I more than anyone else' (e.g. in Poirié 1996: 120, 150; EI: 95, etc.). A strong form of existential guilt pervades, I feel, Lévinas' work: the sense that by my very existence I am usurping another person's 'place in the sun' (Pascal, repeatedly cited, e.g. in Poirié 1996: 115; EI: 120). Such guilt is absent from Buber's work and differs totally from his understanding of existential guilt – which lies 'in remaining with oneself', in avoiding I–Thou relations (Cohen 2004: 241) or with injuring a fundamental 'order of the human world' (Buber 1999c: 116). Yet, despite this unbridgeable gap, I firmly believe that there is much that each can bring to our understanding of therapy and the therapeutic relationship, as the Conclusion will show.

Notes

1 For the distinction between ontological and ontic, see p. 10.
2 When Friedman (D: 99) asks about 'mutuality', he recognizes that Rogers does not believe in the 'full mutuality' of the therapeutic relationship, yet interestingly, according to Anderson and Cissna (1997: 99–100), elsewhere, whenever he quotes this particular exchange he charges Rogers with believing in 'full mutuality at every level'.
3 References for Lévinas are to the titles' abbreviations.
4 For Lévinas, man's 'essence' means his self-centred 'perseverance in being' or *conatus essendi* (this does not have the life-enhancing meaning that it has in Spinoza) and his enjoyment of the world.
5 Face is metaphorical and can stand for other parts of the body.

Further reading

For Lévinas

Lévinas' language is difficult; his own interviews are the best introductions to his thought. In English:

Lévinas, E. (1985) *Ethics and Infinity*, trans. Cohen, R.A., Pittsburgh: Duquesne University Press.

References

Agassi, J. Buber (ed.) (1999) *Martin Buber on Psychology and Psychotherapy: Essays, Letters and Dialogue*, Syracuse NY: Syracuse University Press.

Anderson, R. and Cissna, K.N. (1997) *The Martin Buber–Carl Rogers Dialogue: A New Transcript with Commentary*, Albany NY: State University of New York Press.

Bernasconi, R. (2004) Failure of Communication as a Surplus: Dialogue and Lack of Dialogue between Buber and Levinas, in Atterton, P., Calarco, M. and Friedman, M. (eds) *Levinas and Buber: Dialogue and Difference*, Pittsburgh: Dusquesne University Press.

Buber, M. (1996 [1923]) *I and Thou*, trans. Smith, R.G., Edinburgh: T&T Clark.

—— (1999a [1950]) Distance and Relation, trans. Smith, R.G., in Agassi, J. Buber (ed.) *Martin Buber on Psychology and Psychotherapy: Essays, Letters and Dialogue*, Syracuse NY: Syracuse University Press.

—— (1999b [1956]) What is Common to All, trans. Friedman, M., in Agassi, J. Buber (ed.) *Martin Buber on Psychology and Psychotherapy: Essays, Letters and Dialogue*, Syracuse NY: Syracuse University Press.

—— (1999c [1957]) Guilt and Guilt Feelings, trans. Friedman, M. (1957), in Agassi, J. Buber (ed.) *Martin Buber on Psychology and Psychotherapy: Essays, Letters and Dialogue*, Syracuse NY: Syracuse University Press.

—— (1999d [1965]) The Unconscious (seminar given 1957), trans. Schaeder, G. in Agassi, J. Buber (ed.) *Martin Buber on Psychology and Psychotherapy: Essays, Letters and Dialogue*, Syracuse NY: Syracuse University Press.

—— (1999e [1973]) Correspondence with Hans Trüb, trans. Agassi, J. Buber in Agassi, J. Buber (ed.) *Martin Buber on Psychology and Psychotherapy, Essays: Letters and Dialogue*, Syracuse NY: Syracuse University Press.

—— (1999f) Correspondence with R.C. Smith, in Agassi, J. Buber (ed.) *Martin Buber on Psychology and Psychotherapy: Essays, Letters and Dialogue*, Syracuse NY: Syracuse University Press.

Calarco, M. (2004) The Retrieval of Humanism in Buber and Levinas, in Atterton, P., Calarco, M. and Friedman, M. (eds) *Levinas and Buber: Dialogue and Difference*, Pittsburgh: Dusquesne University Press.

Cohen, R.A. (2004) Buber and Levinas – and Heidegger, in Atterton, P., Calarco, M. and Friedman, M. (eds) *Levinas and Buber: Dialogue and Difference*, Pittsburgh: Dusquesne University Press.

Friedman, M. (1992) *Dialogue and the Human Image: Beyond Humanistic Psychology*, London: Sage.

Lévinas, E. (1991 [1987]) Mourir pour . . ., in Lévinas, E., *Entre Nous, Essais sur le penser-à-l'autre*, Paris: Livre de Poche. (**EN** in text.)

—— (1996 [1974]) *Autrement qu'être et au-delà de l'essence*, Paris: Livre de Poche. (**AE** in text.)

—— (1997 [1982]) *Ethique et Infini, dialogues avec Philippe Nemo*, Paris: Fayard et Radio France. (**EI** in text.)

—— (2000 [1961]) *Totalité et Infini, essai sur l'Extériorité*, Paris: Livre de Poche. (**TI** in text.)

—— (2006a [1993]) La Mort et le temps (Cours donné 1975), in Lévinas, E. *Dieu, la Mort et le Temps*, Paris: Livre de Poche. (**MT** in text.)

—— (2006b [1993]) Dieu et l'onto-théo-logie (Cours donné 1975), in Lévinas, E. *Dieu, la Mort et le Temps*, Paris: Livre de Poche. (**DOTL** in text.)

May, R. (ed.) (1961) *Existential Psychology*, New York: Random House.

Poirié, F. (1996 [1987]) *Lévinas, Essai et Entretiens*, Arles: Actes Sud.

Rogers, C. (1990a [1957]) The Necessary and Sufficient Conditions of Therapeutic Personality Change, in Kirschenbaum, H. and Henderson, V.L. (eds) (1990) *The Carl Rogers Reader*, London: Constable.

—— (1990b [1961]) A Therapist's View of the Good Life: The Fully Functioning Person, in Kirschenbaum, H. and Henderson, V.L. (eds) (1990) *The Carl Rogers Reader*, London: Constable.

—— (1990c [1964]) Toward a Modern Approach to Values: The Valuing Process in the Mature Person, in Kirschenbaum, H. and Henderson, V.L. (eds) (1990) *The Carl Rogers Reader*, London: Constable.

CONCLUSION

The therapeutic relationship, when death enters the therapeutic space

Laura Barnett

For me, this book has grown organically. It started with my interest in the reciprocal relation between existential thought and therapeutic practice and my commitment to raise awareness among therapists of 'the whole ITU event'. Intensive Care brought with it the theme of death in the counselling room. The book started with my own questions, and the theme of personal dialogue which then emerged became an intrinsic part of the book: every contributor's offering, a personal dialogue with their own existential issues and those of their particular client group, and this Conclusion my dialogue with their chapters as well as my own.

I have a sense of having come full circle. In the first chapter I expressed dissatisfaction with the idea of Heideggerian authenticity as the main goal for existential therapy (it is not sustainable and does not concern itself with the moral dimension of choices and decisions, see pp. 20–21). What then is the goal of existential therapy? I have now come to feel that it is maybe only at the end of therapy that one can understand the purpose of a particular piece of therapeutic work. As I look back, I think of M who can now see a point in planning ahead, even if he does not know how many years he has to live; solitary V who realized, in the last days of her life, that her unusual views on life and the world could be interesting and valuable to others (they still remain with me); J who became open to appreciation, warmth and love from others (and who taught me so much in the process). Moments of authenticity occurred, but these were not necessarily the most significant or valuable aspects of our sessions.

While I do believe that it is preferable, for a satisfying life, to learn to confront our mortality and our lack of control over the ground and givens of our existence, to 'own' our values, beliefs and priorities in life and to act upon them (i.e. to be 'authentic'), it is not always sufficient, nor is it necessarily the most urgent goal for therapy. Obstacles may stand in the way preventing us from being open to 'what addresses us' – to the world, other beings, other possibilities, etc. Some clients seem to have an emotion that dominates the way they are 'attuned' to the world (it may be grief, guilt, shame, etc.). For some, life may hold more terror than death. I sometimes visualize it as a briar growing up inside the body on which like experiences tend to attach themselves. To pull this briar up from its roots can become the main aim of therapy, giving clients a fuller sense of their freedom. ('From the roots' does not necessarily imply excavating the past, but discovering a different understanding.) I therefore see the aim of therapy as being different for each client. However, I am not advocating approaching new clients with an aim in mind: paradoxically, maybe the aim of therapy can only be retrospective.

The therapeutic relationship is the heart of therapy. I would like to show how some of the existential concepts encountered so far can illuminate it. We are already 'in relation' before we are born. For Heidegger, being *always already* in relation with others is a fundamental characteristic of human existence; it is an aspect of being-in-the-world. Even indifference and avoidance are ways of relating. Therefore, however 'professional', 'impersonal' and 'distanced' therapists may choose to be, they cannot help but be in a personal relationship with their clients, and vice versa.

The view that body and mind are separate entities was long 'common sense'. This view is frequently linked to the idea of the body as being inferior to the mind, sometimes even as being 'shameful', 'impure' and 'sinful'. Existentialism from Nietzsche onwards offers a revaluation of the body: it emphasizes our embodied condition without attaching any shame to the body.

These two principles alone (being-in-the-world and embodiment) transform the perception of the therapeutic relationship in existential therapy. The other can never be an encapsulated psyche with its intra-psychic and inter-psychic mechanisms, such as repression, transference, etc. Nor can there be a body expressing what has been repressed by a psyche: a person reacts as a whole to the situation of which he or she is a part. The client, like the therapist, is an embodied person-in-relation and has been in an embodied relationship with the therapist from the moment he thought of making contact. Indeed, he may even have been suffering from migraines, stomach upsets or palpitations at the very thought of making that contact. Similarly, in the counselling session, each person will be experiencing the relation in an embodied way: e.g. tightening across the chest; gut wrenching; softness or relaxation, etc.

For the therapist being-there-together involves 'being attuned to' the client with understanding; it involves 'hearkening' to the client, not simply listening to what is being said. Embodiment and Heidegger's concepts of 'attunement' help to make sense, for instance, of the phenomenon that most of us have encountered, whereby the therapist has the sense of experiencing the client's emotion – even an emotion of which the client may be, at that time, still unaware. Our embodied attunement to the other means that we may tune into the other's mood, even if, for the other, that mood lies in the background. We can pick up the sorrow behind the anger, the despair behind the positive attitude, etc. (And this may apply to the client as much as to the therapist!) There is no need for further elucidation, such as recourse to 'stepping into the other's shoes' (empathy) or the intra-psychic mechanisms of psychoanalysis. From an existential perspective, 'mesopathy' (between-feeling) would be more appropriate than empathy (in-feeling): it expresses our ability to sense, in an embodied manner, the interplay of feelings in the room.

The works of Buber and Rogers highlight 'the between' (Buber) that unique embodied therapeutic space that therapist and client create and re-create together. They stress the importance of letting clients feel 'confirmed' and 'prized' in their potentialities; of aiming for a genuine mutuality and reciprocity in the relationship, while remaining aware of the difference of role and of power (e.g. a British therapist with a refugee seeking asylum in the UK automatically creates a power differential); of allowing oneself to be changed by the encounter.

Therapist genuineness and transparency are fundamental elements of the therapeutic relationship in existential therapy and have roots in existential philosophy. Rogers was the first therapist to promulgate the importance of these qualities; Buber could not understand his concept of therapeutic 'transparency' (later 'congruence'). It is not about factual 'self-disclosure' as such – though personal feelings and reactions, where appropriate, may be tactfully divulged as phenomenological feedback. It is about being present, as oneself – rather than as a blank screen, an idealized self-portrayal or playing the role of therapist.

What, I wondered, do I bring of myself into the relationship where death has entered the therapeutic space? While I do not think that it differs from what I usually bring, there may be, I sense, a qualitative difference or a shift in emphasis. Maybe, because of the specific situational inequality between my own physical health and the serious attack on my clients' health/wholeness, what I bring to our encounter may be perceived differently.

In my hospital work, I am more aware of my vulnerability: the vulnerability of my vitality, wholeness and life; a vulnerability that probably opens me more to being changed by our meeting. This may account for the impact on me of some of my encounters with people in the last days of their lives. Alison Diffley speaks of being sometimes 'exquisitely touched' in the course of her work as a palliative care nurse. 'Exquisitely touched' brought to mind those palliative care clients who entered my life, sometimes very briefly (two or three sessions), and changed me, I feel, in some way for ever. I am very aware of my powerlessness to alter some of these clients' dire situations. Yet, as Melanie Lockett reminds me, I need not 'feel helpless. I can express my compassion and be a witness to [their] struggle' (p. 155). This echoes John Heaton's words, working with suicidal clients: 'They may come for many months repeating "You are useless; no one can help me." This is to be respected. . . . The crucial point is that they have a witness, another person, to listen and respond to their misery' (p. 129).

'And how do we stay congruent and at the same time offer containment of feelings that we ourselves experience as . . . overwhelming?' The answer to Ann Chalmers' question (p. 187) is a thread that runs through the book. All the contributors agree that it does not lie in putting up barriers and distancing ourselves.

Rogers' and Buber's insistence on 'empathy'/'making present', however, is unnecessary from a Heideggerian perspective (see above). Melanie Lockett's chapter illustrates the gap between her previous work as a cancer counsellor and her present way of working, coloured by her own recent personal experience of cancer. For me, the change for Lockett was not so much: now I know what cancer feels like, so I can be even more empathic with my clients, but a greater openness to the other, which no longer leaves certain parts of herself (her own anxiety around illness, ageing and death) out of the picture. Adapting Hilary Fife's words, it is the realization that now 'the invulnerability of distance is no longer an option' (p. 158).

Lévinas introduced in philosophy the concept of 'alterity', the total, fundamental otherness of the other person. From a Lévinasian perspective, as a therapist, I understand my client to be different to me and I experience this difference as 'non-indifference'. I cannot change him, nor should I try – to do so would be 'doing violence' to him.

When my client lies before me, ill or dying and I am healthy, I am aware of that difference between us. I am also aware that somehow, by my very existence, in the Pascalian expression that Lévinas likes to cite, I am 'taking another's place in the sun'. I feel called into question to my very core, facing the mystery of death and, in some sense, 'dying together' (Lévinas 1991: 227): together 'awaiting . . . that which is not an *it*', 'death . . . as pure question mark' (Lévinas 2006: 131; 23).

The therapist's position is a very particular one. Sometimes the therapist may be the only person able to be face to face with the dying person (see Smith-Pickard, Chapter 8). In that sense the other defines me: 'The death of the Other who is dying affects me in my very identity of responsible "I" ' (Lévinas 2006: 21).

For Lévinas, my relation to the other is primarily ethical. For us as therapists, it is a reminder that therapy is, at heart, an ethical venture and gesture – 'ethics' should not be something that gets added on in the form of professional regulation. For Lévinas, 'ethics is the spiritual optic'. For him, 'the Infinite' appears in the other's 'face'. For Buber, every genuine encounter is an encounter with the Eternal Thou. Heidegger speaks a secularized, poetic language, yet it is the language of *das Heil*, the holy (e.g. 'being grants', 'thinking is thanking'). All three philosophers express a form of religiosity. In existential therapies, as in other therapies, a spiritual dimension may or may not be felt. This will depend on the co-created relation between therapist and client. However, when death enters the therapeutic space, the therapeutic relationship will be brought face to face with the mystery of existence.

David Horne (p. 61) refers to Koestenbaum's paradoxical phrase 'the vitality of death' and this has been a major theme of this book. Facing up to our mortality and the givens of our existence may be anxiety provoking, but it can also enable us to engage with life in a more fulfilling manner. At the same time, we must remember that this does not simply apply to our clients, it also holds good for us, their therapists. The therapeutic work with clients who have been faced with their mortality is an opportunity for us to confront our own finitude, our own regrets and wasted opportunities, celebrate our joys and strengths, open up to new possibilities and seek to fulfil new dreams.

References

Lévinas, E. (1991 [1987]) Mourir pour . . ., in Lévinas, E. *Entre Nous, Essais sur le penser-à-l'autre*, Paris: Livre de Poche.

—— (2006 [1993]) La Mort et le temps (Cours donné 1975), in Lévinas, E. *Dieu, la Mort et le Temps*, Paris: Livre de Poche.

INDEX

Printed in Great Britain
by Amazon